D0148659

OUR POLITICS, OUR SELVES?

OUR POLITICS, OUR SELVES?

LIBERALISM, IDENTITY, AND HARM

Peter Digeser

PRINCETON UNIVERSITY PRESS   PRINCETON, NEW JERSEY

Copyright © 1995 by Princeton University Press
Published by Princeton University Press, 41 William Street,
Princeton, New Jersey 08540
In the United Kingdom: Princeton University Press, Chichester, West Sussex
All Rights Reserved

Library of Congress Cataloging-in-Publication Data

Digeser, Peter.
Our politics, our selves? : liberalism, identity, and harm / Peter Digeser.
p. cm.
Includes bibliographical references and index.
ISBN 0-691-03716-7 (cl: acid-free paper)
1. Liberalism. 2. Identity (Psychology). 3. Self. I. Title.
JC574.D54 1995
320.5′1′019—dc20   94-23387   CIP

This book has been composed in Baskerville

Princeton University Press books are printed
on acid-free paper and meet the guidelines
for permanence and durability of the Committee
on Production Guidelines for Book Longevity
of the Council on Library Resources

Printed in the United States of America

10 9 8 7 6 5 4 3 2 1

For Beth

Contents

Acknowledgments ────────────────────────────────

MUCH OF THIS BOOK was written with the support of a Summer Regents' Junior Faculty Fellowship from the University of California, Santa Barbara, and with the help of an Eccles Research Fellowship from the Humanities Center at the University of Utah. I would especially like to thank Lowell Durham, Kasey Grier, Lynne Rasmussen, and Rob Showell at the Humanities Center for providing a wonderful environment in which to do research. My 1992–1993 stay in Utah also allowed me to renew my friendship with Peter Diamond and meet Bruce Landesman. I learned a great deal at our luncheon meetings from both of these gentlemen.

The parts of chapter 1 that discuss Foucault draw upon material from "The Fourth Face of Power," *The Journal of Politics* 54 (1992). They appear here with the permission of the University of Texas Press. Some of the discussion of Judith Butler in chapter 5 comes from "Performativity Trouble: Postmodern Feminism and Essential Subjects," in *Political Research Quarterly* 47 (1994). It is reprinted by permission of the University of Utah, copyright holder. Thanks to these journals for permission to use this material.

Despite his deep disagreement with much in this book, Tom Schrock valiantly read and commented upon a number of its versions. His disdain for obfuscation and his relentless pursuit of arguments taught me the virtue of patience and undoubtedly improved the manuscript. A debt of gratitude is also owed to Dennis Fischman, Emily Gill, John Moore, James Read, Stephen Weatherford, and Ross Miller for their helpful comments and criticisms on various parts of this work.

Although I do not know about owing debts to enemies, I certainly owe a debt to friends who disagree. Despite our differences over the relationship between the self and politics, I owe much to Bonnie Honig for her friendship and her boldness of thought (should I say *virtù?*). To another long-time friend, David Mapel, I also owe a great deal. He read and commented extensively on this project and saved me from a variety of blunders, confusions, and meanderings. From both Bonnie and David, I have learned that the most enjoyable part of thinking and doing research is that I get to talk with my friends more often.

If Richard Flathman ever wondered when he would have to stop reading the draft manuscripts of his former students, he never let on. His devotion to careful argumentation, his fair-minded attention to alternative perspectives, and his willingness to respect the interests and

pursuits of his students taught me a great deal about the engagement
of political philosophy. As this book attests, I have also learned much
from William Connolly. I know that I have only begun to respond to
his acute comments and criticisms.

My wife Beth has seen me through course work, comprehensive examinations, a dissertation, job hunting, fellowships, teaching, and the
pressures of publishing. She has read and reread these chapters. All
that I know about the late Roman Empire, I know through her. I owe
her much. It is a pleasure to acknowledge my love and respect for her.
Finally, I would like to thank my parents, Eleanor and Henry Digeser,
for their love and support. In particular, I would like to thank my father who has discovered the life of the mind in his leisured retirement.
Keep at it, Dad.

Santa Barbara, California
May 1994

OUR POLITICS, OUR SELVES?

Introduction _____

Is STATECRAFT SELFCRAFT? Should we look to our souls and selves in assessing the quality of our politics? Is it the business of politics to cultivate, shape, or structure our internal lives? For various critics and defenders of liberal theory and practice, the answer to this last question is a resounding yes. They see the effects of a regime upon our souls and selves as an urgent political concern. The reason for the critics' concern is that liberal culture fragments, debases, or normalizes our selves. Liberal statecraft yields forms of soulcraft that need to be mitigated or rectified. In contrast, others have argued that what makes liberalism valuable is that it cultivates the ideals of autonomy and individualism. In other words, liberalism has been defended precisely because of its salutary effects upon our selves. Despite their differences, both critics and defenders are united by a belief that we have a political responsibility, if not an obligation, to engage in selfcraft.

The current debate over selfcraft extends beyond those who criticize and those who defend the effects of liberalism. Vigorous opposition to the association of statecraft and soulcraft comes from writers who argue that bringing selftalk into politics is illiberal and dangerous. They argue that disputes involving the order and nature of the self have no place in politics. Political theories, legislation, judicial decisions, or public policies should not be justified by appealing to a particular conception of the self or soul.

I believe that the dominant positions in the debate over soulcraft have captured only part of the truth. Those who wish to associate statecraft with soulcraft are correct in thinking that conceptions of the soul or self can have a place in liberal politics. They are, however, mistaken in believing that there is a political obligation or responsibility to foster a particular conception of the self or soul. On the other hand, those who would preclude selftalk from theory and practice are correct in rejecting selfcraft as part and parcel of liberalism. Their mistake is in arguing that selftalk should necessarily be precluded from politics. Somewhere in the middle lies a qualified permission to protect or encourage particular conceptions of human identity. The engagement in self- or soulcraft should be neither ruled out automatically nor considered an essential component of liberal democracy.

I enter this thicket of issues by addressing the concerns of the critics who argue that contemporary liberal democracy produces an objectionable kind of person. In many respects, however, the claim that popular government and culture adversely affect our souls, in a secular sense, is not new. In Book 8 of Plato's *Republic*, Socrates argued that the democratic individual was a jack-of-all-trades, but master of none, unable to distinguish what was necessary from what was not. During the ratification debates over the United States Constitution, the Anti-Federalists argued that the proposed regime would not cultivate properly a citizenry virtuous enough to maintain itself. In *Democracy in America*, Alexis de Tocqueville worried that Americans' excessive love of equality could result in a liberty-destroying individualism. In the twentieth century, thinkers from the far right to the far left—from the fascists to the Frankfurt School— have criticized liberal democracy for producing a deeply objectionable kind of person.

In chapter 1, I explore how communitarians, classical political rationalists, and genealogists have taken up the problem of selfcraft. Each of these positions offers a distinctive account of the effects that a liberal democratic regime has upon our selves or souls. Communitarians charge that this regime fosters fragmented, atomistic, emotivist, shallow, instrumental, disengaged selves. Writers such as Charles Taylor, Alasdair MacIntyre, Michael Sandel, and Robert Bellah have argued that we are alienated from our communities, and that we have fragmented our selves. We have created a culture that excludes heroic virtues, dissolves traditional communities, disenchants the world, and destroys the essential unity of the self.

The Straussians, or classical political rationalists, offer a different although not wholly unrelated assessment of our present situation. According to them, our culture disorders and impoverishes our souls. Leo Strauss, Allan Bloom, Thomas Pangle, and Harvey Mansfield have argued that the liberal regime disorders our souls by failing to teach us to attach much weight to reason and its role in discovering truth. We have been influenced by Enlightenment thinkers who turned reason into the handmaid of our passions, and we have then been corrupted ultimately by German thinkers who argued that reason self-destructs. Reason has been knocked off its perch in our souls. This regime, with its lust for equality, mocks both moral and intellectual virtue.

The final school of criticism that I examine grows out of Michel Foucault's work. Unlike the communitarians who argue that our selves are becoming increasingly fragmented or the classical political rationalists who argue that our souls are being disordered, the genealogists argue that we have become docile, normalized, disciplined subjects. We organize our lives in ways that at once reflect and encourage surveillance by others and that constantly remind us to keep a close eye upon ourselves. We set up disciplinary standards of rationality, responsibility, and normality that in fact presuppose the inevitable production of those who deviate from them. The deviations, the abnormalities, the irresponsibilities, in turn, generate further pressures to crack down and normalize behavior. The liberal individual, although possessing a panoply of rights never before experienced, is produced out of a series of disciplines that are minute, insidious, and pervasive. This chapter concludes by tracing the development and expansion of these themes in the writings of Judith Butler and William E. Connolly.

How should liberal theory respond to these criticisms? In chapter 2, I argue that the critics' claims depend upon both complex empirical (causal) descriptions of soulcraft and normative standards of how we should understand our selves. For the most part, this work concedes the accuracy of empirical descriptions. In light of this concession, I consider the normative standards that support the critics' arguments. At issue is whether we are being harmed by the ways in which our identities are fostered or forged under a liberal culture. This issue requires understanding what being harmed means. Behind the critics' arguments must lie not only a sense of how we are being harmed, but also what it means not to be harmed. In other words, each school of critics must provide a positive conception of the self in order to get critical leverage on the production of modern identity. Chapters 2 through 4 examine the standards that the communitarians, the classical political rationalists, and the genealogists use to judge the effects of liberal democracy. The communitarians appeal to the role of unity within the self; the classical political rationalists appeal to a soul fired by eros and ruled by reason; and the genealogists appeal to a conception of the self as a constructed, complex subject.

An important theme for the critics, then, is that the politics of identity goes all the way down. For the communitarians and the genealogists this means that the self is constituted, at least in part, by the values and demands of its political environment. For the classical political rationalists it means that a preferred conception of ruling is imported into their understanding of the soul. The metaphor of politics elucidates and legitimates the number and ordering of the soul's parts.

In each case, the critics do not offer a persuasive standard for judging the nature of the harm to the self or the soul. More strongly, what each of these schools takes as harmful is deeply contestable. Their alternative conceptions of the self reveal standards of harm that are not compelling. Our judgments about the parts and the ordering of our souls are much less reliable than our large-scale political judgments. Without compelling standards for judging harm to the self, this kind of argument against liberal democracy is weakened significantly.

Can liberal democratic theory simply ignore the effects of this regime upon our internal lives? An important tradition within liberal thought argues that soulcraft should be an essential part of statecraft. Within this tradition, liberal democracy is justified largely on the ground that it can foster purposive, creative, and critically aware individuals. Chapter 5 focuses on that theme by looking at the related concepts of autonomy, authenticity, and autarchy. I assess the philosophical problems and political risks associated with recent understandings of autonomy and authenticity and ask whether liberal regimes have a responsibility to encourage some minimal level of autarchy or agency. Would liberal democracy still be defensible if it stifled or precluded our capacity for choice? Should not liberal democracy, at the very least, produce people with the ability to have desires, formulate interests, and pursue projects? Certainly it is a serious harm to disable or remove the capacity for choice. People do have a right to have their autarchy respected. Nevertheless, there are serious problems with the idea of a right to be autarchic.

Chapter 6 explores in depth the most serious of those problems. A responsibility to cultivate autarchy or agency would require that political institutions and practices could abet such creation. There may be, however, insurmountable difficulties with the claim that autarchy can arise from human practices and interactions. To discuss those difficulties I consider what Foucault calls the direct and indirect constitution of the self. Does either form of constitution provide an account of the construction of agency? In both forms of constitution, agency is not produced but presumed. Without an account of how agency is constructed, its cultivation cannot be a responsibility of liberal government.

My argument thus far is directed against positions that judge liberal democracy by its effects on our selves or souls *and* advance a political responsibility to address those effects. Chapter 7 turns to the central alternative voice in this dispute: liberal politics should not be judged by its soulcraft *and* that liberal theory and practice have no business raising the issue. Here, I examine the familiar liberal position that political practice and theory should be neutral vis à vis these claims. Richard Rorty, Amy Gutmann, Dennis Thompson, and John Rawls offer a series of arguments that can be deployed against the possibility of admitting selftalk into theory and politics. These arguments, however, are inadequate. Appealing to what is shared, avoiding cruelty, establishing the limits of conversation, desiring to surpass the present debate, setting up a requirement of moral validity, revealing the problem of governmental trust, and formulating a duty of civility all fall short of precluding selfcraft.

In the final chapter, I consider the case for a permission to engage in a selfcraft that is qualified by the dangers it can pose to both human agency and freedom. Avoiding these dangers creates the possibility of justifying theories, programs, and policies on the basis of their effects on the self. Under such a permission the state may attempt to establish the conditions that are favorable for the cultivation of particular conceptions of the self. For example, public debate over education, group rights, criminal responsibility, support for the arts, and drug rehabilitation should not preclude talk about the role of reason in our souls or the importance of wholeness and community to our selves or the significance of autonomy for individuals. The expression of dissatisfaction over what people believe to be the effects of liberal culture upon their selves or souls should not be excluded from liberal politics. Statecraft will inevitably be felt as soulcraft. To some extent, liberal politics can address the perceived harms and deeper aspirations associated with claims regarding the self. However, those who seek to place only their own conception of the self within the reach of politics are as mistaken as those who would preclude completely such matters from politics.

1

The Critics

WE ORDINARILY JUDGE the quality of our political life by a complex set of criteria: stability, economic growth, low unemployment, reasonable rate of inflation, rule of law, protection of basic liberties, the justice of distributions, the provision of security, the treatment of the less fortunate, and so on. Some of these standards, such as those related to economic performance, have only recently been seen as state responsibilities. Other standards, such as security, predictability, and stability are part and parcel of what we understand government to be. How these standards are defined, applied, and met varies with time and place. What is a reasonable rate of inflation or an adequate protection of liberty in one place may be deemed unacceptable or tyrannical elsewhere. Even within a given political regime these criteria will be understood and valued differently by different individuals. Pacifists will differ from nationalists in their understanding of security. Free marketers differ from welfare liberals over the appropriate level of state concern for the less fortunate. Debtors and creditors differ over what constitutes acceptable rates of inflation and interest. Civil libertarians differ from law-and-order types over what is an adequate level of protection of civil rights. As ill-defined and conflict-ridden as these criteria are, they remain public standards that we draw upon and apply in political practice. Votes are cast, revolutions are instigated, and regimes are brought down based upon ideas of the quality of political life.

Out of this welter of demands, functions, and expectations, political theorists have attempted to clarify, refine, and (occasionally) establish what criteria should hold in judging the quality of politics. Indeed, some would argue that judging and ranking regimes is the very essence of political philosophy. In contemporary political theory, for example, John Rawls argues that justice is the first virtue of society. By this he means that if a regime is unjust then it does not deserve our respect or obedience. Within his theory of justice, Rawls argues that the principle of equal liberty has more urgency than principles of economic distribution; hence, liberties should not be exchanged for economic advantage. In contrast, Michael Sandel argues that it is a mistake to turn justice into the first virtue of society. Political life involves other human relationships whose quality should not be judged by justice. Conversely, Robert Nozick claims that our political life need only meet and should not exceed the very minimal standard of protecting individual liberty. To employ any other criteria would unjustifiably license state power. Michael Oakeshott has thoroughly refined these concerns by defining the ideal civil association as completely lacking any essential purpose and composed by a formal set of adverbial rules.

As these examples suggest, political theory mirrors our practical judgments to the extent that it is also divided over the definition, weight, and appropriateness of various criteria. But this lack of consensus should not lead us to conclude that there are not better and worse conceptions of these standards. Just as divisiveness need not prevent formation of sound judgments regarding the quality of practical political life, so theoretical divisiveness need not prevent us from judging the quality of criteria advanced by political philosophers.

The problem of soulcraft raises similar concerns. For many critics and supporters of liberal democracy, how a regime affects the self provides a standard for judging the quality of politics.[1] Different schools of thought offer different descriptions and assessments of these effects. These differences raise the question of which, if any, of these approaches employs the best criteria for judging liberal democracy. Indeed, they ultimately raise the issue of whether we should turn to the self in assessing the quality of politics.

The debate over soulcraft actually encompasses two sets of issues. The

---

[1] The ideas of liberal democracy, soul, and self need some clarification. By liberal democracy, I am referring to large-scale, industrialized, representative governments found, for the most part in the West. These regimes usually include some form of market economy as well as characteristics of polyarchy: elected officials, free and fair elections, inclusive suffrage, the right to run for office, freedom of expression, availability of alternative sources of information, and the right to form relatively independent associations (Dahl 1989, 221). Liberal democracy is meant to encompass a large set of formal and informal practices and institutions found primarily, but not exclusively, in the North Atlantic region at the end of the twentieth century.

The idea of the soul and its relationship to the self will be considered in the discussion of classical political rationalism. The immediate problem with the word self is that it has acquired a variety of uses. Consequently, the appearance of the word does not always signal a discussion of something called *the self*. For example, when the term is used as a reflexive pronoun, it may not refer to *the self* at all: a self-cleaning oven does not result in a self that sparkles (Jaeger 1977, 239). Similarly, we must be careful not to see a reflexive usage of the self when applied to humans as necessarily referring to *the self*. Consequently, the question "Can the self be understood?" does not necessarily mean the same thing as "Can we understand ourselves?" It may very well be that understanding ourselves entails understanding our physical and emotional attributes, our ability to endure trials and tribulations, our knowing the relative importance of our projects and desires, and so on. These usages do not imply that there is something called the self that is either the summation or the subject of these characteristics. To help avoid this confusion I will use the word *self* alone when it is meant to express something more than a reflexive pronoun (e.g., my self).

first set revolves around whether a particular kind of person is a necessary prerequisite to sustain a particular kind of regime. For instance, do liberal democracies need to foster certain characters, virtues, or internal orderings in order to maintain themselves? One school of thought argues that statecraft must be soulcraft if a regime is to survive. Recently, this position has found renewed support from thinkers who trace their roots back to an Aristotelian or republican tradition. For example, Allan Bloom, William Galston, Quentin Skinner, Thomas Pangle, and Charles Taylor have all argued that government, for its own sake, must be involved in the cultivation of good citizens. In an opposing camp are those who do not see a particular conception of the self as a necessary condition for government. Liberals in this camp seem to take a certain pride in showing how their conception of government can succeed regardless of the kind of citizen with which it is faced. For example, Kant argues that constitutional government could be run by intelligent devils. In the Federalist Papers, the portrayal of humanity as ambitious, vindictive, and rapacious is used to promote the merits of the United States Constitution. Far from being seen as a failure of democracy, a failure of character is taken as something of a challenge: the worst of characters does not impede the best practical government.

I am concerned primarily with a somewhat different, although related, problem. Instead of asking whether we should judge the quality of our selves by the requirements of citizenship, I am interested in whether we should assess the quality of our politics by its effects upon our souls or selves. Indeed, should such matters be allowed into and have an effect upon liberal politics? The problem of soulcraft that I explore has less to do with finding the necessary prerequisites for securing politics and more to do with what criteria should be employed in assessing liberal regimes.

At issue is whether the effects of political life (broadly conceived) upon our selves should be used in first judging and then conducting politics. There are, however, many ways in which a political regime can be said to effect our souls. Here the problem of soulcraft concerns two kinds of effects. The first pertains to the ways that our internal lives are organized or structured by prevailing institutions, practices, and norms. Do liberal democracies order our internal lives in a troubling or harmful fashion? Or do they provide the necessary conditions for cultivating particular ideals of the self? The second kind of effect concerns the ways in which political life represents or construes what we are ultimately as human beings. The critical issue here is whether liberal regimes encourage a kind of deluded or twisted conception of ourselves that poisons our interpersonal relations and deprives us of the very point of our lives. Because a concern with these effects can be found in a wide variety of positions, they demand a closer look.

At the very least, starting with liberal democracy's critics provides a sense of what many believe to be at stake in the idea of soulcraft. In diverse ways, communitarians, classical political rationalists, and genealogists agree upon the importance of theorizing about the relationship between the political/cultural order and the individual self. In this respect, they offer what could be called a politics of identity.[2] Moreover, they all subscribe to the idea that political theory should be able to track the effects of culture and politics all the way down to the soul. These three positions do not, of course, exhaust the critical possibilities. They do offer, however, distinctive and persistent claims against liberal regimes and represent a significant set of logical possibilities regarding the organization and understanding of the self.[3]

Starting with the critics of liberal democratic theory is also useful because they present an important challenge that deserves a response. In the ongoing conversation about the effects of liberal democracy, it seems that some of the more interesting and striking lines have gone to the critics. This need not be the case, and liberal theory can move beyond the ways it currently engages in this debate. As we shall see, liberalism is itself split between those who argue that crafting the self is an essential component of politics and those who argue that theory and practice should avoid altogether questions concerning the self. This rift is part of a larger set of fractures that run throughout liberalism. Roughly, modern liberalism can still be identified by its commitment to ideas such as freedom, individualism, pluralism, and popular but limited government. These and other commitments, however, give rise to disputes not only over how they should be defined and balanced, but also over how they should be justified. The latter set of disputes points to the

[2] Although the critics' concerns may be encompassed under the idea of a politics of identity, it is clear that this phrase is also used to refer to a much larger set of issues. At the very least, the notion of identity can pertain to a group of social, political, and personal categories that one either takes up or is attached to oneself: nationality, race, sex, ethnicity, class, profession, and so on. Studying the politics of identity can entail looking at how these "subject positions" or spatial/temporal coordinates are used, imposed, challenged, dominated, repressed, and formulated within the political process. If all we are is exhausted by these spatial/temporal coordinates, then the concerns of soulcraft would be wholly encompassed by the politics of identity. Generally, however, soulcraft is concerned with that which bears these identities. What is at stake in considering the problem of soulcraft is something different than what is frequently taken to be the politics of identity. This something else is usually referred to by the terms soul, self, or subject. I owe this point to Dennis Fischman.

[3] From the eighteenth century onward, thinkers such as Rousseau, de Tocqueville, Marx, Nietzsche, Heidegger, Marcuse, Roberto Unger, Alasdair MacIntyre, Charles Taylor, Leo Strauss, Christopher Lasch, George Will, Allan Bloom, Ronald Beiner, and Michel Foucault have all pointed, in one way or another, to the lamentable effects that this type of regime has upon souls and selves. Although my focus upon communitarians, classical political rationalists, and genealogists encompasses a number of these thinkers, it does not respond to the universe of possibilities.

problem of the purposes or ends that a liberal polity is meant to promote. Is such a regime valuable only because it serves as a necessary
condition for whatever is valued by individuals and groups living within
its borders? Or does the regime itself have purposes and ends that stand
beyond contingent individual interests and desires?

For those who see the expression and development of a particular
ideal of the self as a central purpose of government, a liberal polity will
be judged by a standard that will probably exceed the ordinary desires
and interests of many, if not most, people. The position that liberalism
should be deeply suspicious of claims that advance substantive, overarching purposes and goods would also be suspicious of selftalk based
upon such purposes or ends. Settling the larger question of how to justify
liberalism would also appear to settle the question of what role selfcraft
should play in liberal politics. But this is not entirely correct. Even if
liberalism is justified by its ability to enable individuals and groups to
pursue their conceptions of the good life, selftalk may still find a place in
politics. For it is possible that an understanding of the self could be an
important feature of an individual's or a group's conception of the
good. I will argue that within limits the liberal state may be able to provide the conditions for cultivating particular conceptions of the self.

The Communitarians

Over the past ten years something called the liberal/communitarian debate has become a virtual industry within contemporary political theory.
The communitarian captains of this industry include such thinkers as
Alasdair MacIntyre, Robert Bellah, Michael Sandel, and Charles Taylor.
As the communitarians would themselves emphasize, their positions did
not spring up like mushrooms overnight, but are a part of a larger tradition of thought that extends back to the writings of Rousseau, Hegel, and
beyond to classical republicanism. The central themes of the most recent manifestation of communitarianism are that liberal theory is impoverished and that liberal democratic practice is often pernicious in its
effects. The origin of these troubles is found in liberal obtuseness regarding how individuals and political institutions are and ought to be situated in communities. This intellectual impoverishment is manifest in a
conception of the self that is prior to its ends, a notion of freedom that
is negative, an idea of justice as the first virtue of society, a view of rights
as trumps, an understanding of democracy that is merely a decision procedure, a conception of representation that is solely tied to interests, and
a belief that social life is nothing more than the collected sum of individual interests. As the notion of impoverishment suggests, the communi-

tarian critique of liberal theory is limited in many respects. It does not reject the notions of the self, freedom, justice, rights, decision procedures, representation, or individual interests. It approaches them differently. Indeed, it has been suggested that communitarianism is not so much an abandonment of liberal theory, but rather a corrective for its failures and excesses (Walzer 1990).

The communitarian corrective to liberalism has included the ideas that the self is constituted by its ends, that freedom is intimately linked to virtue, that justice is not the first virtue of society, that rights do not necessarily trump all other concerns, that democracy is to be valued because of the participation it demands, that representation can be a transformative institution, and that society also has collective (as opposed to collected) attributes. Liberal theorists have responded to these claims in a number of ways. Some have argued that the communitarian critique misunderstands the presumptions and character of liberal theory (Beiner 1992, 18; Buchanan 1989; Kymlicka 1989, 47–99; Larmore 1987, 118; Rawls 1985, 238, 239 n.21). Others have argued that to the extent that a genuine disagreement exists, the communitarians fail to offer a coherent conception of politics and political ideas (Dahl 1989, 301; Flathman 1987, 81–107; Holmes 1993).

The communitarian critique, however, has always entailed more than an examination of the postulates and presumptions of liberal theory. Just as serious is the charge that the practices and institutions of modern liberal democratic culture have a ruinous effect upon our identities. At one time or another, communitarians have claimed that modern culture engenders fragmented, atomistic, emotivist, shallow, hyperrational, and disengaged selves. Alasdair MacIntyre's *After Virtue* (1984) is the most forceful expression of this kind of argument. MacIntyre argues that our social context is one in which we no longer share a common moral language. At best, our public discourse is a sophisticated set of grunts and squeals signifying emotional rejection or approval. Because we no longer share meanings of good and bad or right and wrong, our moral language has become as emotivist as logical positivists insisted it always was. As things stand, public debate over matters such as war, abortion, the death penalty, and affirmative action can never rise above purely a subjective, emotional level (MacIntyre 1984, 6–22; Bellah et al. 1985, 7).

Within this emotivist social context, MacIntyre argues, we not only lost a shared moral language, we also lost our ability to distinguish between manipulative and nonmanipulative social relations (MacIntyre 1984, 23). Without a common morality, the only remaining criterion for how to treat other people is whether that treatment satisfies preferences and assuages feelings: Does an action yield more squeals of joy than groans of dissatisfaction? This view also suggests that we lack impersonal criteria that allow us to distinguish between using others as means and seeing them as ends. We no longer share a sense of limits defining how others should be treated in the pursuit of our own preferences. We no longer share a set of criteria for judging the ends that individuals should pursue.

The effect of this deracinated, emotivist context upon our selves deeply troubles MacIntyre. We see ourselves as detachable from every and any social context. We have become, to use Taylor's language, punctual, disengaged beings wont to choose whatever alternative pops into our minds (Taylor 1989a, 171–72). Moreover, lacking standards for what we should want means that only a very narrow set of character types are available to us. If we look at our fellow modern humans, MacIntyre suggests, we will see three dominant character types: the rich aesthete, the manager, and the therapist (MacIntyre 1984, 30). MacIntyre describes the aesthete as "those insolent scoundrels of the philosophical imagination, Diderot's Rameau and Kierkegaard's 'A,' who lounge around so insolently at the entrance to the modern world" (73). The aesthete is cynical, constantly threatened with boredom, and more than willing to use others for the achievement of his own, usually desultory, satisfactions. The manager, on the other hand, is a character who sees conflicts of values as beyond the reach of reason. The manager's only concern is efficiency and effectiveness; she is quite willing to use others to secure whatever ends are given to her. Finally, the therapist, like the manager, also takes ends as given and hence also dissolves the distinction between manipulative and nonmanipulative interaction. The central concern of the therapist is effectiveness in "transforming neurotic symptoms into directed energy, maladjusted individuals into well-adjusted ones" (30). In *After Virtue*, MacIntyre argues that we have become these kinds of people largely because of the success of liberal democratic culture. These are the only characters available to us because what has been forged by this culture is an emotivist self (33).

As others have pointed out, MacIntyre's argument suffers from a serious ambiguity: Was he concerned with the lack of community in liberal democratic culture or was he concerned with the quality of the community that exists (Neal and Paris 1990, 422; Walzer 1990, 7–11)? If MacIntyre was arguing that contemporary culture lacked community, then he was also conceding that it is still possible to have a language, a conception of the self, and a form of political life without the communal ties he insists are necessary for human action. This route, obviously, would undermine the communitarian belief that humans are necessarily situated, social animals. If, on the other hand, MacIntyre was pointing to the thinness or impoverished nature of the community, then the communitarians had to concede that even the liberal tradition spawns a community.

This would mean that the communitarians would then have to provide a standard by which this liberal community could be judged inferior to some other community.

A similar ambiguity attended the communitarian critique of the kind of self produced in modernity: Could modernity really foster selves that were emotivist through and through, or is the emotivist self nothing more than a misunderstanding of what we actually are? In the former case we are plastic enough to be disaggregated into fragmented, atomistic creatures. In the latter, liberal democratic culture encourages us to think that we are detached, atomistic individuals, but in actuality we are something quite different. Part of the bracing feature of *After Virtue* was that it seemed to suggest that we really lacked community and that we really were these emotivist beings.

The Impoverished, Unreflective Self

This ambiguity seems to have been resolved in the more recent work of MacIntyre and in the writings of Charles Taylor. MacIntyre's *Whose Justice? Which Rationality?* (1988) and Charles Taylor's *Sources of the Self* (1989a), do not claim that contemporary culture produces a freely floating atomistic self. Rather, they argue that this culture produces a self that is constituted by a unique set of historical traditions and moral sources yet also drawn away from or blind to those traditions and sources. The kind of self modern culture produces is objectionable because it so rarely taps into the deeper, richer, broader aspects of its own identity (See also Bellah et al. 1985, 21). Michael Sandel's work also echoes this sentiment. Although Sandel deals only obliquely with the effects of what he calls the procedural republic, he argues that the liberal understanding of the unencumbered self is not without its consequences. He suggests that "it is as though the unencumbered self presupposed by the liberal ethic had begun to come true—less liberated than disempowered, entangled in a network of obligations and involvements unassociated with any act of will, and yet unmediated by those common identifications or expansive self-definitions that would make them tolerable" (Sandel 1992, 92). The point is that we are encouraged to think of ourselves as atomistic or emotivist beings even though our identities far exceed what commercial, capitalist, bureaucratic societies usually celebrate. In a peculiar way, the soulcraft of liberal democracy is a surface phenomenon. We are being made to appear to our selves in a way that is untrue. It is this appearance that is corrupting or narrowing. It is this understanding that must be brought back into line with what we truly are.

Similarly, the argument is no longer that contemporary liberal democratic culture lacks community, but that it possesses a particularly narrow understanding of community. As in the case of the self, the communitarians argue that our historical traditions reveal the availability of a much richer conception of community, if we only take the time to discover it. In both cases the radical alternative of the communitarian critique has been moderated.

For the moment, it is important to note that this clarification of the communitarian critique also affects how the modern self should be characterized. Instead of rich aesthetes, managers, and therapists, MacIntyre now focuses upon characters with different levels of reflection. To understand this new typology, it is necessary to first understand that in modernity we (i.e., those living in North Atlantic communities) are confronted not with an emotivist culture, but with "a set of rival intellectual positions, a set of rival traditions embodied more or less imperfectly in contemporary forms of social relationship and a set of rival communities of discourse, each with its own specific modes of speech, argument, and debate, each making a claim upon the individual's allegiance" (MacIntyre 1988, 393). The rival intellectual traditions include not only Aristotelianism, Augustinianism, and the Scottish Enlightenment, but also modern liberalism.[4] How you respond to these diverse traditions depends upon who you are and how you understand yourself. Given this situation, MacIntyre's argument implies that there are now four different kinds of characters produced by modern culture (394–98). The first type of person, although not explicitly mentioned by MacIntyre, is the logical endpoint towards which he wants us to strive. Such a character is reflective, self-confident, and immersed in one of these traditions. This kind of individual can be contrasted to a second type of individual who has been raised within one community of discourse, but has not reflected very deeply about what it entails or intimates. When presented with a fuller exposition of this intellectual tradition, he or she will see it as an occasion for self-recognition. A third kind of person is someone who stands outside of all traditions and appears to resemble what MacIntyre had formerly called the rich aesthete. MacIntyre now sees such a person as portrayed more frequently in "modern literary and philosophical texts" than actually existing in everyday life (397). For such an individual to move from one tradition to another would literally require a conversion. But it is the fourth and last character that most interests MacIntyre. This type of person lies "betwixt and between" traditions (397). Such a person's identity is fragmented across intellectual traditions in such a way that he or she draws upon different conceptions of

---

[4] MacIntyre, of course, does not see this list as exhaustive.

justice on different occasions. This kind of individual compartmentalizes the self to prevent conflicts between traditions (397). Because this type has not pledged allegiance to one tradition, however, its representatives are more open to the possibility of being made aware dialectically of their present position and of the greater richness of a particular tradition (398). Bringing them into one tradition may be the intended purpose of *Whose Justice? Which Rationality?* In setting out these kinds of characters, MacIntyre has both clarified and modified what is objectionable about the kind of person produced in modernity.

Charles Taylor has taken a different look at modernity. He argues that the dominant, bureaucratic, capitalist, commercial culture celebrates only one moral source, disengaged reason, and downplays other important moral sources: nature and God (Taylor 1989a, 495–96). As in MacIntyre's argument, this culture stultifies, disempowers, and narrows our selves. In contrast, Taylor does not claim that this narrowed person is objectionable because of the content of his or her beliefs. For our current beliefs in such things as disengaged reason, self-responsible freedom, and instrumentalism are important parts of our modern identity, and should not be dismissed out of hand.[5] Rather, the problem is that the modern self takes these things as the only components of modern identity, which is a mistake not without consequences. Taylor argues that the experiential effects of what he calls an instrumentalist society have been cataloged and expressed in various ways by Schiller, de Tocqueville, Kierkegaard, Marx, Nietzsche, Weber, Rilke, the Frankfurt School, and the student movement of May 1968 (500–501). These effects include an exclusion of heroic virtues, a dissolving of traditional communities, disenchantment, a separation of reason from sense, a fragmentation of community, and a loss of depth and solidity in our surroundings. Taylor summarizes aspects of these effects when he writes that "the individual has been taken out of a rich community life and now enters instead into a series of mobile, changing, revocable associations, often designed merely for highly specific ends. We end up relating to each other through a series of partial roles" (502). In a sense, the self is fragmented across a series of roles and seen as detachable from a more encompassing communal life. As with MacIntyre, Taylor believes that modern iden-

---

[5] Michael A. Mosher chides both Sandel and Taylor for having Hegelian sympathies, but they lack "the master's institutional affirmation of modernity and overlook his claim that institutions must express both commitment *and* reflexivity" (Mosher 1991, 297). While this may be true of Sandel (although I have my doubts), it certainly is not true of Taylor. Taylor does attempt to accommodate both embeddedness and the idea of reflexivity. Consequently, Taylor would agree with the claim that "every definition of a particular self that requires a description of its embeddedness in a specific moral space is not an argument against the 'disengaged' self; for detachment is itself a situated and socially sanctioned practice, which could not survive without roots in a culture" (ibid., 296).

tity far exceeds modern self-understandings. We are selling our identities short. But in Taylor's view, the defenders of modern identity are not the only ones to succumb to this temptation. The critics of modern, instrumental society also tend to overlook important aspects of our identities that have been formulated and celebrated in modernity. The problem with many of the critics of modern identity, and here Taylor may be referring to MacIntyre, is that they ignore the goods that form part of instrumental society and turn only to more expressive, anti-Enlightenment conceptions of the good. Taylor sees these critics of modernity as potentially fragmenting the self in yet another way insofar as they forget theistic sources of modern identity (509–10). For Taylor, the problem is that both critics and defenders of modernity fail to understand the breadth of modern identity. They are unwilling to take on a larger package of goods that constitute who we are (511).

Fragmented Narratives

Despite these differences between communitarians, they all agree that the modern self is alienated from a sense of community. They all see this fragmentation reflected in the unintegrated roles that we adopt and the characters we acquire. A further form of atomization that the communitarians seek to bring to light concerns how we understand our identities across time. MacIntyre claims that there are social obstacles to seeing oneself in terms of a whole life. The problem, according to MacIntyre, is that modernity "partitions each human life into a variety of segments, each with its own norms and modes of behavior. So work is divided from leisure, private life from public, the corporate from the personal. So both childhood and old age have been wrenched away from the rest of human life and made over into distinct realms" (MacIntyre 1984, 204). Unlike the alienation of the self and community or the fragmentation of the self into various roles or parts, this form of fragmentation occurs across time. Modern society discourages us from seeing our lives as a whole. It thus becomes difficult, if not impossible, to engage in the quest for what we see as good in life. It is as if certain things are supposed to happen to you when you are young, different experiences occur when you are an adolescent, and so on into old age. We lack stories that tie these experiences and expectations together. We move from one stage to the next without being able to see the whole, without understanding our pursuit of the good. Life becomes a bland march to death, simply doing one thing and then doing another.

A similar idea is implied by Taylor's notion of the disengaged, unitary, punctual self. This understanding of the self is incompatible with the need to establish a unity over time (Taylor 1989a, 49–51). The punctual self lacks such a need because it defines itself solely through self-awareness. As a tight, unitary center of control, the disengaged, punctual self always knows what it is: it is that which has an immediate knowledge of itself. Story telling is not a component of its self-understanding as it defines itself outside of any social and moral framework. To see oneself punctually is to be unconcerned with drawing one's life together into a grand story.

For MacIntyre, the effect of this fragmentation over time is that it makes it more difficult to realize our excellences or virtues. Without a unified biographical narrative we cannot see our lives as moving towards an ultimate goal or telos. Without an encompassing narrative, Taylor argues that our lives lack meaning and fullness. To the extent that an instrumental society encourages disengaged reason and punctuality, we will be blind to the challenge of crafting our lives into harmonious, unified stories (47–50).

Our Predicament

The communitarians are much less clear about how we have arrived at "our present predicament" (Bellah et al. 1985, 26). The very idea that we are now in a predicament implies that we once were not, and for many communitarians, our present self-understandings are impoverished when compared to what was available in the past. In *After Virtue*, for example, MacIntyre argues that we have pretty much lost the appropriate sense of our selves acquired during the Middle Ages. MacIntyre, showing a strong attachment to the past, offers an apocalyptic tale of a society in which science is blamed for a series of environmental catastrophes. Consequently, its texts are burned and scientists are executed. What remains are merely fragments of a form of knowledge. For MacIntyre, this tale serves as a metaphor for what he takes to be the present state of moral understanding. Medieval communities that were once united by a powerful sense of telos gave way to the fragmentation of the Enlightenment. Perhaps the present disorder of our moral discourse arose out of some great catastrophe—e.g., the wars of religion—that was blamed upon ancient and medieval philosophies and religious teleologies. As per his apocalyptic story, even though we have broken the tablets, fragments of these earlier beliefs and codes are still found in our language.

Not all communitarians are committed to this view of history. Sandel, for example, has avoided appealing to any sort of golden age. Moreover, MacIntyre's more recent work suggests that he has moved closer to Taylor in that he no longer considers the Enlightenment as a kind of second fall from grace. Nevertheless, for both writers, the Enlightenment is still part of a sea change that brought about the thinness of our present culture. Consequently, what remains strong in many communitarian arguments is the notion that a deeper exploration of one's own history will provide a way to recover a better conception of the self. For Taylor, MacIntyre, and Bellah et al., the response to our predicament appears to begin with a form of historical self recovery.

Historical recovery is not the only element in the communitarian explanation of and resolution to "our predicament." Many of the communitarians presume a very powerful connection between philosophic thought and social organization. As Ronald Beiner argues, "MacIntyre, in common with other critics of liberalism, seems to think that we need to get our philosophy right because social reality is a direct or nearly direct reflection of the adequacy or inadequacy of our philosophical beliefs" (Beiner 1992, 76; Holmes 1993, xiv–xv). This assumption animates the claim that the Enlightenment has led to the thinness of our culture. This assumption also accounts for the communitarian attraction to intellectual history. From this perspective, the logical positivists in the first half of the twentieth century were not only describing but (inadvertently?) forging our moral language. Consequently, cleaning up our thinking will go a long way toward improving our social reality.

The idea that improving historical and philosophical thinking are necessary elements for social renewal still does not explain why liberal democracy is implicated in our present situation. Nor does it explain how the present regime generates and sustains our imperviousness to the rich traditions and communities surrounding us. To put it in MacIntyre's terms, how does this regime encourage a fragmentation across intellectual traditions? Or, in Taylor's terms, how do our political institutions and practices encourage the belief that disengaged reason is the sole moral source? For Bellah et al., how is it that we come only to speak with our first language of modern individualism and not with the richer second languages of the republican and biblical traditions? For Sandel, what is it about the procedural republic that encourages us to see ourselves as unencumbered selves when we are actually implicated in webs of duties and relationships that we do not choose? How is this regime implicated in our inability to see our lives as a grand narrative unity? In short, how are we being misled so thoroughly in understanding our selves?

Although communitarians have rarely addressed these kinds of questions directly, it is possible to infer a set of answers from their suggestions for changing the liberal regime. In other words, their recommendations for alternative political and social institutions may also provide a sense of how our present institutions forge these unfortunate self conceptions. The problem is that it is only very recently that communitarians have begun to flesh out alternative institutions. In particular, Bellah et al. in *The Good Society* (1991) and Charles Taylor in "The Politics of Recognition" (1992) have attempted to provide some answers, although in very general terms.

The communitarians suggest that the language of individualism that sustains and fortifies our fragmented self conceptions is itself reinforced by a number of different institutions and practices. There is probably no single explanation for how we got into this "predicament." Rather, the effect of a fragmented self conception is overdetermined. The relevant factors here include such things as the size of liberal democracies and the demands of a commercial economy.

Even though the connection is not as predominant as in earlier republican theories, modern communitarians do link the fragmentation of the self to the impersonal, large-scale character of political institutions. The issue of size actually encompasses a number of concerns, including that of participation and diversity. As the size of a regime increases it becomes increasingly difficult to believe that individual participation makes much of a difference. The result is that apathetic voters and discouraged workers disengage from their surroundings. In addition, increased size may also mean a more diversified population. With more choices and competing conceptions of the good, individuals can be caught betwixt and between different ways of life. Part of the problem with liberalism, for the communitarians, is that it encourages a withdrawal from public life and a proliferation of traditions and moral languages.

While the communitarians, for the most part, have not embraced the notion that small is beautiful, this sentiment is not completely absent from their writings. "What matters at this stage," MacIntyre argues, "is the construction of local forms of community within which civility and the intellectual and moral life can be sustained through the new dark ages which are already upon us" (MacIntyre 1984, 263). In contrast, the more common sentiment is that even if size is a problem, the solution is not to be found in small, homogeneous regimes. Bellah et al. explicitly back away from the claim that communitarianism allows only face-to-face communities (Bellah et al. 1991, 6). Taylor argues that diverse traditions and minority cultures should be recognized and legitimated within the framework of present institutions. Communitarians have attempted to mitigate the problems associated with size by suggesting mechanisms that would increase the quantity and quality of participation. Bellah et al. talk of inspiring vigorous party competition to increase voter participation. More vaguely, they also suggest that "the federal government needs to encourage new institutional arrangements that engage individual citizens and organized groups to become active participants in planning and administration" (143). As with other participatory theorists, the idea of participation is not primarily a mechanism for conveying individual interests into the political process, but a practice that transforms and educates the citizenry (143–44). The key transformative property is that citizens replace their highly self-interested, individualized notion of governing with a concern for the collective good, the commonweal.[6] Participation is meant to connect the individual to the larger community.

In pointing to the effects of commerce, the communitarians can draw upon another very powerful theme found in their republican roots. As with problems associated with size and participation, however, this theme is also altered significantly. For example, modern communitarians do not argue, as did earlier republican theorists, that the luxury that accompanies commerce renders its citizens soft and cowardly. Neither do they argue that it leads to a kind of dependence on foreign goods that deprives the republic of its freedom to act. But they do argue, again as previous republican writers did, that a system of unrestrained markets and capital accumulation results in deep inequalities that fragment society into hostile classes (89, 105). Moreover, a system of free enterprise distracts its participants away from what they hold in common or share and focuses them on individual acquisition and gain. We mistakenly believe that all public virtues are the result of private vices: that the pursuit of our economic satisfactions will inevitably improve the whole (86). The dominance of market relations reinforces the mistaken belief that our traditional ways of life are revocable. In the whirlwind of change that commerce brings, we lose our connections to the past, to the future, and to each other. We see ourselves "punctually," that is, outside of time and without deep linkages to others. Finally, under the tyranny of the marketplace, we engage in tasks and are told to do things with little input and participation of our own. Much of our daily lives is taken up by the anxious pursuit of material advancement, over which we have little control.

In offering a conception of economic democracy, Bellah et al. have attempted to shift us away from our present reliance upon the language of Lockean individualism and to restrain the power of property. They suggest increasing the social ownership of corporate wealth or providing a guaranteed minimum income to furnish greater security for everyone (104). The point is to "give everyone a stake in the increase of productivity in the economy" (104). Furthermore, we need to remind ourselves of the social nature of work and to provide the legal and economic reforms that encourage greater social responsibility on the part of corporations. Bellah et al. seek to "relieve the competitive, anxious self-assertiveness of

---

[6] Sandel is looking for a community that "would engage the identity as well as the interests of the participants and so implicate its members in a citizenship more thorough-going than the unencumbered self can know" (Sandel 1992, 84–85).

this individuated self. . . . What we seek is a more socially grounded person in a more democratic economy" (106). Clearly, the communitarians are not revolutionaries. They respond to what they see as the fragmentation of our selves with the reform of large-scale political and economic institutions.

The Classical Political Rationalists

The second set of arguments that advance the thesis that liberal democracy fosters an objectionable kind of person can be found in the writings of Leo Strauss and his students. United by a desire to recover ancient Greek notions of reason and nature, these political philosophers have been called classical political rationalists by one of Strauss's students (Pangle 1989). On the face of it, this project looks similar to the communitarian endeavor. Indeed, both kinds of critics see present intellectual life as impoverished when compared to the past. Both the communitarians and the classical political rationalists place much of the blame for this impoverishment on the Enlightenment and modern liberal thought. Both look to intellectual history and philosophy to help recover a richer political life in which the notions of virtue and telos are taken more seriously. For the classical political rationalists, in fact, this historical recovery is meant to be a rebirth of classical rationalism. Finally, both see the effects of modernity as reaching into and ultimately distorting or harming our identities.

Despite these similarities, classical political rationalists part company with the communitarians over the source and validation of standards. Unlike the communitarians, the classical political rationalists do not see community and tradition as foundational validations of human action. A community and its standards cannot be self-validated; their validation can only come by reference to the idea of the good community as such. The classical political rationalists argue that we must be open to the possibility that there is a natural standard establishing what is good and bad, right and wrong, noble and base—a transcommunity, transhistorical standard by which to rank any given set of communal norms and practices.[7]

---

[7] Such standards are not entirely absent from communitarian writings. As Connolly points out, Taylor's communitarianism is supported by the perception of a deeper bent or purpose to human life (Connolly 1991, 89). In discussing the idea of a teleological philosophy, Taylor writes, "But if we mean by this expression that there is a distinction between distorted and authentic self-understanding, and that the latter can in a sense be said to follow from a direction in being, I do indeed espouse such a view. And that makes up a big part of my 'ontology' of the human person" (Taylor 1985, 385). This idea of a natural bent or purpose seems to push Taylor's position closer to classical political rationalism.

Second, the classical political rationalists also differ from the communitarians in the language that they use. Not only do they place greater weight upon notions such as nature and natural right, they also focus on the idea of a soul and not the self. Recovering the idea of the soul is meant to reinforce the attempt to understand the given, unchosen character of what we are as human beings. The self is a modern invention, a creature of history and culture (Bloom 1975, 660; Strauss 1968, 261). The preference for soultalk harkens us back to the claim that nature may be able to provide a standard for judging the character and quality of communal life.

Finally, the communitarians focus upon the notion of unity and its loss in modernity. This idea of unity covers several different themes: unity between the self and the community, unity within the self, and unity of the self over time. In contrast, the classical political rationalists appeal to notions of order and hierarchy for critical leverage on the state of the modern soul, one that is portrayed as disordered and impoverished. Our souls are disordered because the relativism regnant in our liberal democratic regime stifles our erotic pursuit of truth. We no longer attach much weight to reason and we have lost a sense of eros: we are effectively deadening the desire to know the whole and experience completion (Bloom 1987, 132–37). We are taught that either there is no such thing as truth about nobility and baseness or that any truth there might be is beyond our faculties. This lament presupposes that there is such a thing as a soul, that the soul has various longings, that these longings can be ordered in a particular way. In short, there is a natural hierarchy to the soul and its pursuits that is disrupted by the institutional structures and cultural milieu of liberal democracy.[8] To understand why this is so, it is necessary to consider the position classical political rationalists have taken vis à vis liberal democratic theory and practice.

Assessing Liberal Democracy

Classical political rationalists make a distinction between the best regime in theory (or "in speech") and the best regime in practice. The distinction is important because it sets out the way Strauss and many of his

---

[8] Strauss wrote, "The different kinds of wants are not a bundle of urges; there is a natural order of the wants. Different kinds of beings seek or enjoy different kinds of pleasures. . . . The order of the wants of a being points back to the natural constitution, to the What, of the being concerned; it is that constitution which determines the order, the hierarchy, of the various wants or of the various inclinations of a being" (Strauss 1953, 126–27). It is important to note that Strauss is taking the idea of *want* very broadly. Reason involves wanting to know something.

students rank and judge political regimes. One of the lessons that Strauss and Bloom have taken from Plato's *Republic* is that the best regime is a regime in which the best rule (Bloom 1968; Strauss 1964). According to Plato, the best regime is one ruled by philosopher-kings. As many classical political rationalists interpret him, Plato argued that this best regime is only best in theory. To attempt to put it into practice would be disastrous. In practice, the best regime is one in which "a wise legislator frame[s] a code which the citizen body, duly persuaded, freely adopts" (Strauss 1953, 141). According to Strauss, the classical writers had a fairly good idea of what this constitution should look like (a mixed regime) and who would best be able to serve as caretaker for and executor of the law (gentlemen). More importantly, what is best in theory remains a standard for judging what is practically best. A regime that comes closer to the best regime given the stubborn realities of politics (the need to convince the people) and circumstance (the level of wealth and stability), will be judged superior to a regime that does not come as close.[9] Consequently, a liberal democracy in a given set of circumstances is worthy to the extent that it approaches the standards set by the best regime.[10] For example, Pangle argues that "the excellences of democracy, like its weaknesses, are clearly viewed, are seen for what they truly are, only when democracy is studied in the light of the standard set by aristocracy" (Pangle 1989, xx).

[9] The theoretical regime plays two important parts in how Strauss and others have understood the possibilities and limitations of politics. Theory provides a standard by which to judge the practical possibilities and also serves as a cautionary tale (Pangle 1989, xx).

[10] What classical political rationalists actually think about liberal democracy has been subject to some dispute. Although there are important differences between Strauss's students over this issue, all would agree that classical political rationalism does not offer an unqualified endorsement of contemporary liberal democratic politics. Critics of classical political rationalism have repeatedly asked whether they have any real admiration for this regime at all. For example, Strauss has been accused of being unfriendly to liberal democracy (Holmes 1979; 1993; Rothman 1962, 352). This charge has also been leveled against Strauss's students, most recently in reviews of Allan Bloom's *The Closing of the American Mind* (Barber 1988; Nussbaum 1987, 25).

On this point, defenders of classical political rationalism admit that they do have something of a problem. After all, democracy is not ranked very highly by any of the thinkers who originally defined rationalism—Socrates, Xenophon, Plato, and Aristotle (Pangle 1989, xii). Even more troubling is that Strauss and many of his students seem to endorse the idea that the best regime is a regime in which the best rule. Because those most capable of ruling are the wise, the best regime is not democracy.

Although classical political rationalists are clearly critical of liberal democracy, they have endorsed its practices repeatedly and see it as far preferable to the fascist or communist regimes that emerged in the twentieth century. Strauss wrote that "liberal or constitutional democracy comes closer to what the classics demanded than any alternative that is viable in our age" (Strauss 1963, 207; 1968, 24). As Hilail Gildin puts it, Strauss offered "unhesitating support" but not "unqualified approval" of liberal democracy (Gildin 1987, 93, 94, 100).

In judging the quality of liberal democracy by how it lives up to standards of aristocracy, the classical political rationalists are, of course, not understanding aristocracy as based upon land or wealth. As they use the term, aristocracy is based on the development of human excellence. More specifically, support for liberal democracy turns on its ability to foster virtue, both intellectual and moral.[11] The idea is that our judgment of liberal democracy, as with any regime, should be based upon the health of the souls that it has a hand in producing. Accordingly, "the healthy soul is the standard for the judgment of regimes and the key to understanding them; the healthy regime is the one that allows for the development of healthy souls" (Bloom 1968, 414).[12] Their criticism of present liberal democratic culture is that it is increasingly hostile to the conception of a healthy soul. At this point, their argument runs along two tracks; first, the regime makes it difficult for human beings to realize their virtues; second, by abandoning a notion of a healthy soul, this regime undermines a necessary condition for its own survival. If the first argument is grounded upon virtue, the second is based upon prudence. For the classical political rationalists, I would claim, priority is granted to an argument grounded upon virtue, for prudence carries weight only to the extent that the regime is worthy of preservation.

If the worthiness of liberal democracy turns on its ability to foster

---

This kind of endorsement is generally interpreted by critics of classical political rationalism as smoke meant to conceal the classical political rationalists' real beliefs. A much simpler explanation is that at the level of theory classical political rationalists generally see alternatives that are superior to liberal democracy, but at the level of practice liberal democracy is the best that we can do.

[11] This is clearly a departure from Plato's view of democracy. For Plato, "democracy is not designed for inducing the non-philosophers to attempt to become as good as they possibly can, for the end of democracy is not virtue but freedom, i.e. the freedom to live either nobly or basely according to one's liking" (Strauss 1964, 132).

[12] It should be noted that to modern ears this seems to be a strange way to justify democracy because it attributes no value to the role of consent. In contrast to other traditional defenses of liberalism (e.g., those of Hobbes and Locke), classical political rationalists do not see consent, either actual or hypothetical, as a sufficient condition to legitimize a regime. However, they do see it as a practical necessity. Strauss, following Plato, tells us that the wise are few and the many are not particularly sympathetic to the wise. Pangle notes that the "primary and simplest" answer as to why the classics believed that consent was important "is that the majority are in virtue of their numbers superior in *strength* to the minority: the nature of political life is such that, in some measure, might makes right—or, at any rate, might cannot be denied a decisive voice" (Pangle 1992, 108). Because of the power of the many, it is unreasonable to assume that any regime will be sufficiently stable without their support. For the classical political rationalists, the notion of consent that is so central to much of seventeenth- and eighteenth-century liberalism is primarily, although not wholly, a concession to practicality.

virtue, then it is useful to clarify the classical political rationalists' arguments by distinguishing between intellectual and moral virtue. Intellectual virtue refers to the quality of the life of the mind. The exercise of intellectual virtue entails the pursuit of what Strauss called "first things" through contemplation, reason, and conversation. The central intellectual virtue is, of course, wisdom and its primary engagement is philosophy. In contrast, moral virtue refers to the quality of our interactions with one another. That is to say, do "we act justly and bravely and display the other virtues, observing what is due to each person in all contracts and mutual services and actions of every kind, and in our feelings too" (Aristotle, *Ethics*, 331)? It appears that all classical political rationalists see the ability to foster both of these virtues as an important criterion for judging a regime. However, there is some dispute within classical political rationalism over whether one of these forms of human excellence is superior to the other. The ranking of these virtues does affect how liberal democracy and the kinds of criticisms leveled against it are judged.

Moral Virtue and Liberal Democracy

All classical political rationalists emphasize the connection between politics and the production of moral virtue. Allan Bloom summarizes this perspective when he writes that a democracy must "produce men and women who have the tastes, knowledge, and character supportive of a democratic regime" (Bloom 1987, 26). More directly, Hilail Gildin argues that "it would be a mistake to conclude that Strauss cared about the fate of constitutional democracy only to the extent to which it was linked to the fate of philosophy" (Gilden 1987, 92). Insofar as liberal democracy is able to foster "political stability and political moderation," it is also seen as worthy (94).[13] Similarly, Stephen Salkever argues that the central virtues of liberal democracy are that it engenders a sense of liberality and independence within the citizenry (Salkever 1990, 218–19). From this perspective, the character of liberal democracy turns on whether it encourages a moderate, liberal people.

The possibility that liberal democracy fosters moral virtue depends upon whether it can provide preconditions such as a necessary level of wealth and political stability.[14] But even these conditions are not suffi-

---

[13] According to Jaffa, "Strauss cared about the fate of liberal or constitutional democracy and about Israel, as a moral and political man, as he cared about the fate of philosophy, as a philosopher. Indeed, *political* philosophy meant precisely the combination of these concerns, rightly understood" (Jaffa 1984, 15).

cient. Within the writings of classical political rationalists, it is not difficult to find assessments of current liberal politics that see it as failing to
sustain and reproduce a morally virtuous citizenry.[15] For these writers,
this "crisis" of morality in the United States manifests itself in a number
of ways: loss of a sense of order, the manipulation of the public agenda
by special interest groups, a lack of a public sense of the good, political
apathy, erosion of labor unions, disintegration of the family, decrease in
the appreciation of serious art, the decay of cities, and the consumption
of drugs (Deutsch and Soffer 1987, 2; Pangle 1992, 79–80). In theorizing
about this state of affairs, classical political rationalists continually return
to two thinkers, Alexis de Tocqueville and Friedrich Nietzsche, who provide the central concepts for criticizing the state of moral virtue within
liberal democratic culture. From Tocqueville the classical political rationalists draw upon the idea of individualism (Bloom 1987, 84, 86, 129;
Mansfield 1991, 209; Pangle 1992, 80; Salkever 1990, 31, 245), and from
Nietzsche they appropriate the idea of the last man (Bloom 1987, 197;
Pangle 1987, 201–8).

According to Tocqueville, individualism "is a calm and considered
feeling which disposes each citizen to isolate himself from the mass of his
fellows and withdraw into the circle of family and friends; with this little
society formed to his taste, he gladly leaves society to look after itself"
(Tocqueville 1969, 506). Tocqueville continues by arguing that "individualism at first only dams the spring of public virtues, but in the long

[14] Perhaps the most important prerequisite for encouraging moral virtue is the existence of a minimal level of economic sufficiency. For whatever reasons, liberal democracies
in the West have been able to provide necessary social and economic conditions for moral
virtue. People who are starving or in the grip of civil strife may find it very difficult, if not
impossible, to develop forms of human excellence such as liberality, moderation, mag-
nificence, truthfulness, and so on. Gildin argues that for Strauss, "If, in an economy of
scarcity, the best that one can reasonably hope for is what Strauss called aristocracy, open
or disguised, then in an economy of abundance the best that one can reasonably hope for
is liberal or constitutional democracy" (Gildin 1987, 98). Salkever argues that "Liberal
Democracy is to be understood not simply as popular sovereignty plus limited government,
but as rule by the kind of people who are primarily concerned with personal independence
and an income adequate to achieve this comfortably, rather than victory or glory or salvation" (Salkever 1990, 218–29). Salkever also alludes to the claim that liberal democracies
attempt to foster and emphasize a set of moral virtues that are different from those found
in religious or warrior communities. Virtues found in warrior cultures such as virility, courage, and intense patriotism are not going to be seen as important to liberal democrats as
moderation, liberality, and thrift. Similarly, virtues found in religious communities (e.g.,
piety, devotion, and celibacy) will not have the same public worth in liberal society. Liberal
democracy, Salkever suggests, will encourage the expression of its own virtues. This regime
will be at its worst when "typically liberal vices, such as stinginess or wastefulness or avarice
. . . predominate" (219).

[15] Salkever seems to be one of the few classical political rationalists who consistently
attempts to moderate these cries of crisis (Salkever 1974; 1987; 1990, 248, 260).

run it attacks and destroys all the others too and finally merges in ego-
ism" (507). Democracies constantly risk fostering highly self-interested,
inward-looking persons. When this happens, the citizenry becomes dis-
connected from past and future generations as well as from any concern
with the public good or the commonweal.

Tocqueville argues that the idea of equality links liberal democracy
and individualism. Democrats, it appears, are susceptible of loving social
and material equality, or what is generally referred to as equality of condition, above all else. This love of equality makes individuals increasingly
concerned with whether they have the same goods as other people.
Tocqueville believes that an unremitting concern with equality of condition pulls people away from the public sphere. Unlike a love of freedom,
the love of equality presents a goal that once satisfied leaves a citizenry
who "owe no man anything and hardly expect anything from anybody.
They form the habit of thinking of themselves in isolation and imagine
that their whole destiny is in their own hands" (508).

One cannot exaggerate the strength of the classical political rationalists' endorsement of Tocqueville's analysis. Harvey Mansfield writes, "If
nothing else, the authority of Tocqueville, whose word is worth far more
than our perceptions (because it is based on his), should prompt us to
fear the onset of *individualism*, as he called the disease" (Mansfield 1991,
209). We have created a mass democracy based upon an extreme form
of egalitarianism. We suffer not from an overbearing majority as the Federalists feared, but "an apathetic or disabled majority that does not claim
its rights or cannot exercise them" (182). The immediate effects of individualism, classical political rationalists argue, are conformism, mass culture, and a disaffection with the political process (e.g., low voter turn-
out). In the long run, an absence of civic virtue or public-spiritedness will
lead to stagnation, anarchy, and despotism.

In *Thus Spoke Zarathustra*, Friedrich Nietzsche describes the kind of
person produced by a comfortable, democratic way of life. Nietzsche
calls this person "the last man." For Nietzsche, the last man is the "most
despicable" of beings. The last man asks "'What is love? What is creation?
What is longing? What is a star?' . . . and he blinks." In a world dominated by the last man, "one still works, for work is a form of entertainment. But one is careful lest the entertainment be too harrowing. One
no longer becomes poor or rich: both require too much exertion. Who
still wants to rule? Who obey? Both require too much exertion"
(Nietzsche 1966, 17–18). The last man is someone who lacks love and
values, but is satisfied with his reasonableness and material abundance
(Pangle 1987, 203–5). The product of democratic egalitarianism and
Greek rationalism, the last man is seen by Nietzsche as representing a
powerful tide of mediocrity and base materialism. What is lost in the

culture created by the last man is any sense of human excellence and hence all conceptions of virtue. For the classical political rationalists, "Nietzsche saw before us the specter of a coming world, centered in Europe, of dwarfed homunculi living lives without dedication, without reverence, without shame, without rank, without the sense of tragedy and nobility bred only in suffering" (Pangle 1992, 81; see also Bloom 1987, 197–98).

Unlike Tocqueville's assessment, classical political rationalists do not unqualifiedly endorse Nietzsche's position.[16] Although writers such as Pangle and Bloom subscribe to Nietzsche's description of a banal, mediocre democratic culture, they do not completely subscribe to his diagnosis of the problem or to his solution. Pangle argues that Nietzsche is "a particularly painful thinker for us, the adherents or friends of liberal democracy" (Pangle 1987, 208). Part of the reason for this pain is that it is unclear how far Nietzsche would go in endorsing either liberal democracy or the reestablishment of moral virtues as a response to the last man.[17] Another part of the pain, as we shall see, is that Nietzsche's diagnosis of the problem goes to the heart of rationalism. As Bloom puts it, Nietzsche "argues that there is an inner necessity for us to abandon reason on rational grounds—that therefore our regime is doomed" (Bloom 1987, 197). Nevertheless, the classical political rationalists draw upon the image of the last man to reveal what can be produced by an egalitarian culture.

Clearly these criticisms point to the cultivation of a particular kind of person by liberal democratic culture. Tocqueville's individualism and Nietzsche's last man, suggest unfortunate, twisted characters who have abandoned a notion of human excellence. For Tocqueville, this excellence would entail an engagement in and a concern with politics while for Nietzsche it entails the capacity for noble action. Instead of directly responding to these charges, I will turn to the classical political rationalist arguments surrounding the state of intellectual virtue, because concentrating on intellectual virtue and the rule of reason brings out more fully problems of the nature and ordering of the soul. Moreover, to the extent that the state of moral virtue is a reflection of an intellectual crisis, the problems surrounding intellectual virtue are more urgent. For example, Pangle argues that although moral virtue is a necessary prerequisite for intellectual virtue, this does not mean that we should ignore philosophic education. Following Strauss, Pangle believes that the deeper crisis of the West is an intellectual one. "What most threatens us

---

[16] In his review of Bloom's book, Benjamin Barber notes that "Nietzsche is at once hero and villain, astute cultural critic of bourgeois culture in the abstract, but nefarious corrupter of American youth in practice" (1988, 63).

[17] This is especially true given Nietzsche's idea of the overman (Pangle 1987, 207).

. . . is not unsettling skepticism, or revolutionary discord, or the excesses of passionate diversity, but rather the deadening conformism to a bloodless and philistine relativism that saps the will and the capacity to defend or define any principled basis of life" (Pangle 1992, 213).[18]

Intellectual Virtue and Liberal Democracy

There is a very powerful theme within classical political rationalism that connects the value of liberal democracy fairly tightly to the pursuit of philosophy and intellectual virtue.[19] Pangle argues that "the highest potential of liberal democracy is its capacity to keep alive and even to revere the model of Socrates, the Socratic dialectic, and the Socratic way of life" (Pangle 1989, xii).[20] In other words, liberal democracy is valuable not only to the extent that it encourages moral virtue, but because it provides a space for philosophy through the development and exercise of wisdom.

How is liberal democracy able to do this? Classical political rationalists could point to a number of things. First, liberal democracy permits the expression of wisdom simply because of the freedoms and rights that it protects. As classical political rationalists frequently point out in their reading of Plato's *Republic*, it is only under a democracy that philosophers get to do what they really want to do (Strauss 1964, 131). Second, these freedoms also allow for the possibilities that the wise can influence the conduct of governance. In a liberal democracy, the wise can come in contact with those who have power through various formal and informal means. By teaching in universities, writing books, advising governmental officials, running foundations and think tanks, the wise may have some effect. Third, liberal democracy can provide an environment for pursuing wisdom through its distinction between the public and the private. This division creates a realm in which philosophers can leave politics behind. For some classical political rationalists, the private life of the

---

[18] For Strauss's description of the crisis as theoretical, see Strauss 1975, 98.

[19] In a defense of Strauss against Myles Burnyeat (1985), David Lawrence Levine perhaps set this position out most clearly: "Strauss's political program can be stated simply: he seeks to renew our appreciation for ancient aristocratic virtues in the face of 'the tide of mediocrity' that is the consequence of our democratization of all things. Like Tocqueville and some of the Founding Fathers, he seeks to found a city within a city, an aristocracy within our democracy. In thus educating his readers, Strauss seeks to be an 'advisor to princes' in their choice of lives and political actions" (1991, 204).

[20] See also Drury's interpretation (1988, 29) and Burnyeat's criticisms of Strauss (1985). This interpretation would be consistent with the value classical political rationalists attribute to the philosophical way of life. Tarcov writes, "Strauss tried to show that Plato as well as Aristotle regarded the theoretical or philosophic way of life as fundamentally different from and absolutely superior to the practical way of life" (1991, 12–13).

philosopher is in fact superior to the public life of the politician. Finally, if the best practical regime is one whose founding laws are written by wise individuals, then the writing of liberal democratic constitutions opens up this possibility. In the case of the founding of the United States, classical political rationalists are somewhat divided over the wisdom of the founders (Wood 1988). One of the central questions is whether these founders attempted to embody in our basic constitutional structures truths and natural right as antiquity understood them. Those who see the founders as thoroughly modern in their approach (relying wholeheartedly upon liberal contractual thinkers) diverge from those who see the founders as deriving this modern regime from classical roots. Pangle offers a clear statement of one side of this matter: "I am inclined to believe that our regime and tradition might well be judged a noble, if flawed, republican experiment, whose flaws and nobility both in key respects surpass those of the republics known to antiquity" (Pangle 1992, 155).

A somewhat more optimistic position is offered by Harvey Mansfield, who argues that "a liberal democracy such as ours is the kind of democracy that makes room for outstanding people—for a 'natural aristocracy,' in Jefferson's phrase" (Mansfield 1988, 34). This sentiment occurs also in Strauss's answer to the question, "What is modern democracy?"

> It was once said that democracy is the regime that stands or falls by virtue: a democracy is a regime in which all or most adults are men of virtue, and since virtue seems to require wisdom, a regime in which all or most adults are virtuous and wise, or the society in which all or most adults have developed their reason to a high degree, or *the* rational society. Democracy, in a word, is meant to be an aristocracy which has broadened into a universal aristocracy. (Strauss 1968, 4)

Whether Strauss believed that this universal aristocracy was possible, he did claim that the purpose of liberal education is to "ascend from mass democracy to democracy as originally meant. Liberal education is the necessary endeavor to found an aristocracy within democratic mass society" (5).[21] Education is essential for fostering this aristocracy, and liberal democracy provides the freedoms necessary for the requisite education.[22] In sum, liberal democracy is a worthy regime in this view if it can be connected to the pursuit of the best life humanly possible.

Why do classical political rationalists believe that contemporary liberal democracy fails to engender intellectual virtue? As mentioned earlier,

---

[21] The idea of founding an aristocracy within democratic mass society implies, of course, that mass society is not going to be converted into an aristocracy.

[22] The connection between freedom and philosophy also leads classical political rationalists to see the purpose of freedom as a freedom to reason (Bloom 1987, 39).

the central claim is that "reason has been knocked off its perch," and thus it has become "less influential and more vulnerable" (Bloom 1987, 260). To knock reason off its perch is to disturb the natural hierarchy within the soul. At the very least, this hierarchy consists of reason having a right to rule passion. This hierarchy, however, is neither automatic nor necessary. It requires some effort and discipline to establish the rule of reason. "Civilization or, to say the same thing, education is the taming or domestication of the soul's raw passions—not suppressing or excising them, which would deprive the soul of its energy—but forming and in-forming them as art. The goal of harmonizing the enthusiastic part of the soul with what develops later, the rational part, is perhaps impossible to attain. But without it, man can never be whole" (71). The formation of what Strauss calls the well-ordered soul (Strauss 1953, 128) takes the right kind of cultivation and education. When this education is success-ful, the individual is able to keep down "his lower impulses" (133). The rule of reason is natural only in the sense that it expresses what classical political rationalists believe is best, given what we are as human beings. It is not natural in the sense of coming without a great deal of effort. The problem is that, because present-day liberal democrats have displaced reason, they have effectively surrendered the pursuit of wisdom.

According to Bloom (using very Foucauldian language), "an archeol-ogy of our souls" can give the story of this displacement (Bloom 1987, 239). In this excavation, Bloom claims to have found a great civilization buried within us, a civilization not in the sense of urban dwellers and great works of art and architecture, but rather in the sense of a well-ordered, reason-governed soul. In the past, the ideas of the soul and intellectual virtue were taken seriously. Today, they are not: "We are like ignorant shepherds living on a site where great civilizations once flour-ished" (239). This great civilization of the soul has succumbed to what Strauss called the three waves of modernity. Machiavelli and Hobbes ushered in the first wave, Rousseau the second, and Nietzsche the final wave (Strauss 1975). My concern here is not with the details of this histor-ical narrative, but rather whether this narrative sheds light on the strug-gle over intellectual virtue in modernity.

In the first two waves of modernity, reason's role in the soul is rede-fined vis à vis the passions. Strauss sets out the transformation this way: "In Hobbes, reason, using her authority, had emancipated passion; pas-sion acquired the status of a freed woman; reason continued to rule, if only by remote control. In Rousseau, passion itself took the initiative and rebelled; usurping the place of reason and indignantly denying her lib-ertine past, passion began to pass judgment, in the severe accents of Catonic virtue, on reason's turpitudes" (Strauss 1953, 252). The self of modern rationalism is no longer a "well-ordered soul." Nevertheless, even from its displaced position, reason can still bring us to certain truths about our natures. For both Hobbes and Locke, everyone with a minimal degree of reasoning power can arrive at the same conclusions about the most desirable form of government.[23]

The classical political rationalists, however, believe that this defining move of modernity disrupts the hierarchical politics of identity that antiquity celebrated. Instead of a justified despotism of reason, the new politics of identity is one of balance. Bloom writes, "Americans are Lockeans . . . following moderately, not because they possess the virtue of moderation but because their passions are balanced. . . . From the point of God or heroes, all this is not very inspiring. But for the poor, the weak, the oppressed—the overwhelming majority of mankind—it is the promise of salvation. As Leo Strauss put it, the moderns 'built on low but solid ground'" (Bloom 1987, 167). This politics of balancing passions, both internal and external, has lowered drastically the objectives of political life. Instead of aspiring towards excellence, modern politics is content with self-preservation. This move away from excellence and hierarchy and towards satisfaction and equality is signaled by a general abandonment of the idea of the soul, to say nothing of the ideal of the well-ordered soul. Machiavelli, for example, is read by Bloom as daring men "to forget their souls" (174), Hobbes is read as blazing a trail to the self "without the psyche" (175; see also Mansfield 1991, 108). Descartes is understood as dismantling the soul (Bloom 1987, 177), and Mansfield reads the Federalists as advocating that it "is not the business of government or of the federal government . . . to cultivate virtue and to improve souls" (Mansfield 1991, 139).[24] These claims give rise to the belief that it is not the responsibility of modern liberal democracy to encourage wisdom directly. At most, one could say that liberal democracy should not prevent the expression and development of wisdom.[25]

The prospects for a truly well-ordered soul are diminished even further in the third wave of modernity. Liberal democratic culture has established an intellectual context that does not merely demote rea-

---

[23] Victor Gourevitch argues to the contrary: "By reducing knowledge or science to construction and by placing it in the service of man's needs and desires, that is to say, by subordinating reason to the passions, Hobbes radically breaks with the one feature that the alternatives he is synthesizing have in common: the view that nature is the standard and that theory—and hence the theoretical or philosophical life—enjoys unqualified priority" (1987, 37).

[24] Mansfield also argues that this move away from soultalk was part of a strategy to free individuals from the enslavement to priests "because it was soul and its invisible virtue which gave the priests their handle with which to manipulate men" (1978, 9).

[25] Mansfield asks whether Hobbes, Spinoza, and Locke "correctly reckon[ed] the cost in human irresponsibility—even to their own project—when men are no longer required or expected to take care of their souls[.] The measures these philosophers adopted to contain religion by diminishing the soul seem also to endanger freedom" (1991, 114).

son, but abandons it altogether. The minimal form of rationalism that Hobbes and Locke supported is "hammered by succeeding generations of philosophic critics, beginning with Rousseau and culminating in Nietzsche and Heidegger—critics who advance powerful arguments contending that rationalism is incapable of providing an acceptably profound, diverse, 'creative,' and 'historical' account of what is truly human" (Pangle 1992, 4–5). The most important player in this third wave is Nietzsche, who argues that our ideals and values are the result of will: Great actions create a cultural horizon within which life is possible. Nietzsche, on Strauss's reading, admits that throughout history the maintenance of these creative acts required an appeal to some foundation—e.g., nature, reason, or God—but now such foundations no longer suffice. We have come to realize that ideals are historical, human artifacts. Nietzsche offers us a historical insight that destroys all known ideals (Strauss 1975, 96). For if reason, nature, and God are nothing more than the result of a human will acting at a moment in time, how could they support and justify action? Nietzsche's answer is that "the realization of the true origin of all ideals—in human creations or projects—makes possible a radically new kind of project, the transvaluation of all values, a project that is in agreement with the new insight yet not deducible from it (for otherwise it would not be due to a creative act)" (96).

What is important here is not how Nietzsche tries to move beyond nihilism, but rather his claim that reason cannot provide the answer for how we should live and what is best. Bloom argues that "Nietzsche surveyed and summed up the contradictory strands of modern thought and concluded that victorious rationalism is unable to rule in culture or soul, that it cannot defend itself theoretically and that its human consequences are intolerable. This constitutes a crisis of the West, for everywhere in the West, for the first time ever, all regimes are founded on reason" (Bloom 1987, 196). The implication is not only that Nietzsche has revealed the fundamental crisis of the West, but that he has set the intellectual context of the present period. His words, such as "values," "overman," and "nihilism," have become our words. His perspective that truth is a matter of perspective, interpretation, and historical position has become our cultural horizon. Nietzsche has nearly established our horizon of meaning.

The ambiguous character of the classical political rationalists' relationship to Nietzsche, which we encountered in the discussion of moral virtue, occurs also in considering the idea of intellectual virtue.[26] On the one hand, Nietzsche's perspectivism would seem to exclude the possibil-

---

[26] Bloom argues that "the reconstitution of man in Nietzsche required the sacrifice of reason, which Enlightenment, whatever its failings, kept at the center. For all the charms of Nietzsche and all that he says to hearten a lover of the soul, he is further away from Plato in this crucial respect than was Descartes or Locke" (1987, 207).

ity that the rule of reason and the possession of Truth are possible. On the other hand, classical political rationalists still see Nietzsche, as well as Heidegger, as philosophers: in undermining reason, they still rely upon reason. There is a sense in which, for the classical political rationalists, the real problem is not what Nietzsche and Heidegger have said, but that what they have said has become dogmatic and certain for us. The intellectual milieu that they have created has closed down more than it has opened up. Nietzsche and Heidegger had to struggle with reason in order to displace it—we simply take its displacement as a given. Classical political rationalism expresses both deep admiration for the work of these men and horror at the intellectual context that they have wrought.

Why is liberal democracy faulted for what the classical political rationalists see as the effects of German philosophy? First, liberal democratic theorists have done very little to respond to these arguments and to fortify even the minimal notion of rationality that is found in Hobbes or Locke. This hesitancy is partly due to liberal democracy's reluctance to take responsibility for the character formation of its citizens. As classical political rationalists correctly point out, a central theme of liberal theory is that matters of the soul are not political matters. When government engages in soulcraft, it "encroaches on the sacred private sphere of basic individual rights to liberty and to the pursuit of happiness" (Pangle 1992, 147). Indeed, "liberalism is necessarily laissez faire with regard to the soul" (Mansfield 1978, 11). In a sense, liberal democratic practice is blamed because it has neglected these matters, thus allowing the disorder and impoverishment of the soul.

This neglect became most evident after the Second World War. Bloom argues that the problem was that the United States "was importing a clothing of German fabrication for its souls" (Bloom 1987, 152). Nowhere is this more evident than in the universities where, Bloom believes, the dominant intellectual milieu absolutely rejects the possibility of absolutes. The great liberal virtues of openness and toleration amount to an unwillingness to respond to positions that undermine the possibility of liberal democracy. Liberal culture is becoming dogmatic in its dismissal of positions (such as Strauss's) that attempt to open the possibility that there are absolute truths.

The second reason that liberal democracy should be held responsible for the effects of German thought is that there is allegedly a logical connection between the Enlightenment's abandonment of a classical notion of reason and the form of historicism celebrated, for example, by Heidegger. That is, unlike classical rationalism, modern rationalism self-destructs. The self-destruction of reason may be the "inevitable outcome of modern rationalism as distinguished from pre-modern rationalism" (Strauss 1965, 31). The thrust of this claim is that what eventually flows from the pens of nineteenth- and twentieth-century Germans was already implicit in the writings of seventeenth-century Englishmen.[27] Furthermore, as was true of communitarianism, corruptions of philosophical thought ultimately reveal themselves in corruptions of action.

For the classical political rationalists the only hope for liberal democracy lies in whatever premodern threads it has running through it. For Strauss, "above all, liberal democracy, in contradistinction to communism and fascism, derives powerful support from a way of thinking which cannot be called modern at all: the premodern thought of our western tradition" (Strauss 1975, 98). Only by attempting to recover a premodern conception of reason can liberal democracy encourage human excellence. This recovery, Strauss suggests, is a "pressing duty" for liberals. They must "counteract the perverted liberalism which contends 'that just to live securely and happily, and protected but otherwise unregulated, is man's simple but supreme goal' . . . and which forgets quality, excellence, or virtue" (Strauss 1968, 64). Reason, it would seem, must be restored to its rightful place. As West notes, "Strauss refused to join Nietzsche and Heidegger's farewell to reason. Instead, he wondered whether the disillusionment with reason did not rather stem from the specifically modern understanding of reason. The thinkers who originated the modern project to solve the human problem had rejected the classical understanding of reason" (West 1991, 157–58).[28]

Scholarship and education constitute a central pillar of the recovery of reason. Indeed, classical political rationalists have driven much of the recent debate in the United States over the character of higher education. The best example of this, of course, is Bloom's *The Closing of the American Mind*. Pangle also argues that "the reform most needed as regards the spirit of higher education is the reform of the spirit of higher education, since it is higher education, or the practitioners of higher education, whose outlook is likely to dominate in the long run" (Pangle 1992, 182).[29] Furthermore, in order to be ready for a philosophic education, it is necessary to prepare the ground through appropriate civic and moral education (164). While a liberal education does not guarantee an endorsement of the rule of reason, they believe it does offer the best hope for a rebirth of classical rationalism (Gildin 1987, 100–101).

[27] It is extremely important to note that for both Nietzsche and Heidegger the source of modern nihilism is found deep within the roots of Greek rationalism.

[28] Tarcov, however, notes that "Strauss . . . recognized the danger that the return to classical political philosophy he proposed might be turned into a search for classical recipes for contemporary political concoctions" (1991, 10).

[29] Pangle believes that "American education is today in the throes of an awesome cultural deracination, not only from its own, but from the entire Western—that is, predominantly European—cultural legacy" (1992, 79).

Genealogical Perspectives

The final set of positions that I am going to examine have been loosely termed genealogical. In setting out these positions, I will turn to the work of Michel Foucault and two authors whom his writing has influenced: Judith Butler and William Connolly. Like the communitarians and the classical political rationalists, the genealogists are also troubled by the ways in which our identities are forged in the late twentieth century. As with the other positions, the genealogists construct their criticisms in a distinctive language and conceptual framework. For the communitarians, the ideas of community, the self, wholeness, and narrative are central. For the classical political rationalists, the notions of reason, natural right, the soul, and virtue are key. The constellation of ideas that frame the genealogical position include concepts such as difference, the subject, contingency, resistance, performatives, and discipline. These terms play important roles in how Foucault, Butler, and Connolly each conceive of the production of modern identity.

Genealogists judge the quality of our political life (as well as other social institutions and practices) in part by what it does to our selves. They argue that the modes of governing ourselves (both formal and informal, statist and nonstatist) unavoidably involve soulcraft. Moreover they are highly critical of the forms of selfcraft that have accompanied much of modern and late modern life. However, unlike classical political rationalists who see modern soulcraft as abandoning nature, genealogists see it as constantly reinforcing the ideas of nature and hierarchy. For the genealogists, the problem with modern soulcraft is that it freezes, settles, and naturalizes what is ultimately fluid, changing, and contingent. The hierarchically ordered, naturally given soul that the Straussians seek to recover is, for the genealogists, already and continually imposed upon us through the ideas of the normal individual, a natural gender duality, delinquency, and normal sexuality. Moreover, the genealogists appear to be formulating an ethic establishing a political responsibility to respond to the unfortunate effects of modern soulcraft.

A central feature of this third approach to the problem of soulcraft is its subscription to Nietzsche's notion of genealogy.[30] In an essay on Nietzsche, Foucault argues that the idea of genealogy "rejects the meta-historical deployment of ideal significations and indefinite teleologies. It opposes itself to the search for 'origins'" (Foucault 1984a, 77). By ideal

---

[30] It is not uncommon to use the terms postmodern or poststructural to refer to the kinds of positions that these thinkers adopt. As others have pointed out, however, these labels are frequently used to bundle together positions and elide differences that are deep and persistent (Butler 1992a, 5; Flax 1990, 188; Mouffe 1992, 369–70).

significations, Foucault is referring to notions such as truth, the self, Man, good and evil—terms that are taken frequently to possess a meaning that stands outside of time and place (i.e., an ideal meaning). Genealogy rejects the idea that these terms are absolute, unchanging markers for understanding the past, instead treating them as the effects of historical processes and ideological forces. Similarly, Foucault's conception of genealogy rejects the notion that progress, development, or the final revolution provide an ideal goal towards which history continuously strives. These are those unfortunate "indefinite teleologies" he repudiates. The final aspect of genealogy is its opposition to the search for "origins," which Foucault sees as a search for the pure essence of something. It is a search "directed to 'that which was already there,' the image of a primordial truth fully adequate to its nature" (Foucault 1984a, 78). In this instance, "origins" does not refer to a thing's first appearance or acceptance; rather, it is connected to the search for essences or natures.

If these are the kinds of things that genealogy does not do, what does it do? Whereas the classical political rationalists recoil from Nietzsche's historicism, the genealogists embrace it thoroughly. Foucault argues that when the genealogist listens to history, "he finds that there is 'something altogether different' behind things: not a timeless and essential secret, but the secret that they have no essence or that their essence was fabricated in a piecemeal fashion from alien forms. . . . What is found at the historical beginning of things is not the inviolable identity of their origin; it is the dissension of other things. It is disparity" (Foucault 1984a, 78–79). In Foucault's historical writings, he uses the idea of genealogy as Nietzsche used it in his history of morals. Foucault attempts to provide a study of the emergence and acceptance of a variety of human practices that we take to be self-evidently true or natural. Distinctions such as sick/healthy, good/bad, normal/abnormal, and mad/sane, are obvious targets of genealogical reflection. The objective of genealogy is to uncover the disparate elements and the contingent events that have gone into the formation of these ideas and practices. The genealogist takes the claims that these distinctions and concepts are part of human nature or are set out by divine command not as stopping points but as so much wool pulled over our eyes.

As we shall see, both Connolly and Butler rely upon a genealogical approach in their understandings of modern identity. For example, according to Butler the purpose of a feminist genealogy is to "trace the political operations that produce and conceal what qualifies as the juridical subject of feminism" (Butler 1990c, 5). According to Butler, "genealogy investigates the political stakes in designating as an *origin* and *cause* those identity categories that are in fact the *effects* of institutions, practices, discourses with multiple and diffuse points of origin" (viii).

The central "identity categories" to which she refers here are woman, gender, and sex. The genealogist, opposed to essences and natures, will not see these terms as simply given, possessing the same meaning across time and space. They are not self-evident or ontologically solid. Genealogy attempts to show that at the origin of these terms is not a unitary identity or one pure essence or truth, but a motley combination of things.

The Disciplinary Subject

Even though genealogists use the words *self* and (occasionally) *soul*, their analyses frequently rest upon the idea of the *subject*. What does this term mean? Clearly, the word *subject* serves a number of purposes in Foucault's histories and analyses.[31] One such purpose is that *subject* paradoxically expresses the way in which human beings have become objects of scientific inquiry. Under the watchful eye of the human sciences, we are subjects in the same way that interest groups or political parties are subjects studied by political scientists. Psychology, medicine, and the social sciences have provided us with powerful understandings of ourselves that yield conceptions of what is healthy, normal, and rational as well as what is unhealthy, abnormal, and irrational.

At another level, Foucault's *subject* is opposed to being merely an object. In this sense, we are subjects in having desires, wants, and projects— as opposed to being merely the objects of somebody's desires, wants, and projects. We are subjects by possessing subjectivity. In much of his work, Foucault is concerned with the "different modes by which, in our culture, human beings are made subjects" (Rabinow 1984, 7). The implication is that our subjectivity is not biologically necessary, naturally essential, or ontologically ordered. Being a subject is not part of the furniture of the universe; thus subjects have a history or a genealogy. For example, in the first volume of his *History of Sexuality*, Foucault considered how pleasures were produced by all the talk about sexuality in the last century. We become subjects within a larger set of social practices and discourses.

At a third level, Foucault uses the term *subject* to express our liability or amenability to being subjugated. There is a sense in which Foucault infuses the other two uses with this meaning, giving them a pejorative con-

---

[31] Foucault writes, "There are two meanings of the word *subject*, subject to someone else by control and dependence, and tied to his own identity by a conscience or self-knowledge" (1983, 212). This distinction, however, does not fully account for the ways he uses the term. It does resemble another distinction Foucault makes between the direct and indirect constitution of the self, which will be discussed in chapter 6. For a general discussion of the variety of meanings of the word *subject* see Heller 1992, 269–70.

tent. In other words, Foucault believes that there is something about the effects of the human sciences and the construction of our subjectivity that is subjugating.

What does Foucault's genealogy tell us about the character of our subjectivity and the modes by which it is produced? In modernity, one of the most important of these modes of production is a mild, minute, and insidious form of power that Foucault calls disciplinary power. The result of this power is the disciplinary subject. To understand what Foucault means by the disciplinary subject we must briefly consider his idea of disciplinary power. Unlike understandings of power in which As get Bs to do something they do not want to do or have no "real" interest in doing (Dahl 1957), Foucault's disciplinary power forges the As and Bs (Digeser 1992). Moreover, this form of power does not emanate from one source or from the top down. Rather, it has emerged through the techniques and goals of a variety of institutions and practices. For Foucault, the emergence of this power can be traced to the way we have organized armies, ordered the work place, structured schools, designed hospitals, conceived of prisons, and developed the human sciences. According to Foucault, a diverse set of strategies and mechanisms constitute the human subject. Unlike older forms of power that work directly on the body through torture, chains, locks, and public executions, disciplinary power involves unending examination and observation. Its crowning achievement is a self that seeks constantly to order and organize itself. The social practices that set up the standards for health, normality, and rationality form the template for the organization of the self.[32]

Subjects are not only social constructions, they also do not naturally fit whatever identities are inevitably imposed upon them. Becoming a subject, for Foucault, entails its own form of violence. This violence appears most clearly in our responses to those who are other, those who fail to live up to established standards. To fall outside the range of acceptability is to experience immense social pressure to conform, standardize, and normalize. Foucault suggests that under modernity our social norms have become ever more rigorous, well defined, and encompassing. In so doing they become increasingly difficult to meet and hence generate their own failures. These failures, in turn, seem to legitimize a further and tighter enforcement of the norms. The constant possibility of failing to act normally, rationally, and responsibly leads to a self perpetually engaged in reexamination and discipline.

The disciplinary power that forges the disciplinary subject is both to-

[32] Although there is a sense in which disciplinary power is a central, all-encompassing feature of modern practices and institutions, Foucault also says that "nothing, you see, is more foreign to me than the quest for a sovereign unique and constraining form. I do not seek to detect, starting from diverse signs, the unitary spirit of an epoch, the general form of its consciousness, a kind of *Weltanschauung*" (1991a, 55).

talizing and individualizing (Foucault 1983, 213). It is totalizing in the sense that it brings all aspects of life under its gaze and prods the thoughts, beliefs, actions, morals, and desires of individuals towards the norm. Foucault describes our present situation as one in which we are rendered "normal" and docile through constant observation, threat of exclusion, and self-discipline (Foucault 1977, 227).[33] In *Discipline and Punish*, Foucault asks, "Is it surprising that prisons resemble factories, schools, barracks, hospitals, which all resemble prisons?" (228). The mechanisms of discipline and surveillance first mold the soul and then inscribe conceptions of health, sexuality, and propriety upon the body.

Disciplinary power is individualizing because it is focused constantly upon the various ways in which we actually carry out or potentially can fall short of the governing standards of normality. As the notion of what a normal body, sexuality, attitude, or disposition is becomes more evident, it also becomes easier to identify those who do not fit. One is individualized by falling outside the norm, by not living up to its standards. As Connolly argues, "The sign of a normalizing society is not . . . that everyone becomes the same, but that more and more people deviate in some way or other . . . opening themselves through these multiple deviations to disciplinary strategies of neutralization" (Connolly 1991, 150). The expression and perpetuation of this notion of individuality can be seen in the idea of "permanent record," a file that is never closed:

> In a system of discipline, the child is more individualized than the adult, the patient more than the healthy man, the madman and the delinquent more than the normal and the non-delinquent. In each case, it is towards the first of these pairs that all the individualizing mechanisms are turned in our civilization; and when one wishes to individualize the healthy, normal and law-abiding adult, it is always by asking him how much of the child he has in him, what secret madness lies within him, what fundamental crime he has dreamt of committing. (Foucault 1977, 193)

[33] Foucault's notion of the totalizing aspects of disciplinary power resembles Iris Young's account of the logic of identity. Drawing upon Theodor Adorno, Young writes, "The logic of identity expresses one construction of the meaning and operations of reason: an urge to think things together, to reduce them to unity. To give a rational account is to find the universal, the one principle, the law, covering the phenomena to be accounted for. Reason seeks essence, a single formula that classifies concrete particulars as inside or outside a category, something that is common to all things that belong in the category" (1990, 98). As with the totalizing aspects of power, this urge to find unity and identity has the effect of generating difference. Young argues that "the irony of the logic of identity is that by seeking to reduce the differently similar to the same, it turns the merely different into the absolutely other" (1990, 99). In this limited sense, one could say that the Foucauldian approach is opposed to a politics of identity.

The engagement of both totalizing and individualizing techniques, whether in the name of health, knowledge, truth, or reform, results in the production of the modern disciplined subject.

Resistance is an important term in understanding the formation of the disciplined subject. According to Foucault, resistance always accompanies the exercise of power. Because we are not naturally suited to be one kind of person or another, there is always something about us that resists the imposition of form. We can never be made to fit perfectly into any standard of normality, rationality, or sanity. Complete success in any attempt to forge a particular self is impossible. The dream of disciplinary power is a normal, disciplined self, but the reality will always be checkered by resistance.

Evidence of this resistance can be seen both externally and internally. Externally, individuals who do not fit the norm of modern, rational, responsible, well-ordered subjects are marginalized, and this marginalization forges an identity that serves as a target for more control. As our standards for normality become more rigorous, the production of resistance becomes easier to observe. For example, a tightening of the standards of normality can be seen in the conceptual transformation of the madman from a divinely inspired prophet to a sinner to someone who is ill. The direct target here may be prisoners, deviants, or the sick, but the rest of us become indirect targets. Someone else's marginalization serves as a lesson for us, and we discipline our selves accordingly. Foucault's model for this process is the panopticon, Jeremy Bentham's ingenious prison design in which the jailer can, in a moment, see the status of the prisoners without the prisoners knowing that they are being observed. The perpetual possibility of surveillance forges a self-disciplined prisoner even when the jailer is not in the watchtower, and those desires or wishes that express an internal resistance to this discipline are self-capped and self-controlled. Disorderly, irrational, or irresponsible thoughts are the responsibility of the disciplined self, because we never know when someone may be looking. We become our own jailers and perpetuate disciplinary practices through our own actions.

Disciplinary Power and Liberal Democracy

How is liberalism implicated in the production of disciplinary individuals? Foucault offers little systematic discussion of this relationship. It is clear that the formation of the subject is an effect of a variety of practices that extend beyond the traditional concerns of liberalism. Foucault's discussion of psychiatry, army organization, and the clinic are not specifically linked to liberal politics and culture, and indeed, even his idea of the pastoral state (a state that is concerned with the well-being of each individual) can be applied to modern regimes other than liberal democracies. From this perspective, it appears that liberalism can be held responsible for the disciplinary individual only as much as any form of social organization that has incorporated modern ethical and scientific practices.[34]

On the other hand, Foucault's writings suggest a complex set of connections between disciplinary power and modern democracy. At one point, he argues that "this democratisation of sovereignty was fundamentally determined by and grounded in mechanisms of disciplinary coercion" (Foucault 1980b, 105). Disciplinary power undergirds liberal democratic institutions: "the representative régime makes it possible . . . for the will of all to form the fundamental authority of sovereignty, the disciplines provide, at base, a guarantee of the submission of forces and bodies. The real, corporal disciplines constituted the foundation of the formal, juridical liberties" (Foucault 1977, 222). The freedoms guaranteed by the rule of law and the liberal state require and presuppose the construction of a rational, responsible, disciplined individual. The egalitarian, noncoercive, public, liberating aspects of liberal democracy are accomplished through a nonegalitarian, coercive, private, disciplinary form of power.

Foucault suggests not only that disciplinary power supports liberal democracy, but also that liberal democratic institutions mask and intensify disciplinary pressure. He writes that "we should not be deceived by all the Constitutions framed through the world since the French Revolution, the Codes written and revised, a whole continual and clamorous legislative activity: these were the forms that made an essentially normalizing power acceptable" (Foucault 1980a, 144). The notion of the rule of

[34] Colin Gordon extends this interpretation by arguing that Foucault, in his lectures from the late 1970s and early 1980s, saw the liberal welfare state as even further removed from disciplinary mechanisms. The panopticon is no longer key: "We live today not so much in a Rechtstaat or in a disciplinary society as in a society of security" (Gordon 1991, 20). Liberalism "affirms . . . the necessarily opaque, dense autonomous character of the processes of population. It remains, at the same time, preoccupied with the vulnerability of these same processes, with the need to enframe them in 'mechanisms of security'" (20). Mechanisms of security here refer to matters of social welfare as well as ways of looking at populations that include cost/benefit analysis and a willingness to tolerate a wide band of activity. Gordon also argues that the "disciplinary 'private law' of the factories is in part subordinated to the public norms prescribed in health and safety legislation, in part opened up to collective negotiation with organized labour, and, for the rest, underwritten in the interests of public order as a necessary branch of public law" (33). Nevertheless, Foucault still seemed to think techniques of discipline exist, but they are focused "largely on the organization of its own staffs and apparatuses" (27). Gordon goes so far as to suggest (confirming Jürgen Habermas's suspicions) that Foucault's perspective "may be libertarian, but it is not anarchist" (6).

law, so central to the idea of liberal democracy, has helped extend the reach of disciplinary power into our souls. According to Foucault, "the great continuity of the carceral system throughout the law and its sentences gives a sort of legal sanction to the disciplinary mechanisms, to the decisions and judgments that they enforce" (Foucault 1977, 302). Through the sanction of the law, we come to see the normalizing practices as normal and reasonable. For example, modern criminal law greatly magnifies the normalizing tactics of psychiatry. Foucault presents the law as becoming less concerned with what the defendant has done and more concerned with establishing who the criminal is: his or her nature, background, what psychological mechanisms are at work, and why someone would commit such and such a crime. Judicial authority is fixed upon the offender, not the offense (Foucault 1988a, 140). Its imprimatur makes reasonable and necessary the close interrogation and definition of the offender.

Foucault also suggests that disciplinary power can itself be conveyed by the specific actions of the government. For example, Foucault claims that the object of the state's police power has changed from peace and justice (presumably less disciplinary objectives), to the physical well-being, health, and longevity of the population (Foucault 1980d, 170). With the augmentation of police powers, disciplinary techniques flow more easily into the population as a whole. Indeed, the population itself becomes an explicit object of regulation by the state. This form of "bio-power" concentrates upon the importance of monitoring birth rates, death rates, sexual practices, and public health. All of these things allegedly come to define norms and standards necessary for the totalizing and individualizing aspects of disciplinary power.

The self, then, is forged into a disciplined subject. The production of this self also entails masking or redescribing this activity. The norms and standards that govern this production not only receive the imprimatur of the state, they are also portrayed as natural or given. This naturalization, for Foucault, is accomplished through the various sciences. Truth, knowledge, and power are all connected. Psychoanalysis creates an inner truth or a law of sex that must be discovered and lived up to. The health professions ferret out a conception of how the healthy body must appear and act. Jurists and criminologists establish the standard of rationality. Liberal theorists advance an autonomous, interest-driven individual with broad capacities to choose and control his or her destiny.[35] What is his-

---

[35] David Gruber argues,

If Foucault's insights are valid, liberalism's flaw is not that it has been inefficacious in pressing its agenda on behalf of individuals against modern tendencies that repress individuality and obstruct its potential, but that its rhetoric and its practices are themselves tragically and completely implicated in the burdensome network in which we find our-

torical, contingent, and a function of power is portrayed in this culture as natural and necessary, with the disciplined, normalized self fitting perfectly into our being—without resistance and without remainder. The reality is that everything that does not fit is repressed and rejected, and those repressions and rejections are never finally complete.

The Paradox of Difference

Writers such as Connolly and Butler have picked up and expanded the themes of discipline and naturalization. In so doing they enlarge the arguments regarding how these things are connected to contemporary selfcraft and how we should respond to them. One description Connolly offers of the effects of disciplinary power is in terms of what he calls the paradox of difference: "To possess a true identity is to be false to difference, while to be true to difference is to sacrifice the promise of a true identity" (Connolly 1991, 67). The possession of a "true identity" for Connolly means believing that one's own identity is the right one and those who refuse or resist it are not living up to their natures. It implies that there is a definite human ideal. Accompanying this belief is the temptation to remonstrate, reform, or restrain those who are different. In Connolly's terms, this failure to respect other ways of life is false to difference.

In contrast, being true to difference entails a belief that there is no natural or definite answer to the being of humans: no form of identity exhausts what we ultimately are, and the identities we possess are deeply contingent. But the possession of even a contingent identity requires that we distinguish what we are from what we are not, that we create and define difference. To be true to difference, then, is to acknowledge the deep contingency of identity and to be reluctant to construe what is different as a failure or an evil or as something to be reformed. It does not mean that difference possesses a reality that identity does not. The tragic element of this half of the paradox is that to be true to difference is to abandon the possibility that there actually is a true form of identity.

In the relationship between identity and difference, modern disciplinary power is exercised in the "multiple drives to stamp truth" upon the norms and standards that define our identities (67). The idea of a natu-

---

selves. His observations on the intertwinement of liberalism's individuality with its apparent opposite suggest that the current task for thinking and for action is not yet another attempted revivification and return to the individual, but instead is the rejection of, and resistance to, the individualities that we are, one crucial element of which is liberalism's programs and rhetoric. (1989, 615)

ral identity (e.g., a responsible, rational, self-disciplined, self-interested agent) establishes a norm to live up to or to fall below. As Foucault argues, pursuing that identity in ourselves and in others means the deployment of social pressures and individualizing techniques of disciplinary power. For those who fail to live up to the standards of a true identity, their difference is their misfortune.

If difference is the prime target of disciplinary power, a disciplinary society is one that attempts to resolve the paradox of difference in favor of the truth of identity. In this case, the practical resolution of the paradox means that difference need not command our respect. As we are reassured of the truth of our identities (intrinsically good, rational, normal, coherent, healthy, civilized, safe), we ignore the possible costs of constituting a set of differences as "intrinsically evil, irrational, abnormal, mad, sick, primitive, monstrous, dangerous." Connolly wants to convince us that the failure to respect difference is the same as not being true to difference. In order for this argument to work we must come to believe that difference commands respect. Why should we be concerned about difference?

Connolly here draws on both ontological and genealogical arguments. The ontological argument builds on Foucault's notion of resistance. Connolly argues that life always exceeds whatever identity is imposed upon it:

> internal and external nature contains, because it is neither designed by a god nor neatly susceptible to organization by human design, elements of stubborn opacity to human knowledge, recalcitrance to human projects, resistance to any model of normal individuality and harmonious community. . . . Each worthy design of the normal self, the common good, and justice, while realizing something crucial to life through its patterns of connectedness and interdependence, encounters resistances that inhibit its transparency, coherence, and responsiveness and impede its harmonization with the other elements of life to which it is bound. (31)

For Connolly, the source of resistance is this stubborn opacity that eludes any imposition of a true identity. He frames this idea with the neologism "ontalogy" (Connolly 1993b, 146–51), which is meant to express our inability fully to understand the self given its lack of an organizing purpose or principle. Our being is "a-logos"—there is an excess or multiplicity to the self that can never be fully contained and ordered. Like an inexhaustible unconscious, or a conception of being that transcends identity, Connolly's notion of recalcitrance means that every attempt to craft or resign oneself to one's identity is to cover over other aspects of one's being. Every unveiling is always a veiling.

Clearly, Connolly's ontalogical claim is also normative: Not only does the subject exceed its identity, but that excess should be respected in oneself and in others. "There is more in my life than any official definition of identity can express. I am not exhausted by my identity. I am not entirely captured by it, even though it is stamped upon me—and even though it enables me. This fugitive difference between my identity and that in me which slips through its conceptual net is to be prized; it forms a pool from which creativity can flow and attentiveness to the claims of other identities might be drawn" (Connolly 1991, 120). But is this not just a more complex way to make a claim regarding the truth of identity? Connolly acknowledges that one could *call* this a true identity, but to do so would go far beyond the well-crafted, limited identities that we normally celebrate as true. Just how far it departs from our usual notion of a true identity brings us to his genealogical arguments.

To cultivate the belief that there is nothing necessary about the facets or features of identity, Connolly relies upon genealogy. Genealogy erodes the claim that there is a necessary order to the self. As we have seen, it attempts to reveal the fragmentary character of what was once thought of as a unified whole. As Foucault argues, "Where the soul pretends unification or the self fabricates a coherent identity, the genealogist sets out to study the beginning—numberless beginnings, whose faint traces and hints of color are readily seen by a historical eye" (Foucault 1984a, 81). Genealogy reinforces the sheer contingency of our identities.

The appeal to genealogy challenges attempts to resolve the paradox of difference in favor of the truth of identity. It is meant to instill in us suspicion of any move that sees these entrenched contingencies as natural: "The demand to *ethicize* or universalize the entrenched contingencies on the grounds that they flow from a true identity is a recipe for repression of difference; by treating alternative types of sexuality as immoral, deviant, or sick, it calls upon you to purge any such dispositions lingering in yourself and to support the treatment or punishment of others who manifest them more robustly" (Connolly 1991, 177). The costs of purgation, treatment, or punishment come to light once one has understood the contingent features of identity. Before turning to the question of how we should respond to the effects of disciplinary power, I will briefly take up Judith Butler's argument.

Naturalization

Foucault, as we have seen, is concerned with the production of normalized, disciplined selves. Connolly has similar concerns with true identity and the paradox of difference. In contrast, much of Butler's work has focused upon the pressures to naturalize or reify the categories of gender, sex, body, and self. Her argument is directed towards not only larger societal pressures, but also the demands within feminist theory and practice to draw upon a substantive, essentialist conception of women. In addition, she has taken issue with the desire found within gay and lesbian communities to establish coherent identities (Butler 1993, 113–18). In short, Butler wants to resist the pressures that impose coherence or a nature upon our identities, whatever their source.

In the case of feminism, the pressure to naturalize identities comes from the belief that a such a conception could provide transcultural, transhistorical solidarity as well as legitimize the epistemological standpoint and unique experiences of women. But it is also the case that within the culture itself, the pressure to naturalize our identities is overwhelming. There are, Butler argues, enormous demands to stick to the dominant conceptions of gendered and sexed identities. These demands exist in the form of severe forms of punishments for those who do not fit those roles. She argues that "the category of sex imposes a duality and a uniformity on bodies in order to maintain reproductive sexuality as a compulsory order. . . . I would like to suggest that this kind of categorization can be called a violent one, a forceful one, and that this discursive ordering and production of bodies in accord with the category of sex is itself a material violence" (Butler 1992a, 17). Similarly, the drive to establish a coherent identity is one that pervades society, but it has also shown up in gay and lesbian politics. Even if we do not subscribe to the idea that nature sets a standard for our identities, we may still believe that identity should be coherent. The criterion of coherence means that identities should express an internal consistency and jettison whatever does not fit. For some identities the standard of coherence is a way to establish solidarity in the face of a larger society that rejects and denigrates those identities. Clearly, however, the demand for coherence could be made of any identity, regardless of its social position. Indeed, Butler suggests that this demand can play a role similar to naturalization, especially when it is used by the dominant identities. For example, not merely a natural, but a coherent conception of heterosexuality requires jettisoning or denigrating whatever homosexual desires or impulses we may possess.

The claim that feminists make a terrible mistake when they subscribe to a naturalized conception of gender or sex is not new (Di Stefano 1990, 65). Butler's version of this argument is that the more firmly grounded or well-established the category of woman is, the more exclusive and oppressive it becomes. For example, the belief that this category creates a natural solidarity among more than half of the human population is taken to be not only troublesome, but dangerous. It ignores or disciplines differences between women (race and class) and excludes those (e.g., lesbians and bisexuals) who may contest the natural grounding of the category. In other words, feminism replicates the forms of exclusion and domination that already exist.

Just as unsettling, if not more so, is Butler's distrust of coherence. The problem with coherence is that there are "tacit cruelties that sustain coherent identity, cruelties that include self-cruelty as well, the abasement through which coherence is fictively produced and sustained" (Butler 1993, 115). Any coherent conception of identity falls short of the complexity of our lives. Sustaining that coherence requires that we reject that excess both in ourselves and in others. According to Butler, the standard of coherence presumes that "what a 'subject' is is already known, already fixed, and that that ready-made subject might enter the world to renegotiate its place" (115). Once we have accepted the standard of coherence, we are less likely to see connections between ourselves and others. And the more we multiply coherent identities (coherent heterosexuality, coherent lesbian, coherent gay identities) the more difficulty abject identities will have in organizing politically. The factionalism that Madison celebrated, Butler regards with deep suspicion. That kind of pluralism serves "the regulatory aims of the liberal state" (116). The drive for coherence is but an insidious effect of liberal pluralism to divide and pacify: "When the articulation of coherent identity becomes its own policy, then the policing of identity takes the place of a politics in which identity works dynamically in the service of a broader cultural struggle toward the rearticulation and empowerment of groups that seeks to overcome the dynamic of repudiation and exclusion by which 'coherent subjects' are constituted" (117).

What is distinctive about Butler's position is the way it attempts to nullify essentialism and the presumption of a fixed, pregiven subject. Butler argues that the categories of gender, sex, and the self are not expressive of our nature, but are the result of socially governed performances and practices. For example, gender is not expressed but performed. Just as a promise does not exist before individuals invoke certain social practices and words, our genders are not already present prior to their being performed. However, unlike making a particular promise, which is a discrete act involving the will, gender is an unending, constant affair, one that is only occasionally chosen. The case of gender does resemble promise making to the extent that a promise requires an encompassing set of practices that are themselves kept alive by being invoked repeatedly: the saying of certain words, the exchange of certain signs, the doing of particular deeds all provide a context for specific promises. A promise could not be a single event and make sense; it needs an institutional and conventional context to work.

Similarly, "doing" gender cannot be a singular act. It draws upon a larger set of norms and conventions that identify certain behaviors and ways of being with particular genders. For Butler, what is important is not merely the performative character of gender and the hegemonic form of the conventions that direct those performances, but also the source of the authoritative character of those regularized norms. Our individual actions must appeal to or "cite" these norms in order to be appropriately gendered. The action or gesture must be within the given sets of gestures and actions that are part of the sanctioned repertoire.

The harms and cruelties associated with the dominant identities have led Butler to consider why one set of norms and conventions have an authoritative character and others do not. Is there an original authorization that sanctions these practices? How have we come to see a binary division of gender and sexuality as natural? These kinds of problems have broadened the scope of Butler's analysis. In order to understand the possibilities and limitations of displacing our currently gendered practices, she attempts to understand their foundation or grounding. Butler argues that in the case of gender, we seem to believe that our practices are ultimately grounded in certain undeniable facts: the sexed body, sexuality, psychoanalytic laws, or the nature of matter. These "facts" are meant to put an end to the matter of justification and legitimize our gendered practices. These things appear as the origin and justification of those practices.

Butler argues, however, that how we actually authorize our gendered practices is more complex. Far from being a pregiven source of authority, these foundations are the product of our repeated attempts to ground our conventions. "In other words," she writes, "it is precisely through the infinite deferral of authority to an irrecoverable past that authority itself is constituted. That deferral is the repeated act by which legitimation occurs. The pointing to a ground which is never recovered becomes authority's groundless ground" (108). What does this mean? Perhaps one place to begin is with an assumption that may underlie the argument: we are driven to seek an ultimate justification for our norms and conventions. If this were not true, then it is unlikely that a practice of appealing repeatedly to the ground of authority would ever develop. Second, Butler suggests that any ultimate justification for the authority of our conventions can potentially generate an infinite regress (108). The reason why this may be true is that any justification that we give drawing upon conventions, norms, or even language itself will generate simply another search for their legitimacy. What, I think, follows is a third claim that "perpetual deferral" means that our ultimate justification must therefore be found in whatever exists beyond our conventions (for if it was just another convention, then we could ask what justifies *that*). A fourth element of the argument is that we create a practice of justification by repeatedly assuming the existence of a grounding that is perpetually out of reach. The practice, however, can work only if we repeatedly assume that whatever is perpetually deferred is somehow related to what we are doing (or trying to justify). In a sense, I suppose, we make that grounding in the image that is necessary for the conventions we want justified. This ultimate justification may be the solid facts of the body, or God, or "I," or psychoanalytic laws. Once that grounding is secure in our justificatory practices, then a reversal takes place, for that which was constructed out of our conventions and practices is now portrayed as their source and legitimacy. What Butler calls the practice of citation, "effectively brings into being the very prior authority to which it then defers" (108–9). To bring this discussion back to the problem of identity, the ultimate justification of our identities is not found in some pregiven, irresistible fact about ourselves. Instead, it is found in a grounding that we have constructed and placed in that original position. Not only is the self a result of performances that are demanded and deeds that are done, but those performances are themselves the results of prior performances. Performativity goes all the way down.

These very general comments do not encompass the complexity of Butler's position. An important further element is her claim that the production of gender, sexuality, and a coherent identity is not done without rejecting bodies that are monstrous, genders that are not straight, and identities that are complex. This part of the argument will be considered again in chapter 4.

Parodic Subversion and Agonal Democracy

As we have seen, the genealogists are attempting to contest the disciplining of difference and the naturalization and ordering of identity. They do this through the practice of genealogy and by emphasizing such notions as performativity, multiplicity and contingency. In Foucault's writings, however, there is very little talk about solutions. In one interview he said, "My point is not that everything is bad, but that everything is dangerous, which is not exactly the same as bad. If everything is dangerous, then we always have something to do. So my position leads not to apathy but to hyper- and pessimistic activism" (Foucault 1984b, 343). At most, Foucault sees his writings as giving

> some assistance in wearing away certain self-evidences and commonplaces about madness, normality, illness, crime and punishment; to bring it about, together with many others, that certain phrases can no longer be spoken so lightly, certain acts no longer, or at least no longer so unhesitatingly, performed; to contribute to changing certain things in people's ways of perceiving and doing things; to participate in this difficult displacement of forms of sensibility and thresholds of tolerance—I hardly feel capable of attempting much more than that. (Foucault 1991b, 83)

Despite these rather modest ambitions, the genealogical response to modern sociality is frequently criticized as either entirely too amorphous or desultory. Because it provides little guidance on how to proceed politically, it is taken to be at best an immobilizing and at worst an entirely destructive enterprise.[36]

Both Butler and Connolly have gone farther than Foucault in attempting to respond to the production of modern identity. According to Butler, what is needed, particularly with regard to issues of gender, is "a politics of performative gender acts" based upon what she calls parodic subversion (1990a, 281). Connolly's response to the pressures of disciplinary society is to conceive of a politics that attempts to maintain both sides of the paradox of difference.

Given the performative character of gender identity and the citational features of sexuality, Butler believes that the legitimacy or natural feel to our gendered actions requires that they be repeated and reexperienced (277). If this is true, then the best response would be to refuse to play one's part. This alternative, however, is not available because it suggests that there is an agency that can stand independent of social practice and history. A general refusal would require being able to step completely out of the practices that sustain and enable one's identity. It would presuppose the very conception of the self that Butler's genealogical position precludes.[37]

Ruling out a general refusal, however, does not rule out more limited responses. Butler suggests that the "possibilities of gender transformation are to be found in the arbitrary relation between such acts, in the

---

[36] The standard charges against postmodernism, according to Jane Flax (1992, 446), include: feminism is irreconcilable with postmodernism; postmodernists are a- or antipolitical; they are relativists; they leave us with only the notion of power; they render agency impossible; they write in an obscurantist manner; and they present an all-or-nothing choice. For a criticism of the consequences of Butler's argument see Di Stefano 1991 and Jones 1993. For a discussion of the problems associated with Connolly's agonistic democracy see Digeser 1992. As Colin Gordon notes, the central objections to Foucault's notion of power include the claim that it fails to address the relations between society and the state, it precludes the possibility for individual freedom, and that it leads to an "overall political philosophy of nihilism and despair" (1991, 4). For an argument that takes issue with the consequences of Foucault's argument for feminism see Hartsock 1990. For other criticisms of the political consequences of Foucault's work see Fraser 1985, Habermas 1987, and Walzer 1986.

[37] In contrast, Kathleen Jones interprets Butler as providing us with "fantasies of autogenesis" (1993, 9). This interpretation seems off the mark. In an interview, Butler said that "there is a bad reading [of Gender Trouble], which unfortunately is the most popular one. The bad reading goes something like this: I can get up in the morning, look into my closet, and decide which gender I want to be today. . . . my whole point was that the very formation of person, presupposes gender in a certain way—that gender is not to be chosen and that 'performativity' is not radical choice and it's not voluntarism" (Kotz 1992, 82–83). The question about Butler's position is not whether she ignores our situatedness (Jones 1993, 9), but whether she allows enough room for agency.

possibility of a different sort of repeating, in the breaking or subversive repetition of that style" (271). It appears that the act of repetition always contains some slack that allows for interpretation. How one repeats one's role is constrained, but not completely determined.[38] Our gendered performances are not mechanical processes or algorithms, but rule-governed practices. Consequently, the response to a set of gender roles can come from our interpretations of the provided scripts. The metaphor of the theater is useful in understanding the possibilities and limitations that Butler sees in responding to the rigid naturalization of gendered identities. Butler writes that "just as the script may be enacted in various ways, and just as the play requires both text and interpretation, so the gendered body acts its part in a culturally restricted corporeal space and enacts interpretations within the confines of already existing directives" (277). But what can be done with these scripts? Butler's enigmatic answer is to devise a strategy that is "a thoroughgoing appropriation and redeployment of the categories of identity themselves, not merely to contest 'sex,' but to articulate the convergence of multiple sexual discourses at the site of 'identity' in order to render that category, in whatever form, permanently problematic" (Butler 1990c, 128). By the articulation of "the convergence of multiple sexual discourses at the site of 'identity,'" Butler appears to mean that one combines and substitutes the various kinds of performances that are available. In the case of gender identity, Butler looks to the possibilities of drag as a performance that "subverts the distinction between inner and outer psychic space and effectively mocks both the expressive model of gender and the notion of a true gender identity" (137). In a sense, one engages in a close imitation of the socially approved roles, but in such a way as to call them into question. If naturalization is the problem, then parody provides a response. A subversive performance such as drag is useful in revealing that every performance of a gendered action or quality is an imitation of an imitation. There was never an original, natural gender, against which all of our actions are merely copies. For Butler, being able to engage in parodic performances opens up the possibility for new roles that subvert the natural or essential conceptions of sex and gender.

Butler argues that while parody such as drag can be subversive, it need not be. In the case of drag, parody may point to the constructed character of gender, but it may also reinforce the dominant norms. The de-

---

[38] At times, Butler seems to open up this space for agency (e.g., 1992a, 12–13), and at other times she appears to close it down as when she argues, "Performativity has to do with repetition, very often with the repetition of oppressive and painful gender norms to force them to resignify. This is not freedom, but a question of how to work the trap that one is inevitably in" (Kotz 1992, 84). Is this not freedom because freedom is impossible? Or is it not freedom because freedom is found elsewhere?

naturalization of sex is not a sufficient condition for displacing the prevailing conventions of sex and gender, but she does appear to believe
that it is a necessary condition (Butler 1993, 125). Without an understanding of the performative or citational quality of our identity categories we will continue to deny the cruelties and harms of our current
norms and conventions. The spell of the illusion, Butler's argument suggests, can be broken only by reconceiving what we are. Breaking this
spell may not be enough to change things, but until we can understand
that sex, gender, and the self are human arrangements and not independent forces, we are less likely to dispute or change them.

The political ramifications of Butler's response are fairly open-ended.
Its immediate effect dispossesses feminism and gay and lesbian politics
of a natural, coherent identity that can serve as a rallying point or foundation for political action. Parodic proliferation "deprives hegemonic
culture and its critics of the claim to naturalized or essentialist gender
identities" (Butler 1990c, 138). However, instead of subverting feminism
entirely, Butler believes that her approach subverts a kind of feminism
that demands that the word *woman* signify an essential set of characteristics. But Butler also believes that her argument does not have a necessary
set of political consequences. She acknowledges that a variety of strategies could come from her position (Butler 1990a, 280; 1992a, 8). She is
hopeful, however, that a kind of coalition or democratic politics can be
developed that allows for more fluidity of human identities (Butler
1990b, 339). This spirit of hope is embodied in her claim that

> If identities were no longer fixed as the premises of a political syllogism, and
> politics no longer understood as a set of practices derived from the alleged
> interests that belong to a set of ready-made subjects, a new configuration of
> politics would surely emerge from the ruins of the old. Cultural configurations
> of sex and gender might then proliferate . . . within the discourses that estab-
> lish intelligible cultural life, confounding the very binarism of sex, and expos-
> ing its fundamental unnaturalness. (Butler 1990c, 149)

Connolly also seeks a proliferation of identities and discourses. His
response to disciplinary power consists of devising a politics that will give
expression to the paradox of difference. Connolly's goal is to try to keep
both sides of the paradox alive. While he argues that there are enormous
pressures to resolve the paradox in favor of the truth of identity, he does
not want to resolve the paradox in favor of difference. Connolly refuses
to invert the hierarchy largely because arguments supporting either the
truth or the contingency of identity rest upon equally shaky epistemological grounds. Despite this skepticism towards establishing the truth of
either position, the central political problem is to relieve the disciplinary
pressures that impose a notion of a true identity.

According to Connolly, one way to relieve this pressure and keep both sides of the paradox alive is through what he calls an agonal form of democracy, in which those who wish to be true to identity and those who wish to be true to difference oppose each other in a spirit of respect and forthrightness. It requires that neither side attempt to purge the other, and yet "robustly pursue" their respective agendas: one attempts to foster and enable what it sees as the truth of being, the other tries to create enough space to protect the "elemental rights to diversity" (Connolly 1991, 87). Connolly believes that the mechanism of a lively competitive democratic politics can partially relieve normalizing pressures.

Ultimately, the ability to sustain this kind of politics requires that the culture of genealogy is widespread enough such that difference is respected. Agonistic democracy requires the cultivation of a virtue of agonistic respect. This means that both those who wish to be true to difference and those who wish to be true to identity must share an ethos of self-restraint when facing their opponents. Genealogy plays an important role in cultivating respect because it reveals the shaky grounding of all claims regarding identity and difference. The point of this revelation is not to drive us away from groundings and foundations but to show us the difficulties that would attend any attempt to resolve the paradox of difference. Connolly notes, however, that genealogy is not sufficient. Revealing the contingent character of identity "can lead either to repression of the experience of contingency it enables or to a passive nihilism" (Connolly 1993a, 372). In the former case, the realization that there is nothing guaranteeing the correctness of our identities may foster a desire to hold tightly to whatever elusive sense we have of ourselves and view as a threat those who are different. Disbelief in a true identity does not necessarily lead to a respect for difference. Without a sense that we possess a true identity, moreover, we may simply give up on life. Passive nihilism suggests an exhaustion that is incompatible with the agonistic, competitive quality of Connolly's conception of democracy.

Aside from genealogy, what is also needed is a willingness to work on the self. In order to avoid repressing the experience of contingency and passive nihilism, Connolly makes a plea for cultivating the self in a particular way: "The goal is to modify an already contingent self . . . so that you are better able to ward off the demand to confirm transcendentally what you are contingently" (373). As a response to the predominant normalizing and naturalizing forms of soulcraft, Connolly offers an ethic of cultivating the self. In a sense, genealogy merely provides an opportunity for this ethic. We must still work on our selves in order to respect and care for difference. In coming to understand the contingency of our own identities we must continually resist the temptation to portray difference as evil.

Is there an obligation to foster this ethic of care for difference? Clearly, genealogy is meant to convince us of the strength of an ont*a*logy over ontology. In so doing it attempts to cultivate an alternative self understanding. But an alternative understanding of the self is not itself a form of soulcraft. Furthermore, in quoting Nietzsche's idea that we have to learn to think and feel differently, Connolly argues that Nietzsche is merely soliciting or requesting and not commanding (372). To the extent that he agrees with Nietzsche's position, then, Connolly does not present an obligation to take up an ethic of care. There is no imperative to work on the self one way as opposed to another.

Even if the genealogical position presents no imperative to engage in a particular form of selfcraft, certain features of this position do challenge the effects of contemporary liberal culture. First, genealogists argue against ignoring the effects of politics and culture upon ourselves. Second, they still see it as appropriate to judge the quality of politics in part by those effects. Third, Foucault, Butler, and Connolly explicitly or implicitly set out an imperative to foster a culture of genealogy and reveal the contestable character of all claims to a true identity. Finally, the ideas of parodic subversion and working on the self reveal a request or plea to counter the harm of naturalized self understandings.

Having said this, it may be the case that I too hastily dismissed an imperative or obligation to engage in selfcraft. For at least in Connolly's argument the desirability of an agonistic democracy seems to point to something stronger than a plea or a request. If we should work towards an agonistic democracy, then we should also employ the necessary means. As noted above, a culture of genealogy is not enough to support this form of democracy. What is also imperative is that people cultivate a particular kind of self. Connolly's position implies a political responsibility to "revise vengeful sensibilities that have become fixed" (372–73). And although this political responsibility may not pertain to everyone (after all, Connolly wants to maintain both sides of the paradox of difference), it is applicable to those who take the results of genealogy seriously. In talking about an ethical sensibility, Connolly is offering a guide for human activity. In establishing the importance of agonistic democracy, he confers an imperative element onto that guide.

Foucault's desire for us to hesitate about our discourse, Butler's celebration of parodic subversion, and Connolly's conception of agonal democracy are highly abstract, not to say thin, responses to the disciplinary and naturalizing features of modern society. A similar sort of complaint can be made against many of the alternatives offered by communitarians.[39] Nevertheless, the quality of the critics' responses can be distin-

---

[39] The agenda of classical political rationalists, particularly with regard to the reform of higher education, is somewhat more tangible (Bloom 1987; Pangle 1992). Similarly, the students of Strauss have generally been political conservatives. It is less clear whether there

guished from the strength of their criticisms. Perhaps they have inadequate solutions, but that does not necessarily detract from their analyses
of the effects of current liberal political culture.

Comparisons and Contrasts

In important ways, these critics differ over what they take to be the condition of our souls or selves. The communitarians argue that the problem with the dominant form of soulcraft is that it fragments the self. For
the classical political rationalists it disorders and dulls our souls; for the
genealogists, the problem is that we are constantly subjected to disciplinary and naturalizing pressures. Contemporary political, economic, and
social institutions fixate upon the production of docile, normalized, disciplined subjects.

When we turn to the ways in which these claims are grounded, additional differences emerge. For the classical political rationalists, there is
a metaphysical grounding to their arguments that the genealogists attempt to circumvent and soften. The classical political rationalists argue
that they are trying to discern what we are. There is a truth to be discovered about the psyche that can provide critical leverage against the production of modern identity. Liberal politics goes wrong if it prevents us
from living up to naturally given standards of human excellence. From
the genealogical position, it is precisely this kind of move that is so troubling about modernity. The classical political rationalists' appeal to nature and even the communitarians' presumption of harmonious wholeness are part of the problem and not part of the solution. The desire for
the truth about the soul or the self is what the genealogists want to resist.
Instead of talking about a human nature, the genealogists talk about the
ways in which our subjectivity is constructed. To the extent that genealogists stake out an ontological position, they see it as tentative and always
subject to subversion.

Finally, the differences between these perspectives and the level of
mutual acrimony should not be underestimated. For the genealogists,
the communitarians and the classical political rationalists represent the
dangers and disciplines that are lodged and repressed in much of contemporary political theory. For the communitarians, the genealogists
seem to be advocating the very fragmentation they seek to heal. And
although the communitarians are sympathetic to aspects of the classical

---

is a conservative political agenda that necessarily follows from Strauss's line of thought,
although Shadia Drury has tried to make this argument (Drury 1988).

political rationalist analysis, some have found it too contemptuous of modernity (Taylor 1991a, 15) or dependent upon a "bizarre conspiracy theory" (Bellah et al. 1991, 167). For the classical political rationalists, the communitarians are merely fellow travelers of modernity and the genealogists are Visigoths within the walls of Rome.

Despite these differences, there are a few patches of common ground, the most important of which is a willingness to judge the quality of political and cultural life, at least in part, by their effect upon our identities. All of these positions share a postulate that a great deal can be said about our selves or souls (although they differ over the standing of what is being said). Each of these positions presumes that our self understanding is good enough to identify the harms resulting from contemporary liberal democratic culture.

Second, all of these positions hold a view of the Enlightenment as a time when a number of bad philosophical moves were made. This was also when liberal theory was developed and advanced most significantly. For the communitarians, this period saw the emergence of the disengaged, fragmented, punctual self. For the classical political rationalists, this was when reason's first demotion was concretized in political thought. For the genealogists, this was the beginning of modern normalization as well as the establishment of the master narratives of progress and "Man."

Third, despite their criticisms, all three schools of thought remain more or less entwined in the liberal democratic project. As we have seen, the communitarians can be portrayed as providing a corrective to the excesses of liberal theory. The classical political rationalists tend in practice to be conservative defenders of this regime.[40] The genealogists are more ambivalent. At times they appear to reject liberalism completely (Foucault 1980b; Gruber 1989). At other times, they appear to want to reform and adjust it (Gordon 1991; Connolly 1991).

Fourth, all of these positions are willing to say not only that politics affects our selves or souls, but that there is something about our selves or souls that is deeply political. For the communitarians this means that the self cannot be extracted from its constituting political and social environment. For the other perspectives, there is a sense that the metaphor of politics can usefully describe the organization of the soul and the constitution of the subject. Political terms such as constitution, regime, ruling, enslavement, anarchy, and order reveal a kind of internal politics that reflects a preferred conception of an external politics. For the classi-

[40] This emphasis on the ways in which these positions are both critical of and drawn into the liberal democratic project can be contrasted with Stephen Holmes's approach in *The Anatomy of Antiliberalism* (1993). For Holmes, the battle lines between "us" and "them" are quite clear.

cal political rationalists, modernity has enacted a kind of coup against reason, one which has either installed a pretender to the throne (desire) or left us in a state of complete anarchy. In contrast, the genealogists see a self that organizes a form of authority or sovereignty to which it has no right. Thus, all of these positions share a sense that something can be said about the number and ordering of the parts of the self or the soul. The unity or wholeness of the communitarians can be contrasted to the well-ordered structure of the classical political rationalists' soul. These positions can, in turn, be contrasted to the fragmented, multiple subject offered by the genealogists.

Finally, all three of these schools of thought see political organizations and social institutions as responsible for counteracting the effects of the present regime on our souls or selves. For the communitarians and classical political rationalists this means that the polity should not adopt a laissez-faire attitude towards our souls. Communitarians argue that government should make the attempt to foster less atomistic, less fragmented selves. For the classical political rationalists, democratic government should ennoble our souls by cultivating reason, moral virtue, and a natural aristocracy. Similarly, the genealogists argue that we would be better off understanding our selves in certain ways as opposed to others. Moreover, they believe that transforming our political life may have the effect of cultivating or reinforcing those preferred self understandings. Indeed, transforming our self conceptions may also spur favorable changes in our political life. Whether or not genealogists would see it as an imperative, it is clear that they too are advocating a form of soulcraft.

Throughout these discussions I have yet to consider why these critics believe that the effects of certain social and political practices are harmful to our souls or selves. The next three chapters will explore and assess the criteria for moral harm implied by each school of thought.

2

The United, Unified, and Unitary Self

Preliminary Considerations

The critics' descriptions of the effects of two hundred years of liberal democracy are not without plausibility. When taken on their own, these criticisms have an undeniable coherence and fascination. When they are taken together, however, they all cannot be right. For example, the communitarian argument that our selves are fracturing in all sorts of ways is incompatible with the genealogical claim that we are increasingly normalized and disciplined. Similarly, the classical political rationalist argument that we have lost all order and hierarchy in our souls is incongruous with the genealogical argument that the demands of order and hierarchy dominate this regime. Finally, the communitarian description that we are betwixt and between traditions conflicts with the classical political rationalist description that we are firmly situated in modern rationalism (at best) and German nihilism (at worst).[1]

These contradictory opinions regarding the cultivation of modern identity point to the importance of empirical evidence for the three sets of critics. They are, after all, offering descriptions of the effects of liberal democratic culture. Included within these descriptions are fairly complex causal connections between democratic institutions and culture on the one hand and the quality and character of our internal lives on the other. But these claims are not entirely empirical. The normative force of the critics' descriptions rests upon philosophical arguments regarding what constitutes harm to our selves, and more deeply what constitutes the self. Finally, the critics presume that these concerns should be rectified or mitigated through politics.

A comprehensive analysis of the critics' claims would require a close examination of these empirical, philosophical, and political elements.

---

[1] Perhaps, at some level, there is a way to reconcile these descriptions. The genealogists could argue that the fragmentation and fracturing that the communitarians and classical political rationalists bemoan is caused largely by the excessive drive to fit everything into harmonious unities and clear hierarchies. The classical political rationalists, in turn, could argue that what the genealogists see as the normalized character of contemporary society is actually the normalizing effects of the tyrannical majority. Nevertheless, even if these criticisms could be reconciled, the problem of how liberal democratic theory should respond would remain.

To a large extent, I proceed on the assumption that the descriptions and causal relations embedded in the critics' arguments hold. I am less interested in establishing or criticizing the accuracy of their descriptions than with the norms and standards that they use to make their cases. Nevertheless, it is important to say something about the empirical problems that their positions raise. The first part of this chapter briefly examines some of these empirical issues and the idea of harm. The bulk of the chapter, however, focuses upon the communitarian critique.

Empirical Problems

The empirical content of the communitarian, classical political rationalist and genealogical criticisms emerges most clearly when we look at how they describe who is doing what to whom. For the communitarians and the genealogists at least this equation would exclude very few people living in liberal regimes. For example, when the communitarians argue that we have lost the ability to tell narratives that connect our lives into wholes, they are referring to you and me. Although some individuals may have retained this ability, they are exceptions. Similarly, for the genealogists, the effects of disciplinary power range throughout society and into the most minor behaviors and actions.

In contrast, the classical political rationalists' focus upon the status of reason leads to a somewhat different assessment of who is being affected. In a regime that depreciates the pursuit of wisdom, the immediate harm is to those souls able to engage in this pursuit. In addition, the relativism fostered in this regime sours and discourages those capable of forming an intellectual elite. Classical political rationalists argue that those who know how to think and philosophize can make a valuable contribution to the conduct and quality of politics. Moreover, to the extent that one of the beliefs that supports liberal democracy is the existence of "self-evident truths," then the depreciation of reason and nature may ultimately undermine the regime itself.[2]

Despite these claims, the critics have devoted varying amounts of attention to showing whom this regime has adversely affected. Of the three schools of criticism, the communitarians may have done the most in trying to support their description with empirical evidence. Drawing upon the civic republican tradition, Bellah et al. argue in *Habits of the Heart* that the state of the middle class is important for the success of free institutions. The focus of their study involved interviewing over two hundred

---

[2] On the other hand they also argue that unbridled discussion can erode the beliefs and opinions that hold society together. These two claims do not necessarily conflict insofar as thinkers need not say everything.

white, middle-class Americans over the course of five years (Bellah et al. 1985, viii–ix). Although they do not claim to have talked to "average" Americans, they do claim to have portrayed a certain segment of the American population during the early 1980s. As extensive as their evidence is, it still leaves open important questions about whether the values celebrated in this regime affect all members of liberal societies equally. Does the problem of soulcraft mean different things depending upon gender and race?[3] Or, more broadly, does liberal democracy have the same effects on Germans and Australians as it does on Americans? Are these various societies affected differently, or does liberal democracy homogenize these differences? Finally, in an increasingly interdependent world, do questions of soulcraft know any boundaries?

Clarifying who or what is the cause of the critics' complaints is also extremely important. Liberals could argue that the blame for whatever we have become should not be placed (if it is to be placed anywhere) at liberal democracy's door. These criticisms, they may claim, make too easy an association between liberal government and such things as modernity, bureaucracy, capitalism, science, and popular culture. Liberal democracy is not simply an amorphous malevolent force, but rather a set of political institutions and practices that are distinguishable from economic, cultural, educational, moral, and social institutions. To bundle these all together and equate modernity with liberalism is to paint with too broad a brush. Furthermore, to say that a liberal democratic regime permits certain disturbing practices is not the same as saying that it endorses such practices. We can certainly distinguish between endorsing and not prohibiting. Liberal democratic regimes allow various educational practices, forms of aesthetic expression, and ways of life, but that is not the same as offering its imprimatur to these things.

To be fair to the critics, some of their brushes are broader than others. As we saw in chapter 1, they do postulate connections between our identities and institutions that a liberal would understand as explicitly political. Moreover, the blending of economic, cultural, and bureaucratic effects into politics is also intelligible. At the very least, although these social institutions and politics are not logically connected (e.g., liberal democracy need not be bureaucratic), liberal democracies will tend to be commercial, bureaucratic, and technocratic into the near future. Thus wholesale criticisms of these institutions (such as Taylor's notion of an instrumental society) serve as criticisms of the liberal democratic regime.

Part of what is at issue here is the notion of *regime*. An Aristotelian would claim that political association is the most sovereign and inclusive

[3] Why Bellah et al. focused upon whites is not clear.

of associations. This does not mean that there is no difference between politics and these other things. Rather, it means first that political life will include economic, familial, and cultural practices and associations and not vice versa. But it also means that "core political principles shape the character of every aspect of the community" (Galston 1991, 292). On this view, to see liberal democracy as a regime is a way of referring to all of these things together. But if politics shaped all other associations, one of the significant tenets of liberal government would have been abandoned, as a central theme of liberalism is the protection of areas of life from the power and influence of governments and leaders. Whether the description does hold is, of course, an empirical matter. Critics of liberalism are more willing to accept an expanded notion of politics and regime than are defenders. Nevertheless, let us proceed with a conception of regime that includes political, social, and cultural practices.[4] Even under an expanded conception of regime, the idea of a political responsibility to take up the problem of selfcraft runs into serious problems.

In an enlarged understanding of regime, the prevailing intellectual milieu is part of the regime. For both the communitarian and classical political rationalist critics the impoverished nature of that milieu is an integral part of the problem. For MacIntyre and Taylor the proof that our identities have been significantly foreshortened can be found in their perception that intellectuals no longer draw upon our rich historical traditions. For MacIntyre the argument comes very close to claiming that our traditions are fragmented because intellectuals disagree over matters of fundamental importance. Similarly, for Taylor our modern tradition is impoverished because intellectuals do not take nature and God seriously. In other words, the culture that is fragmented and narrowed may be the culture of academia.

A similar argument exists in classical political rationalism. For example, Strauss's three waves of modernity (Strauss 1975) is a story about the decline of our intellectual life, not an appeal to what is generally called social history. Another example comes from the beginning of *Natural Right and History* where Strauss argues that "whatever might be true of the thought of the American people, certainly American social science has adopted the very attitude toward natural right which, a generation ago, could still be described, with some plausibility, as characteristic of German thought. The majority among the learned who still adhere to the principles of the Declaration of Independence interpret these principles not as expressions of natural right but as an ideal, if not an ideology or a myth" (Strauss 1953, 2).

---

[4] There is something too neat about a response to the critics that defines liberal democracy out of the problem. Yet a powerful version of this kind of response exists, one that turns upon the idea of neutrality; it will be considered in chapter 7.

Parts of the argument of both the communitarians and the classical political rationalists depend upon their characterization of the current intellectual milieu. At one level, this is an empirical question about what intellectuals believe. Perhaps Strauss is correct in asserting that most social scientists now see the principles of the Declaration of Independence as an ideology or myth. On the other hand, his claim is not self-evident. Similar problems face the communitarian claims that these are the central traditions we have available to us or that intellectuals ignore the moral sources of God and nature. Who are these intellectuals? How many of them believe what? Do numbers matter here? Does one Voegelin or one Strauss have a greater effect in defining the intellectual milieu than ten minor Rortarians?

Properly characterizing the intellectual milieu, however, is merely the first of many empirical hurdles that these critics must jump, for what must be demonstrated next is that this intellectual context and the larger political/social context are both connected to our self understandings. Classical political rationalists believe that there is a very close connection between deracinated intellectuals and the common person. Their presumption is that what happens in the university may ultimately have very real effects on the person in the street. This presumption, however, is reasonable only if there is sufficient evidence linking the prevailing intellectual milieu in academia with what everybody else is thinking. Unfortunately, this connection is usually based upon anecdotal evidence. Allan Bloom, for example, draws from his own experience as a professor at a few select universities.[5] But he also talks about the influence of German ideas on Woody Allen movies (Bloom 1987, 145–46), on a cab driver whom he encountered in Atlanta (147), and upon Louis Armstrong's singing "Mack the Knife" (151). At the very least, this is not enough to demonstrate a clear linkage between German nihilism and American popular culture.

All of this leads up to the question of what is being done to us. The study by Bellah et al. paints a particularly disturbing portrait of Americans as a people who know very little about themselves and why they do what they do. It many respects, it is a kind of cultural analog to what many voting studies have already told us. It is less certain, however, whether Bellah's interviews contribute to a picture of our souls. For example, they note that their interviewees found it difficult to articulate why they thought things such as political participation or marriage were

[5] Bloom sees his students as having "an unordered tangle of rather ordinary passions, running through their consciousness like a monochrome kaleidoscope" (Bloom 1987, 156). Earlier, Bloom observes that "students these days are, in general, nice. . . . They are not particularly moral or noble" (82). Finally, Bloom says that "The young are exaggerated versions of Plato's descriptions of the young in democracies" (87).

important. They attributed this inarticulateness to the sort of shallowness that the language of liberal individualism imparts. But what if most people, in most places, throughout most of history, could not provide articulate reasons for accepting and participating in significant social and cultural roles and institutions? Could inarticulateness regarding these matters simply mean that most people accept their lives as they find them and that they are not highly reflective and thoughtful? Or, more troubling, perhaps Bellah et al. confuse inarticulateness with the subscription to liberal individualist values, assuming, in effect, that these values cannot lend intelligibility to life (Yack 1988, 158). Furthermore, people may be even less articulate in integrated, tradition-saturated societies. Questions regarding why one chooses a particular occupation or marries instead of remaining single would be highly peculiar in a society that clearly defined and regulated everyone's station and its duties (Holmes 1993, 93). Inarticulateness may itself be evidence of a rich traditional life rather than of an impoverished liberal existence.

As Robert Dahl notes, "to determine the relation between regime and personal qualities is a formidable task, and modern social scientists have so far made little advance over the speculations and conjectures of Plato, Machiavelli and Mill" (1989, 92). This difficulty does not entail the absence of any and all data. Bloom, for example, appeals to particular kinds of data, as does Connolly. Connolly notes that with regard to the genealogical portrayal of the disciplinary society,

> Those who want aggregate measures can count the number of people today whose primary job is to control, observe, confine, reform, discipline, treat, or correct other people (think of the police, military personnel, welfare agents, therapists, state security agents, private security agents, advertising firms, prison officials, parole boards, nursing home attendants, licensing agents, tax officials, and so on) and the various clients, patients, delinquents, misfits, troubled souls, losers, subversives, and evaders who provide the primary objects of these practices. And they can compare this index—after sorting out the complex dimensions that make every aggregate comparison extremely coarse—with its counterpart a hundred (or even fifty) years ago. (1991, 188–89)

It would, of course, be interesting to see what these aggregate measures look like. Connolly believes, however, that the answer is clear: our society has become increasingly disciplined. This conclusion does seem plausible, but one would also have to consider not only the absolute numbers of people involved in these professions but also their number relative to the size of the population. For example, it is not self-evident that the opportunity for observation and self-discipline are far greater today than in the seventeenth-century Massachusetts Puritan communities.

The importance of historical evidence is, of course, central to Foucault's work. Rejecting a priori conceptualizations, Foucault attempts to show the slow emergence of disciplinary power in a variety of institutions. As important as this work may be, it is not unimpeachable (Fraser 1985, 175; Kent 1986), and its applicability to the late twentieth-century welfare state is questionable (Gordon 1991). Furthermore, although Foucault's evidence may go some distance in advancing the case for disciplinary power, it may not be enough to reveal the disciplinary subject.

The question of effects, however, is complicated by those liberal democrats who argue that the consequences of liberal democracy are to be celebrated and not depreciated. For example, J. S. Mill, Walt Whitman, George Kateb, William Galston, and Stephen Salkever are all of the opinion that liberal political institutions and culture can promote human flourishing. The constitution of the self is such that it is consonant with the demands and ways of life that a liberal democratic culture offers. For example, Mill argues that a system that encourages liberty will also encourage the formation of character and individuality (1975). Whitman believes that democratic culture provides a setting for the disclosure of "democratic individuality," which entails "self-expression, resistance in behalf of others, and the receptivity or responsiveness (being 'hospitable') to others" (Kateb 1990, 546).[6] Kateb also suggests that "democratic culture is (or can be) the soil for the emergence of great souls whose greatness consists in themselves being like works of art in the spirit of a new aristocracy" (545). Salkever argues that liberal democracy's central virtues are moderation and liberality or generosity, virtues that allow for a kind of human flourishing (1987). William Galston argues that liberal government fosters rational self-direction, duty-bound behavior, and individuality (1991, 229–31).

The question that these defenders of liberal democracy raise is whether the critics' descriptions are at all accurate. Of course, the defenders' arguments also depend heavily upon empirical evidence. Without such evidence, all of these arguments amount to nothing more than hypotheses (232–33). But the problem may be deeper than a lack of empirical evidence, for it will not tell us whether the state should look after the health of souls or what constitutes the normative standards of harm that the critics use. So despite these empirical problems and given these conceptual concerns, let us proceed as if the critics' descriptions were accurate.

[6] Kateb argues that Whitman reaches for "a religious conception of soul as unique and unalterable identity, whether immortal or not," but then suggests that "such substantialist talk about the person or the soul gets in the way of Whitman's most democratic teaching" (Kateb 1990, 561, 562).

Obligation and Harm

For each set of critics, the political responsibility to mitigate or remedy the effects of "liberal selfcraft" is based on the nature of those effects. As discussed, communitarians, classical political rationalists, and genealogists attempt to bring to light or unmask a form of harm that liberal theorists should acknowledge and address. Indeed, if the critics are correct in claiming that various liberal democratic institutions and practices are harming us, then their claims do acquire a degree of urgency, because the idea of preventing harm remains a powerful element in justifying political action within liberal thought.

Since the notion of harm is so important to the critics' arguments, the problem of its meaning and identification becomes central. Defining *harm*, however, is notoriously difficult. Initially, it will be enough to emphasize that harm is a contrastive notion: we understand that something is being harmed because we have a sense of what not being harmed means. In the absence of this latter sense, the meaning of harm becomes unmoored and questionable. In other words, the idea of being unharmed is a necessary component for judging harm. Because of this relationship, the critics' assessments of the kinds of persons that liberal democracies foster must draw upon an understanding of what an unharmed self or soul looks like. Without a convincing account of this preferred alternative, criticisms of liberal democracy and arguments favoring a state responsibility to engage in soulcraft lose their footing. The contrastive character of harm is enough to get the argument going. This problem of defining harm, however, will come up again in chapter 8 when I consider whether a more expansive conception of harm can strengthen the critics' arguments.

In this and in the next few chapters, my approach moves the argument away from considering liberal democracy's effects directly and instead examines the standards that critics use to judge these effects as harmful. In some cases, I argue that the critics do not offer a coherent standard of harm. In other cases, I argue that what the critics take as harm is not necessarily so. If such standards are lacking, or if alternative self-conceptions are just as plausible, then the strength of the critics' concerns is significantly weakened.

The difficulty in applying the notion of harm to the organization of the self also plagues some of liberalism's defenders. There are liberals who judge the quality of politics on the basis of how it affects our selves. The point of discussing both critics and defenders of liberalism is to defeat the case for a political responsibility to engage in selfcraft, although defeating the case for a responsibility seems to draw us to the opposite extreme. If there is no requirement to engage in selfcraft, perhaps there is a prohibition against doing so. Defeating the latter argument requires examining the arguments offered by liberal neutralists, for these are thinkers who argue that liberal theory and politics should not admit certain concerns, such as selfcraft, within its purview. Effectively responding to liberal neutralists will bring us closer to the conclusion that the engagement of selfcraft should be nothing more and nothing less than a qualified permission.

Communitarianism and Forms of Unity

Given what communitarians say about fragmentation and being betwixt and between traditions, the idea of wholeness or unification is clearly an important standard in their judgment of liberal democracy. Their criticisms imply that the self is or should be singular, encumbered, deep, engaged, and united. This idea of unity assumes a number of different roles. It delineates the deepest relationships between the self and the community (the united self), it sets out the organization of space within the self (the unified self), it describes the number of parts of the self (the unitary self), and it plays an important part in portraying the self over time. The first three senses of unity have acquired ambiguous functions in the communitarian critique of liberal democracy. Claims regarding the unity of self and community and the internal organization and number of parts of the self are of only modest use to the communitarians. In contrast, the communitarians do retain a fairly strong notion of maintaining the self over time. My response to this demand for a diachronically unitary self will validate partially the communitarian position and yet also open up the possibility for a more fragmented conception of identity over time. In other words, the identity of the self as a unity makes sense, but so does the possibility of talking about future and past selves. Because seeing one's life as an all-encompassing whole is not what necessarily matters to us, a politics that attempts to foster a greater conception of a life as a whole can be advanced only at the cost of other conceptions of oneself in time.

Uniting Self and Community

Michael Sandel's idea of the intersubjective self best expresses the first notion of unity. Sandel claims that "in certain moral circumstances, the relevant description of the self may embrace more than a single, individual human being, as when we attribute responsibility or affirm an obligation to a family or community or class or nation rather than to some particular human being" (1982, 62–63). Taylor expresses this unity with the idea of a "we-identity" as opposed to an "I-identity" (1989b, 170). For both writers, the intersubjective self is not a collection of individual identities, rather it is an "I" that is also a "we." Our we-identity is a real unity, not in the sense of being a convergence of individuals, but in the sense that individuals participate in something that extends beyond their bodies. The holism in this claim of unity is a standing reproach to a liberal society that is seen as denying any reality beyond individuals who value mobility, property, and other rights. Communitarians argue that such a society is both deeply impoverished and has pernicious effects.

Critics of the communitarian position have credited it with a conception of unity that is both deep and broad, and have read it as ambitiously claiming a oneness that will harmonize all our social relations. Connolly sees the communitarians as holding that "our mutual rights, duties, and aspirations will be harmonized more effectively as we are brought to greater self-consciousness of their preconditions and implications" (Connolly 1991, 88). Others such as Patrick Neal and David Paris argue that the relevant distinction between communitarians and liberals here is not that liberals deny all shared social relations while communitarians affirm them, but that for liberals these relations are only contingently related to identity, while communitarians see them as essentially related (Neal and Paris 1990, 425). By "essentially related," Neal and Paris mean that there is no Cartesian ego standing behind these relationships. As MacIntyre says, "I am brother, cousin and grandson, member of this household, that village, this tribe. These are not characteristics that belong to human beings accidentally, to be stripped away to discover 'the real me'" (1984, 32). Because we are essentially related, to see our selves as contingently related is a fundamental misunderstanding. It is, once again, a misunderstanding that the communitarians believe has grave consequences.

In a certain respect, these portrayals inadequately express the communitarian view of the self. Although Neal and Paris are correct to focus upon the notion of an essential relationship, Sandel, Taylor, and MacIntyre have qualified that relationship in a number of important ways. Sandel, for example, rejects the claim that our identities are solely whatever our families, city, class, nation, and culture have imparted to us. Rather, he distinguishes what we are from what we have, a distinction that drives a wedge between the self and its constituent elements.

In denying the claim that we are solely a set of communally given endowments, Sandel rejects what he calls the radically situated self. He argues that "any theory of the self of the form 'I *am* x, y, and z', rather than 'I *have* x, y, and z, (where x, y, and z are desires, etc.) collapses the distance between subject and situation which is necessary to any coherent conception of a particular human subject. This space, or measure of detachment, is essential to the ineliminably *possessive* aspect of any coherent conception of the self" (Sandel 1982, 20). The notion of distance is fundamental here. It prevents us from being "submerged in a circumstance that ceases to be ours" (183). Sandel relies heavily upon the metaphor of drowning to highlight the importance of distance, for if I am unable to "distinguish what is mine from what is me, I am in constant danger of drowning in a sea of circumstance" (57). It is for this reason that Neal and Paris's idea of essential relationships is, on its own, inadequate: it fails to capture Sandel's notion of distance.

Nevertheless, the idea of distance still means that at a certain level, the community constitutes the self. For Sandel, this constitution is a necessary, but not a sufficient condition for possessing an identity. It is not a sufficient condition because such a powerful notion of unity between the self and communal characteristics would be disempowering and because it would render the notion of the continuity of the self impossible. For Sandel, the notion of disempowerment is connected to a kind of dispossession that occurs when there is no distance between the self and its ends. In this kind of situation, "I am disempowered in the sense of lacking any clear grip on who, in particular, I am" (57). Distance is necessary to recover a distinction between one's identity and all the attributes, desires, aims and projects that have been impressed upon oneself.

A strong notion of unity also implies that "just *any* change in my situation, however slight, would change the person I am" (20). Sandel argues that "this distancing aspect is essential to the continuity of the self. It preserves for the self a certain dignity and integrity by saving it from transformation in the face of the slightest contingency" (55). In other words, the radically situated subject, implied by a strong notion of unity, changes as the situation changes. Sandel's notion of the self weathers these kinds of changes by granting it an element of integrity and durability over time.

How this distancing is achieved can be found in Sandel's conception of cognitive agency. His argument suggests that when we become aware of our selves in the world we are already equipped through our upbringing with a whole set of ends, desires, interests, projects, notions of what is good, and so on. We face the problem, however, "that the self, being unbounded in advance, [is] awash with possible purposes and ends, all impinging indiscriminately on its identity, threatening to engulf it" (152). In response, we forge our identities by sorting out the limits or boundaries of the self through an act of cognitive agency. This process amounts to trying to discover who we already are. It is not a question of choosing ends, but of reflecting upon ends that we already have. "The relevant question is not what ends to choose, for my problem is precisely that the answer to this question is already given, but rather who I am, how I am to discern in this clutter of possible ends what is me from what is mine" (59). I take this given bundle of desires and projects and through an act of reflection declare that this collection is *mine* and not simply *me*. Through the act of reflection, something becomes "more an attribute and less a constituent of my identity" (58). This is "a subjectivity less fluid if never finally fixed" that, in the course of a lifetime, is able "to participate in the constitution of its identity" (152, 153).

As a kind of primordial unity, the radically situated subject is ultimately disempowered. In order to have an identity, we must create some space between what we possess and what constitutes us originally, but the boundaries that we create through distance and reflection are not given in advance. In other words, what I will come to affirm as mine depends upon a combination of the ends that are provided antecedently and upon the reflection in which I engage. The boundaries of my self will be established by what I affirm as my own.[7]

If the ideal of unity in Sandel's work is compromised significantly by his conception of distance, it appears to be reinforced by his idea of the intersubjective self. But even here the notion of distance prevents a slide into radical situatedness. The intersubjective self results from one possible way of drawing the boundaries of the self. This self is not intersubjective merely because the origins of its ends can be found in family, religion, nation, friends, and so on. Rather, it is intersubjective because I take the ends and purposes of others as my own. By so doing, I can interpret what is happening to other individuated bodies as also happening to me. For example, in some families, an attack upon one member is an attack upon all. This kind of community is based upon individuals reflecting upon their antecedently given ends. There is nothing a priori about the intersubjective self; it emerges only after particular boundaries are carved in the clutter that constitutes me.

Whatever community exists, whatever unity is available between self and other is mediated by cognitive agency. According to Sandel,

> Even an enlarged self, conceived as a community, has its bounds, however provisional its contours may be. The bounds between the self and (some) others are thus relaxed on the intersubjective account, but not so completely relaxed as to give way to a radically situated subject. The bounds that remain

---

[7] What Sandel means by "my own" here is heavily qualified. Because the source of our attributes is found in the community, Sandel argues that the possession of attributes is a form of guardianship. "To say that I am the guardian of the endowments I bear is to imply that they are owned by some other subject, on whose behalf, or in whose name, or by whose grace I cultivate and exercise them" (Sandel 1982, 97). One problem with this view is that if the ultimate owner of my endowments is the community and the self can be intersubjective, then guardianship looks more like my left hand lending my right hand money than some kind of external relationship.

are not given by the physical, bodily differences between individual human beings, but by the capacity of the self through reflection to participate in the constitution of its identity, and where circumstances permit, to arrive at an expansive self-understanding. (144)

The boundaries between self and other should never be completely relaxed because of the importance of distance to identity. The fact that the boundaries of our identities are not given to us, but must be reflected upon and acknowledged by us further diminishes the importance of unity. The point of cognitive agency is to allow "self-command" (59) over what is already given to us.

Nevertheless, Sandel argues repeatedly that drawing these boundaries is not a matter of choice but of reflection. Thus he distinguishes sharply between a voluntaristic conception of agency and the cognitive conception. But Sandel refuses to say that we *choose* how to draw our boundaries because he reserves the notion of choice for an activity performed by a highly abstract, antecedently given, Kantian subject. In a sense, we could not choose how to draw these boundaries because voluntaristic agency is illusory.[8]

But clearly there are elements of choice built into Sandel's idea of cognitive agency, and they reinforce the distance that he believes necessary for identity. First, could we not choose to engage in a very superficial level of reflection? We could, for example, identify with only those influences imparted to us by a particular community or by our parents

---

[8] Sandel offers a number of accounts for what a voluntaristic conception of agency would entail and finds them all wanting. On the first account, it may be possible for choice to be based upon existing wants and desires, but then we must ask whether those wants and desires are themselves chosen. If they are not chosen, but are simply there because of nature or nurture, "such a 'choice' would involve less a voluntary act than a factual accounting of what these wants and desires really are" (Sandel 1982, 162). At most, agency would entail matching existing given wants and desires to the best means of satisfying them. There is, in this description, an inward weighing of alternatives, something that Taylor calls weak evaluation. The self acquires this weak role of reading the scale to see which desire weighs in more heavily and then engineers the best means for accomplishing the given end.

A second conception of choice is that the self not only weighs its desires, but also considers the desirability of the desires. But the idea of the self as a simple weigher of alternatives would not necessarily disappear here either. On what basis, Sandel asks, would we judge the desirability of the desires? If it is on the basis of other given desires and interests, then the original problem is replicated.

The only way out of these problems is to appeal to a third conception found in the existentialist notion of radical choice. On this account, the sovereign self simply picks one of the desires arrayed before it. But is this a matter of choice? The problem here is that choice acquires such an arbitrary quality that while one could still see it as an act of will, it is one based solely upon caprice. In this account, choice is rendered so thin as to be meaningless.

and refuse to consider the rest. Indeed, perhaps we could choose not to engage in reflection at all. Finding ourselves awash with so many influences and so much cultural clutter, we may give up trying to carve out our identities and simply fade into our circumstances. Like a kind of Zelig, we could take our social cues solely from our immediate circumstances and think little about how these things connect to our past or to our future.

Second, the fact that our ends are given to us by a larger community does not mean that those ends will inevitably cohere. Upon reflection I may find that the preservation of life is of utmost importance to me, as is the preservation of the community that imparted that value. In a given set of circumstances, I may have to choose whether the ends of pacifism outweigh protecting that which fosters pacifism. Because not all ends fit together into a harmonious whole, we may have to choose our identities as well (see also Honig 1993, 178).

Third, as Will Kymlicka notes, the inability to jump outside of social influence does not preclude our ability to rethink and revise our ends (1989, 15). The problem here is not merely the harmony of our ends, but that our beliefs about our ends change. It is always possible that what we now see as worthwhile will be seen as foolish in the future. Because changes in information and culture change our beliefs, the notion of cognitive agency is compatible with the choice to revise our ends.

Finally, Sandel offers a conception of what he calls the intrasubjective self that also opens space for choice. There will be times when the "appropriate description of the moral subject may refer to a plurality of selves within a single, individual human being, as when we account for inner deliberation in terms of the pull of competing identities, or moments of introspection in terms of occluded self-knowledge, or when we absolve someone from responsibility for the heretical beliefs 'he' held before his religious conversion" (1982, 63).[9] As I understand it, the intrasubjective self could result from a situation in which the various boundaries we draw happen to carve out distinct identities. For example, I could identify myself not only with a particular religion but also with a larger culture (Honig 1993, 177). If these two identities do not mesh, then I may be forced to choose between ends. This kind of situation occurs more frequently as society becomes increasingly pluralistic. In any case, a tight unity between self and community is rendered impossible.

If we take seriously Sandel's arguments about the need to reject the radically situated self, then our identity demands that we distinguish

[9] Of these examples, it is unclear why the notion of conversion should be seen as a case of an intrasubjective self as opposed to two different selves at two different times.

what we are from what we possess. If the "essential relationships" that constitute our identity are thus merely preconditions, then we can be neither wholly transcendental, Kantian, noumenal selves nor radically situated subjects and still have a conception of the self. But this characterization says very little about the actual fragmentations and divisions that liberal democratic culture produces. Sandel's position contains no logical or moral necessity for seeing ourselves intersubjectively or as individuated by a particular physical body or as internally fragmented. These options are all possible because the way we draw the boundaries of the self is shot through with contingencies, including the level of reflection in which we decide to engage, the coherence of the ends that have been imparted to us, the coming to light of new information that revises our beliefs, and the coherence of the traditions that influenced us. It is not clear what leverage Sandel's position can provide against the cultivation of our identities by liberal democracies.[10]

Both Taylor's and MacIntyre's later work also softens the unity of self and community significantly. MacIntyre, for example, argues that conflict lies at the heart of any tradition. Moreover, conflict cannot be surpassed or avoided: rather, it is something that constitutes and enriches tradition (MacIntyre 1988, 12).[11] On top of disagreements within traditions, there are disagreements between those traditions that constitute Western intellectual life. Disagreement seems to be as much a part of establishing a tradition as agreement.

Although Taylor argues that "a democratic society needs some commonly recognized definition of the good life" (1989b, 160), his argument in *Sources of the Self* undercuts the possibility of such a commonly recognized definition. At one level Taylor argues that we do agree upon the importance of the standards of freedom, self-rule, justice, and benevolence. He believes, however, that we also disagree deeply over the moral sources that support these claims.[12] The theistic moral source that once provided an overarching unity has been irrevocably shattered (Tay-

[10] In fairness to Sandel, it should be pointed out that *Liberalism and the Limits of Justice* does not attempt to provide leverage against the actual production of identity by liberal societies, but against certain theoretical arguments regarding the presumptions of liberal political philosophy. The former argument, however, is suggested in his article "The Procedural Republic and the Unencumbered Self" (1992).

[11] Contrast, for example, the claims found in the second chapter of *After Virtue* that bemoan the interminable character of contemporary moral debates with the claims in *Whose Justice? Which Rationality?* that argue that fundamental conflicts are hidden by a rhetoric of consensus (1988, 2) and that conflict is central to defining an intellectual tradition (12).

[12] It seems arguable that there is even agreement over these standards of freedom, justice, and benevolence. For Taylor's argument, however, agreement over these things is not as significant as agreements and disagreements over their sources.

lor 1989a, 496). In its place we are left with multiple moral sources (e.g., God, disengaged reason, nature, authenticity) that can conflict with one another. Indeed, Taylor argues that they can lead to genuine moral dilemmas over how to promote our conceptions of what is good. There is no longer a coherent set of moral sources that supports whatever public agreement exists.[13] Taylor claims that the goods that flow from these sources are all genuine, but they cannot all be advanced in human action necessarily. This diversity of moral sources "can be the basis . . . for a cruel dilemma. . . . But a dilemma doesn't invalidate the rival goods. On the contrary, it presupposes them" (1989a, 511).

The communitarian argument that the self is constituted by a set of given, essential relationships remains. Nevertheless, those relationships do not preclude wrenching, difficult choices that show that whatever initial unity may exist between the self and the community will inevitably be disturbed as individuals reflect upon and choose between the diversity of available ends and goods. In a certain respect, even the communitarians are not recommending that we fuse our selves with a given pluralistic culture. To do so would be simply to validate the fragmentation and conflict of the larger society. On the other hand, the communitarians do not appear to believe that even sticking to one tradition (MacIntyre) or one moral source (Taylor) will yield a harmonious whole (at least on earth). The stubborn or ineliminable conflicts that flow through our identities suggest that unity of self and community could occur only by accepting the fragmentation of the whole culture, or by closing oneself off to the diverse moral sources that also compose our identities. Taylor's aspirations for unity without any kind of remainder seem chastened significantly by his exploration of the sources of modern identity. Even for communitarians a self fully united with its community can no longer serve as a standard for judging modern identity. The relationship of the self to the community is so heavily qualified by the conceptions of distance (Sandel), conflict (MacIntyre), and dilemmatic choice (Taylor), that it does not offer a standard for judging the effects of liberal democracy. The drive to unity, however, has not completely disappeared from the communitarian position. This drive is apparent in Taylor's understanding of the organization of internal space, to which I now turn.

[13] Taylor argues that "underneath the agreement on moral standards lies uncertainty and division concerning constitutive goods" (1989a, 498). But even in this disagreement, there is still a kind of agreement. He writes, "my aim was to outline certain modes of thought and sensibility which are either so widespread in the modern West—perhaps I might better say North Atlantic region—that they are the object of a wide consensus; or else so deep-lying that they actually underpin the contending sides in a dissensus" (Taylor 1991b, 237).

The Unified Self

Taylor argues that the major facets of modern identity include a sense of inwardness, an affirmation of ordinary life, an expressivist notion of nature, and the idea of epiphany. All of these facets emerged at a particular time in human history, so in this sense they are all contingent. For us, however, they provide the moral horizon or social context within which we understand who we are. Very briefly, in the case of inwardness, Taylor argues that we see ourselves as creatures with inner depths. At first we saw these depths as ways to understand the good or as a way to approach God (Taylor 1991a, 26–27). Now, however, we believe that there is something special or unique about each one of us that can be found only through introspection. Looking inward is no longer solely a path to God, but a path to our voices, our own way of life.

A second facet structuring our identity is the value we attribute to ordinary life, by which Taylor means all those things "we need to do to continue and renew life" (1989a, 211). We are more willing to connect what is valuable to our everyday existence than to draw upon a larger cosmic order or a divine conception of history. According to Taylor, we have come to value everyday relationships and the relief of suffering above the pursuit of perfection and our role as citizens.

A third facet of our identities entails the Romantic conception of seeing nature as a moral source. According to Taylor, "In the philosophy of nature as source, the inexhaustible domain is properly within. To the extent that digging at the roots of our being takes us beyond ourselves, it is to the larger nature from which we emerge. But this we only gain access to through its voice in us" (390). Finding that voice allows us to know nature and give it expression in our lives, for each of us has a nature to express. By looking inward we find that original path, that unique measure, that authentic core that makes our lives our own.

Finally, Taylor talks about the importance of being brought into the "presence of something which is otherwise inaccessible, and which is of the highest moral or spiritual significance" to our identities (419). This is the notion of epiphany, which Taylor argues is not so much a religious as an aesthetic experience in the twentieth century. Art, for example, can bring us into contact with a transcendent moral source. "The epiphany is our achieving contact with something, where this contact either fosters and/or itself constitutes a spiritually significant fulfillment or wholeness" (425).

Taylor's primary purpose in *Sources of the Self* is to trace these facets of modern identity back to various moral sources or "constitutive goods."

These moral sources of the self include God, a conception of disengaged reason, and a Romantic conception of nature. As I suggested in chapter 1, Taylor believes that much of the crisis of modern identity revolves around the suppression of one or more of these moral sources and hence of one of the facets of our identities.[14] Central to Taylor's account of moral sources and their relationship to identity is a fairly deep claim regarding the unity of the self. Here the unity in question is not between the self and something else—rather it describes the organizational space of the self (the unified self) and is related to claims regarding the number of parts the self possesses (the unitary self).

Taylor claims that the unification of the moral self "was a precondition of the transformation which I will describe as an internalization. . . . Without the unified self which we see articulated in Plato's theory, the modern notion of interiority could never have developed" (120). And without the idea of interiority, it is difficult to see how the moral sources of disengaged reason and an expressivist conception of nature could have emerged. But what does Taylor mean by a unified self? Clearly, if we are to take our cue from Plato, it does not mean that the self consists of just one part. If the self were simply one thing, it would be a "unitary self." In contrast, the unified self is not one thing, though it is found in one place or location. Plato unified the self or the soul in the sense that in his work it designates "the unique locus where all our different thoughts and feelings occur" (118). Taylor contrasts this Platonic move with an earlier Homeric view of the "agent" in which action, thought, and feeling emanate from a variety of bodily locations. Taylor argues that Plato also conceived of the mind as one space, portraying reason as capable of mastering the other parts of the soul (119). The self is unified only in the sense that there is one location in which everything of importance occurs or should occur. This Platonic move is so powerful that if we experience ourselves as being composed of a plurality of locations, then something has gone wrong: "a plurality of loci is an experience of error and imperfection" (120).

The idea of a unified self does not necessitate a unitary self. This is true of Plato's view of the soul: rule *by* reason is not a rule *of* reason

---

[14] Taylor also sees other tensions within modern culture and groups them into three areas. The first concerns the debates over and differences derived from the moral sources themselves. The second concerns the dominance of instrumentalism and proceduralism, and the third concerns the issue of whether our moral terms can themselves exact a cost. In the last chapter of *Sources of the Self*, Taylor looks at each of these tensions very briefly. The first leads to genuine dilemmas, which seem to be part of the modern condition. The second can be mitigated by advancing theistic and expressive sources of morality. The third is left hanging, although Taylor seems optimistic about our abilities to respond to the costs of morality (1989a, 518–19).

alone. The unified self need not mean a drive to univocality.[15] Within the space that composes the mind, there may be other parts (as in Plato) or other voices. These kinds of claims soften the notion of unity that serves as a necessary precondition for Taylor's notion of inwardness.

As important as the unified self is to our identities, it provides very little critical leverage against the self-understandings that a liberal democratic regime forges. Unless one thinks that this culture fosters or should foster something like a Homeric conception of agency in which there are multiple locations of the self, Taylor's idea of a unified self provides little critical traction.[16]

Taylor's idea of a unitary self is somewhat more complex. Although he does not use it as a standard against which to judge modern identity, he does see the unitary self as impoverished. Taylor argues that "an escape from the traditional idea of the unitary self was a condition of a true retrieval of lived experience" (462). He then offers at least two different notions of the unitary self. One conception takes disengaged reason as its sole moral source; the other takes the Romantic ideal of nature as its sole moral source. Both of these conceptions of the self are incomplete. The general problem is that the unitary conception of the self fails to give alternative moral sources their due. Exploring the problems that Taylor associates with the unitary self shows yet another way in which the theme of unity plays an ambiguous role in the communitarian position.

The Unitary Self

One way to understand a unitary conception of the self is through the notion of disengaged reason, by which Taylor means a type of reason that is detached from an external, substantive criterion or measurement. As developed by Descartes, disengaged reason turns upon procedures that are derived from thinking itself. Instead of viewing the success of reason in terms of its ability to reveal Platonic forms, disengaged reason constructs orders of ideas according to certain canons. For Descartes, reason permits and expresses what Taylor calls self-sufficient certainty: "What I get in the cogito, and in each successive step in the chain of clear and distinct perceptions, is just this kind of certainty, which I can generate for myself by following the right method" (156).

---

[15] It is less clear whether seeing our identity as connected to one place is necessary for a notion of inwardness. There may very well be other cultures that have inward-looking, contemplative practices that do not subscribe to a unity of place within the person.

[16] It is unlikely that even Sandel's notion of the intrasubjective self is one with multiple locations. Its internal struggle seems to occur in one location and not, for example, in a tension between the stomach, the liver, and the lungs.

In his pursuit of self-sufficient certainty, Descartes pushed for a disengagement that would not only separate reason from any substantive, Platonic criterion, but would also disengage the self from the body and the world. According to Taylor, "Descartes took the step of supposing that we *are* essentially disengaged reason; we are pure mind, distinct from body, and our normal way of seeing ourselves is a regrettable confusion" (Taylor 1991a, 102). A conception of the disengaged subject, then, accompanies disengaged reason.

The disengagement that Descartes began is carried to fruition with the Lockean punctual self. As we saw in chapter 1, this self is wholly identified with its ability to choose and alter its environment. The self is that which is not only distinct from all of its ends, but also what is capable of transforming them. The punctual self is unitary in the sense that it *is* this one thing that is capable of control and creation.

Because of this disengagement and distance, the punctual self opens the possibility for radically scrutinizing and remaking traditions, habits, feelings, and politics (Taylor 1989a, 175). According to Taylor, this understanding of the self encouraged human dignity, human rights, personal commitment, and political freedom. But Taylor also associates the punctual self with all aspects of an instrumental society: It shores up social contract theories, instrumental relationships to nature, bureaucratic approaches to public administration, and proceduralism. Lockean instrumentalism encourages us to see our selves as disengaged, unitary, free agents. It is this unitary notion of the self that encompasses the primary strengths and weaknesses of classical liberalism.

In Hegelian fashion, Taylor's communitarianism seeks to surpass yet preserve the achievements that flowed from disengaged reason. An important step in this dialectic comes with the Romantic movement. For this movement called into question the punctual self, but it did so by offering an antithetical unitary conception of the self. In effect, the Romantics claimed that the disengaged self was not a true unity. Its instrumental stance towards the world divided us from nature, its atomistic view of society separated us from one another, and its objectified view of the self fragmented our selves into reason and feeling (413). Ultimately, as Schiller and Tocqueville presented the argument, the instrumental view of the human condition undermined "the very basis of cohesion which a free, participatory society needs to maintain itself" (414). What the Enlightenment had put asunder, the Romantic movement sought to reunite: "And so among the great aspirations which come down to us from the Romantic era are those towards reunification: bringing us back in contact with nature, healing the divisions between reason and sensibility, overcoming the divisions between people, and creating community. These aspirations are still alive: although the Romantic religions of nature have died away, the idea of our being open to nature within us and without is still a very powerful one" (384).

At the very least, Taylor is sympathetic towards the kind of criticism and form of unity that accompany the Romantic movement. But this sympathy is, once again, tempered by a desire not to "occlude the complex connections in the modern understanding of the self between disengagement and self-responsible freedom and individual rights, or those between instrumental reason and the affirmation of ordinary life" (504). More important, Taylor's writing suggests that a modern, more fragmented notion of the subject can encompass the achievements of the Lockean punctual self and the Romantic expressivist self. In its pursuit of the "true retrieval of lived experience," modernism has abandoned the idea of the unitary self in both of its forms. As it is expressed in modern art, poetry, and philosophy, "the liberation of experience can seem to require that we step outside the circle of the single, unitary identity, and that we open ourselves to the flux which moves beyond the scope of control or integration" (462).

Taylor sees the movement away from the unitary, disengaged self and the unitary, expressive self as opening yet another dimension of human life and experience. Still, he does not completely abandon the aspiration for unity. He sees the modern displacement from the self to "the flow of experience" as potentially giving rise to "new forms of unity, to language conceived in a variety of ways—eventually even as a 'structure'" (465). But what these new forms of unity are exactly is unclear, for Taylor does appear to celebrate the modern impulse to fragment the self in the pursuit of a new understanding of inwardness.[17] Taylor's reminders that the self is multifaceted only hint at this move away from unity (29), which is more strongly established in his claim that we can never fully articulate our identities (34). If our identities always exceed our articulations, then a unitary conception of the self could never be actualized.[18]

Taylor rejects the adequacy of both the punctual self of disengaged reason and the expressivist self of Romanticism. At most he allows that disengaged reason might be seen as "an achievement worth aiming at for certain purposes, something we manage to attain part of the time, even though constitutionally our thought is normally embodied, dialogical, shot through with emotion, and reflects the ways of our culture" (Taylor 1991a, 102). The kind of fragmentation that Taylor finds depicted and

---

[17] The problem with some forms of modernism, according to Taylor, is not their abandonment of the unitary self, but rather the abandonment of the possibility of epiphany. Taylor argues that writers such as Derrida and Foucault have taken the negative claims of modernism, "while neglecting its opening to epiphany" (1989a, 488).

[18] This looks very much like Connolly's position, which will be taken up again in chapter 4.

valued in modern art also opens up the possibility of experiences that are "otherwise inaccessible." In recognizing this possibility of epiphany, Taylor argues that we also recognize that we live on different levels: "The epiphanic and the ordinary but indispensable real can never be fully aligned, and we are condemned to live on more than one level—or else suffer the impoverishment of repression" (Taylor 1989a, 480). In both its Lockean and Romantic formulations the impoverished punctual self reveals only a small part of the self. A better understanding of the self, one which accompanies the notion of epiphany, is that it is multileveled. This preferred, multileveled understanding has to be "won against" both the controlling punctual self and the expressivist natural self.[19]

For Taylor, the unitary self represents a form of misunderstanding. From what he says about the character of modern identity, it is unlikely that we could ever become such a self. The unitary self is troublesome given the moral framework that defines modernity, for within that framework the punctual and the expressivist self fall far short of what we are capable of understanding our selves to be. Taylor's argument is not that these punctual or expressivist views are completely wrong, but that they are grossly inadequate.

Taylor's position can provide communitarians with a critical standpoint on the cultivation of modern identity only to the extent that our prevailing practices encourage us to misunderstand ourselves as unitary selves. In this regard, his argument parallels Sandel's rejection of the unencumbered self and the radically situated self. As with the unencumbered self, Taylor criticizes the punctual self for being entirely distinct from whatever ends and conceptions of the good it possesses. As with the radically situated self, Taylor is suspicious of Romantic expressivism because it eliminates the capacity for distance and choice. To the degree that liberal writers subscribe to the unitary self in either of its forms, Taylor's position provides significant critical leverage.

When we turn to contemporary liberal theory, it is not clear to what this leverage amounts. A great deal depends upon what Taylor means by defining the self in relation to its constitutive concerns. Or, to put it in Sandel's language, how encumbered do we have to be? Taylor's, Sandel's, and MacIntyre's communitarianism converge on the belief that we are not so encumbered, constituted, or tradition bound that we are unable to reflect upon and choose our ends and purposes (if not our traditions and moral frameworks). A constituted or encumbered self must still make room for human agency. But at the same time, liberal writers

---

[19] Taylor writes, "The recognition that we live on many levels has to be won against the presumption of the unified self, controlling or expressive" (1989a, 480). Here Taylor seems to refer to the self of disengaged reason and the self of Romanticism and not the notion of a unified self as it is contrasted to a Homeric view of agency.

have also acknowledged (and in some cases reaffirmed) the importance of context and circumstance to agency, meaning, and human understanding (Flathman 1987; Rawls 1985). Although it would be inaccurate to say that liberals and communitarians now agree on this major point, it would be hard to find a liberal theorist who argued that the self was nothing more than a neutral, punctual entity. What liberals do emphasize is that however constituted the self may be through language and community, we possess the capacity to judge and reconsider our ends and purposes.

Liberals and their critics are suspicious of the unitary self. But that suspicion does not mean that liberalism must also accept Taylor's account of the moral sources of the self or MacIntyre's account of the prevailing intellectual traditions. Nothing about the content of our situation or how we understand the notion of good follows from a rejection of the punctual self. The claim that our agency must be situated does not dictate how we ultimately respond to that situation.

For Taylor the problem with the punctual self is not merely that it ignores the constituted character of the self, but that it precludes seeing life as a whole (1989a, 50). The identity of the punctual self is what it always is. This tight center of control requires neither past memories nor future projects to sustain its identity. Indeed, for both Taylor and MacIntyre the atomistic self is unacceptable in part because of the need to view our lives as a whole over time. It is their belief that a rejection of the punctual self does point us to a more substantive position regarding the nature of the self.

Identity and Time

Even with their emphasis on the importance of community, communitarians have backed away from an overwhelming unity between the self and the community. This unity no longer holds the promise of the wholeness and harmony that the communitarians wanted to recover in a fragmented and pluralistic liberal culture. Perhaps it is in part because of the importance of wholeness and harmony to the communitarian project that they strenuously retain the idea of an individual's unity over time. I will now consider why the diachronic problem of identity is so important, how it provides the communitarians with critical leverage, and finally whether there is a defense against their criticisms.

Taylor argues that "we must inescapably understand our lives in narrative form, as a 'quest'" (52). To understand this claim and how it relates to the problem of identity over time, we must further explore Taylor's conception of the good. He believes that we understand who we are in relationship to our pursuit of what is good. Our identities are framed by what we understand as important to us and by the kinds of commitments and projects that we make and pursue (27). This framing occurs most importantly within and through our associations and identifications with states, communities, religious groups, families, political parties, friendships, and moral commitments. We can decide who we are only within these larger frameworks.[20] Unlike the punctual self, our identities are inevitably situated in frameworks in which, for the most part, we happen to find ourselves. Within a complex moral, linguistic, cultural, and social context the situated character of our particular identities is not simply given to us. Instead, we must work out our identities and give sense to our lives with the background conditions and tools that these frameworks provide. In so doing we make all kinds of evaluative contrasts in figuring out our conception of the good. We appeal, in other words, to terms such as good and bad, higher and lower, noble and ignoble, courage and cowardice. If we completely lacked any sense of where we stood or if we could not use these evaluative terms, we could not engage in social life or discourse or determine what is good or how we should live (27). In short, our identities are deeply, but not completely, situated because our understandings of the good are embedded in larger social frameworks. For Taylor, the web is not so tightly woven that critical assessment of, deviation from, or outright rejection of a moral framework is impossible.

Taylor notes that we enact our pursuit of the good over the course of time and in the face of the changes and challenges that fortune brings. Our commitments, projects, and intentions are exposed constantly to the contingencies and vicissitudes that accompany a movement through time. As beings in time, pursuing what we see as good, "the issue of the direction of our lives must arise for us." Taylor writes, "in order to make minimal sense of our lives, in order to have an identity, we need an orientation to the good, which means some sense of qualitative discrimination, of the incomparably higher. Now we see that this sense of the good has to be woven into my understanding of my life as an unfolding story. But this is to state another basic condition of making sense of ourselves, that we grasp our lives in a narrative." As beings in time, the only way we can make sense of our pursuits of the good is through narrative. To understand our orientation to the good and hence understand our present identity, we must both account for how we got wherever we are and describe where we are going. Thus, for Taylor, story telling is part of what it means to be beings who must make sense of their identity within

---

[20] Taylor defines a framework as "that in virtue of which we make sense of our lives spiritually. Not to have a framework is to fall into a life which is spiritually senseless. The quest is thus always a quest for sense" (1989a, 18).

a moral space. We cannot help producing narratives whenever we are faced with the question of who we are. Narrative is not "an optional extra" (47). Indeed it not only makes our own actions intelligible, but others' actions as well. Along similar lines, MacIntyre argues that "it is because we all live out narratives in our lives and because we understand our own lives in terms of the narratives that we live out that the form of narrative is appropriate for understanding the actions of others" (1984, 212).

The connection between narrativity and the intelligibility of human action is relatively unproblematic. To understand what we are doing now requires a sense of either what went before or what will come after: An event that was singular or momentary, without connection to past or present, would be puzzling, if not unintelligible. But this general claim that we must tell stories is not very illuminating. It seems to require nothing more than a minimal level of narrativity that could be satisfied by telling very specific stories within a very narrow time horizon. A narrative could begin in the recent or distant past and extend into the distant or near future. A minimal narrative could be as simple as saying that "I get up every morning at this time," or it could be as entailed and complex as an epic poem. The description and self-justification of our specific intentions, commitments, and projects rely upon all kinds of stories. The assumption that we are narrative creatures does not mean that we will tell very interesting, very encompassing, very consistent, or very accurate stories. At the least, the communitarians are successful in arguing that a minimal level of narrativity is essential to understanding our selves.

The claim that a minimal level of narrativity is a necessary condition for intelligibility, however, is a weak tool for analyzing an ongoing set of human activities. To the extent that any social life is intelligible to its practitioners, this narrativity condition, by definition, must be met. We must draw upon a minimal level of narrativity no matter how shallow or disengaged we conceive our selves. In many respects, the claim that we cannot avoid telling stories resembles the communitarian claim that human beings are situated in a social and linguistic context. Although this claim perhaps tells us something about our selves, it reveals nothing about the content or the character of that context.[21]

Taylor and MacIntyre, however, go beyond the claim that a minimal

---

[21] Martin Löw-Beer sees Taylor as showing that living without biographical narrative would be unbearable: that is, it would be existentially impossible (1991, 225–26). Taylor responds that a life without narrative would not be merely unbearable, it would be unintelligible. Narrative points to what is involved in living our lives as agents (1991b, 250). Both writers, I suggest, blur the distinction between a minimal level of narrativity that is required for intelligibility and a large-scale biographical narrative that they see as essential for a meaningful life.

form of narrative is a necessary condition of intelligibility. Both argue that human life should be understood as a more encompassing narrative that extends from birth to death. MacIntyre makes this move by arguing that a minimal form of narrativity is always embedded in longer, deeper stories: "Each of the shorter-term intentions is, and can only be made, intelligible by reference to some longer-term intentions. . . . Hence the behavior is only characterized adequately when we know what the longer and longest-term intentions are and how the shorter-term intentions are related to the longer. Once again we are involved in writing a narrative history" (1984, 207–8). The point here is not just that we are writing narrative history, but that we are driven to write a story that is increasingly more encompassing in order to make sense of the minimal narratives that we tell every day. For MacIntyre, these more encompassing narratives are also necessary prerequisites for our capacity to be virtuous. MacIntyre claims that to possess virtue is to be able to act virtuously in a variety of circumstances. To call an individual virtuous requires "a unitary life, a life that can be conceived and evaluated as a whole" (205). Without a strong conception of identity, it is impossible to assess whether one is truly virtuous or merely does virtuous things.

Taylor's move from the minimal form of narrativity to the drive for unity over a whole life is less clear than MacIntyre's. Even though Taylor argues that we should consider ourselves as a whole, he does not see such wholeness as a prerequisite for virtue. Instead, he sees it as an essential concern: "We want our lives to have meaning, or weight, or substance, or to grow towards some fullness. . . . But this means our *whole* lives. If necessary, we want the future to 'redeem' the past, to make it part of a life story which has sense or purpose, to take it up in a meaningful unity" (1989a, 50–51). This concern prompts Taylor to reject positions, such as Derek Parfit's, that argue that talking about previous and future selves is defensible. According to Taylor, to accept Parfit's position that what happened in our childhood could have happened to another self is "to accept a kind of mutilation as a person; it is to fail to meet the full challenge involved in making sense of my life" (51). The fuller notion of narrative that Taylor advocates here grows out of a deeply seated desire to craft a life as a unity from birth to death. The goal is to craft a story of one's whole life as a quest for the good, in which even the errors and mistakes of the past can be redeemed as we learn our lessons and progress. To fail to accept this challenge is to be a coward: it is to be afraid to look at life squarely and to try to tell a story about it. To take up the challenge, however, opens up the possibility of redeeming wasted time by incorporating it into a larger narrative. This larger narrative can yield the goods of fullness and meaning. Like MacIntyre's notion of virtue, fullness and meaning depend upon the ability to tell the longest story about oneself.

The idea of an all-encompassing unity over time may be Taylor's way of compensating for the cruel dilemmas and choices that multiple sources of the good present.[22] As we have seen earlier, Taylor argues that the moral sources of God, nature, and disengaged reason can lead to genuine dilemmas in choosing actions and commitments. Taylor suggests that viewing a life as a unity can indeed redeem wasted time and retrieve the remainders that these cruel choices create. Perhaps the pursuit of salvation in one's youth can be spun into a story in which that pursuit ultimately led to the sort of expressive fulfillment that Romantic writers describe. If this retrieval is possible, then the opportunity costs of pursuing salvation can be recovered by describing how that pursuit served as an important stepping-stone for one's orientation towards nature. Taylor's conception of a life as a quest allows us to say that even our dumbest decisions taught us something important. Diachronic unity softens significantly the tough choices that we make in life. As long as we can tell a story, to do may not mean to forgo.

In chapter 1, I considered the social obstacles that MacIntyre sees to these large-scale biographical narratives. Because our lives in the liberal democratic regime are partitioned into distinct segments, it becomes impossible to view them as wholes. This fragmentation makes it more difficult to realize the virtues that MacIntyre celebrates or the fullness that Taylor desires. The value associated with unity over time provides a standpoint from which to criticize current social and political organizations and institutions. The problem with our instrumental culture is that it encourages us to partition our lives (MacIntyre) and disengage our selves (Taylor). It inhibits our capacity to craft our own stories.

It is important to remind ourselves of the extent of the damage that modern liberal culture is allegedly causing here. When MacIntyre notes that "to think of a human as a narrative unity is to think in a way alien to the dominant individualist and bureaucratic modes of modern culture" (1984, 227), he cannot be claiming that these modes of life rule out the minimal form of narrativity discussed earlier. After all, both Taylor and MacIntyre suggest that narratives are not optional extras. What must be optional, in some sense, is accepting the challenge to unify a life. In other words, it must be possible not to see our lives as well-crafted unities. This possibility means, however, that even the liberal democratic regime cannot disable our abilities to tell minimal narratives: that is not an option as long as we remain agents who have intelligible interactions. Rather, the communitarians must argue that liberalism makes it more difficult to tell the kind of story that makes sense of a whole life.

We can fill out the communitarian critique by noting possible political effects of our inability to see the importance of large-scale stories. Per-

---

[22] I owe this suggestion to Bonnie Honig.

haps by devoting little effort to seeing life as a whole, we become less able
to tell stories in which our pursuit of the good is connected to the ongoing experiences of the community or the planet. How can we be concerned with the effects of our actions seven generations into the future
when we see no reason to connect them to our own personal future?
Moreover, to lack the desire to craft a comprehensive unity over time is
to lack concern with the historical sources of the goods we pursue. And
so the past becomes less and less important and our moral sources become more inaccessible. Finally, the communitarians could claim that
the great issues of our day—the environment, deficits, health care, development, economic planning—seem to demand a larger time horizon
than our disengaged, punctual self-understandings permit. The public
effect of a liberal instrumentalist society may not only be the deprivation
of the goods of fullness or wholeness, but an inability to understand the
depth of the problems we face.

Narrative and Identity

Are the communitarians correct about the importance of an all-encompassing narrative unity over time? If so, it would appear that insofar as
liberal democratic culture blinds us to this kind of narrative, it also mu-
tilates us in fairly deep ways. Taylor's and MacIntyre's claims that we
should be telling longer stories seems to provide a vantage point from
which to criticize our current self-understandings. Is fostering large-scale
biographical narratives a defensible criterion for judging the effects of
contemporary communities? Assessing that criterion moves the argument away from the community as such and towards the ways in which
communitarians judge a community worthy of respect.

As with the Romantic criticisms of disengaged reason and the punctual self, the desire for a rigorous unity over time does have a certain
resonance. But just as the Romantic unitary conception of the self was
narrowing, so this concern with unity over time may be. As we have seen,
Taylor abandons the unitary notion of the self in favor of one that permits greater flux. He accepts a kind of synchronic multiplicity in order to
provide for a wider set of human experiences. Perhaps the best way to
respond to the demand for diachronic unity is to use the same arguments that the modernists deployed against the Romantic demand for
synchronic unity. As Taylor framed it, that argument is that the unitary,
expressive self of the Romantics closes us off to the fragmentation of
lived experience. In response, he suggests that we "step outside the circle
of the single, unitary identity, and that we open ourselves to the flux
which moves beyond the scope of control or integration" (1989a, 462).

Does lived experience over time require us to move away from the drive to unity over time? Presumably the flux of experience occurs not only at a moment but also through time. To open ourselves to this experience could require stepping away from the demand to construct an all-encompassing narrative. If Taylor is convinced by the modernist reply to the Romantics, he should also be convinced by a modernist reply to his own conception of narrative unity.

Taylor, however, refuses to make this move, even when he discusses how modernity has attempted to reconfigure the idea of time and hence the notion of narrativity. For Taylor, scientific, disengaged reason promotes an objectified view of the world that, in turn, has yielded a "spacialization" of time (463). Time, from the rational scientific viewpoint, is something that passes in discrete moments independent of any lived experience. Taylor sees modernity, however, as attempting to recover a notion of "lived time" in which the experience of events is seen to be as real as the discrete moments of our rational understanding of time.

Taylor notes that this idea of "lived time" changes how we regard story telling. In the writings of Proust, Eliot, and Pound, Taylor sees a new form of narrative emerging in which events can be united by cutting across discrete, spacialized time. This notion of "lived time," in fact, avoids the celebration of fragmentation. According to Taylor, both Eliot and Pound are reaching for another kind of unity, one that extends "across persons, or across time" (465). As long as time is involved, Taylor still wants to hold onto unity. Perhaps lived time still permits the quests and biographical narratives that Taylor sees as necessary for our identities.

Instead of reconsidering the notion of time, however, one could reconsider the importance of identity. If identity is what is important to us, then we will be concerned with preserving whatever remains the same over time. MacIntyre's and Taylor's conceptions of narrative focus upon how that sameness encounters and responds to the world through various happenings. The attraction of their conceptions of narrative is partly due to the importance that we attribute to identity. If identity is not what matters to us, however, their conceptions of narrative would be less compelling.

Derek Parfit provides an alternative perspective by arguing that what matters to us is not identity strictly conceived, but rather what he calls "relation R": psychological connectedness and/or psychological continuity (1984, 262). Strictly speaking, identity is an all-or-nothing relationship with the property of transitivity. If, for example, A at five years old is the same person as B at twenty-five and B at twenty-five is the same as C at sixty-five, then A and C are the same person. Through a series of intriguing thought-experiments, Parfit argues first that a kind of Cartesian ego standing above and beyond our thoughts, desires, and intentions is indefensible. Second, Parfit claims that instead of identity, what really matters is sustaining a sufficient bundle of psychological attributes, abilities, memories, intentions, commitments, and desires over time.

Parfit depicts what he calls a reductionist conception of the self. According to him, we say that A at one time is the same person as B at another time, not because there is some further fact about us, some unchanging Cartesian ego that sustains identity, but because there are enough psychological connections between A and B. Moreover, because these psychological connections can alter over time, the idea of continuity can be a matter of degree. Unlike the strict conception of identity, continuity need not be a transitive relationship. A may be the same person as B (i.e., A may have enough psychological connections with B) and B may be the same person as C. However, under Parfit's conception of relation R, A may not be the same person as C, even though one can trace a kind of psychological continuity over time between them.

For both MacIntyre and Taylor, narrative unity over time rests upon the claim that there is personal identity in the strict sense and not simply psychological connectedness. This assumption puts them in something of a bind because neither of their positions appeals to the kind of Cartesian ego that could sustain identity over time. MacIntyre repeatedly repudiates the modern conception of the self as independent of all social roles. Taylor not only rejects the punctual self as a gross misunderstanding of ourselves, but paradoxically frames the self much as Parfit does: our identities are largely composed of a series of commitments and pursuits. Taylor argues that unlike our heads and our hands, our selves are not given. Of course, both Taylor and MacIntyre appeal to the importance of social context in constructing these commitments and pursuits, but it is not clear why this context would make much of a difference to Parfit's claim.

Yet, MacIntyre is quite blunt about the significance of a reductionist position to his own project:

> Derek Parfit and others have recently drawn our attention to the contrast between criteria of strict identity, which is an all-or-nothing matter . . . and the psychological continuities of personality which are a matter of more or less. . . . But what is crucial to human beings as characters in enacted narratives is that, possessing only the resources of psychological continuity, we have to be able to respond to the imputation of strict identity. I am forever whatever I have been at any time for others—and I may at any time be called upon to answer for it—no matter how changed I may be now. There is no way of *found-*

ing my identity—or lack of it—on the psychological continuity or discontinuity of the self. The self inhabits a character whose unity is given as the unity of character. (1984, 216–17)

What is intriguing about this position is that even though MacIntyre does not posit some further, transcendental fact about ourselves, he still must impute a strict conception of identity. One way to understand his position is to use Nietzsche's terminology: personal identity is a necessary fiction for his narrative. Personal identity does not exist prior to the telling of a long story. It is written into the story itself: "The concepts of narrative, intelligibility and accountability presuppose the applicability of the concept of personal identity, just as it presupposes their applicability and just as indeed each of these three presupposes the applicability of the two others. The relationship is one of mutual presupposition" (218). In other words, as long as we desire to tell these kinds of stories we will be in the business of constructing the notion of a strict identity.

Despite his protestations, MacIntyre's solution is, in fact, consistent with Parfit's position. To put MacIntyre's notion of narrative unity over time into Parfit's notion of psychological continuity, one could say that there must be at least one continuing thread throughout one's life: the desire to tell a story about a whole life and create a fiction of personal identity.[23] This thread is not strong enough, of course, to bear the weight of an identity claim.[24] But, according to the communitarians, it is still something that we should want. Why? For MacIntyre the thread or larger narrative is necessary both for the smaller intentions to make sense and to enable large-scale assessments about the virtuousness of our lives. For Taylor, sustaining this thread is desirable because it is a necessary condition for a kind of courage, it allows the redemption of lost time, and it opens us up to a fuller, more meaningful life. With all of these good effects, how could one possibly deny the importance of this strong notion of unity over time?

[23] Martin Löw-Beer argues that Parfit's position "overlooks the importance of personal narratives in shaping our lives" (Löw-Beer 1991, 220). In a sense, I think this is correct, but Löw-Beer fails to demonstrate that Parfit's position cannot incorporate the importance of, at least, a minimal form of narrative. Perhaps narrativity is already embedded in what we mean by an intention, project, or commitment. That is, it is embedded in the psychological connections that compose Parfit's relation R. Löw-Beer sets out a more interesting claim when he argues that if one reads Parfit's description of persons as being informed by utilitarianism, he is actually committed to dissolving all distinctions between individuals and constructing a "super-person." Once again, although Parfit is a utilitarian, he does not see his view of persons as inspired by utilitarianism (in fact Löw-Beer believes that his own reading is forced, [221]), nor does his utilitarianism seek to construct a super-person. Relation R does not render the distinction between persons irrelevant.

[24] This would mean that our identity over time is based upon a desire for such an identity.

The Benefits of Relation R

Perhaps the best strategy is to accept the possible importance of the communitarian account, but also to suggest both that it has no monopoly on plausibility and that it carries costs that the communitarians do not consider. At the very least, MacIntyre's conception of intelligibility is far too demanding. MacIntyre claims that our lesser intentions cannot be rendered intelligible unless they are placed in a more encompassing narrative. Yet actions and intentions are, in fact, intelligible both to ourselves and to others with fairly abbreviated, implicit narratives. In our day-to-day actions and interactions we rarely engage in a large-scale narrative construction to explain what we or others are doing. MacIntyre glosses over the difference between asserting the necessity of a minimal narrative to make an action intelligible and the claim that an intelligible and virtuous life requires large-scale narrative. It is not true that only those who can tell life-encompassing stories can act intelligibly. From the opposite perspective, telling a larger story may not greatly help us understand a mundane action or experience. Reaching for one's life story with every bite to eat could become rather tedious.

The deeper argument supporting the communitarian position is that to abandon this project of constructing a whole life is to accept a kind of defeat. If we took Parfit seriously and opened ourselves to the possibility that who we are today may not be who we once were or who we are going to be, then we will have closed ourselves off to certain experiences (e.g., fullness, meaning, substance, virtue). But seeing ourselves as constructed, well-crafted unities may also close ourselves off to certain important experiences of the human condition. Parfit clearly believes that, at least in his case, his view does provide him with something that a nonreductive vision of the self cannot. Parfit writes,

> Is the truth depressing? Some may find it so. But I find it liberating, and consoling. When I believed that my existence was a such [*sic*] a further fact, I seemed imprisoned in myself. My life seemed like a glass tunnel, through which I was moving faster every year, and at the end of which there was darkness. When I changed my view, the walls of the glass tunnel disappeared. I now live in the open air. . . . Other people are closer. I am less concerned about the rest of my own life, and more concerned about the lives of others. (Parfit 1984, 281)

Parfit suggests that with his reductionist view we become more concerned with the quality and character of our individual intentions and projects than with whether there will be some grand and glorious 'I' to experience them. This kind of experience also lessens our resentment toward death. The aspiration to find a strict identity over time may be an attempt to establish a final secular breakwater against time. The communitarian urge to tell a unifying story across a life may also be an urge to tell a story that will endure outside of time. Taylor suggests as much when he writes, "the modern aspiration for meaning and substance in one's life has obvious affinities with longer-standing aspirations to higher being, to immortality" (1989a, 43). But this urge to unite a life may make the ending all the more final and resented. In contrast, Parfit claims that if we see that what matters to us is not something that stands above and beyond our experiences, but the experiences themselves, then death can never be a complete or final break: "there may later be thoughts that are influenced by mine, or things done as the result of my advice. My death will break the more direct relations between my present experiences and future experience, but it will not break various other relations. This is all there is to the fact that there will be no one living who will be me. Now that I have seen this, my death seems to me to be less bad" (Parfit 1984, 281).

The move away from an all-encompassing narrative may also better account for our own practices of responsibility. These practices are, in many respects, connected to and diminish with the passage of time. Statutes of limitations, the excuse of youthful indiscretions, the hope that people can change, the virtue of forgiving and forgetting, all seem to be more in line with Parfit's relation R than with the communitarian construction of strict identity. Finally, Parfit's position can accommodate the communitarian position, but not vice versa. Parfit writes that "on the Reductionist view, the unity of our lives is a matter of degree, and is something we can affect. We may want our lives to have more unity, in the way that an artist may want to create a unified work. And we can *give* our lives greater unity, in ways that express or fulfill our particular values and beliefs" (446). Because of the importance of the strict conception of identity to their notion of narrative unity, the communitarians cannot conceive that any value could be derived from a lesser concern for identity. For this reason alone, Parfit's position offers a better account of the diversity of human experience than what the communitarians provide.

The Costs of Unity

The communitarians argue that the drive to an all-encompassing identity opens us up to a fuller notion of virtue and meaningfulness (although Parfit's account of relation R does not rule out the possibility of virtue). Nevertheless, they fail to consider the direct costs that this notion of identity may also incur. One possible cost is that an intense concern with constructing a life that stands as a whole may stultify growth and change. The communitarian project may make us less willing to do anything that pushes against or challenges our current narrative identity. After a certain point, we may become less willing to disturb the narrative we have constructed. The push to unity may ultimately stifle creativity, growth, and maturity. A second and related cost is that the valorization of unity may lead us to reject others who move away from or do things that fail to fit in their own life stories as we understand them. The problem with valorizing identity is that change becomes so much harder to accommodate and accept. A third danger within the communitarian position is that it may intensify self-loathing, particularly if one cannot construct the harmonious, redemptive kind of story that Taylor and MacIntyre assume will be told. It is not clear that every action can be or should be redeemed by a story. In this case the drive to unity may itself be a waste of time and may demonstrate an unwillingness to let go of the past. In some cases forgetting may be as important as recovering. On the other hand, if we construct personal identity when we create a biographical narrative, as MacIntyre suggests, what criteria do we use to judge the accuracy of our stories? Does not the coming together of personal identity, responsibility, and narrative not suggest that our stories will always be stories of success? Does this make things too easy? For Parfit, the drive to unity may be directed by an aesthetic criterion. It is unlikely that the communitarians would see this as sufficient. Finally, the push to create a well-crafted unity over time is itself akin to the self-centeredness that the communitarians attribute to modern culture: I become less concerned with other people and more concerned with my own story. The communitarian desire to create biographical narratives may simply replicate atomistic self-understandings.

The argument here is not that the communitarian drive to unity is a wholly unacceptable way to conceive of human experience. In fact, this notion of unity may have the kind of resonance that Taylor's other conceptions of the good possess. I am claiming, though, that this view of life over time entails direct costs that its proponents fail to address, and that this view rules out different ways of conceiving oneself in time and hence closes down other worthwhile human experiences and possibilities.

Communitarians argue that liberal culture fosters an objectionable kind of person. The standards they use to make this determination center on the concept of unity. Liberal selves look so objectionable in large part because unified selves look so good. Communitarians, however, have qualified the unity of the self and community so heavily that a liberal self capable of choosing and rethinking its conception of the good appears an intrinsic part of their project. The problem is somewhat different with the punctual or expressivist self. If anything, Taylor seems to suggest that modern life has cultivated a multileveled self and not a unitary self, a development he celebrates.

What appears to remain most objectionable about liberal democratic selfcraft is that it fosters a diachronically fragmented self. The compartmentalization of liberal culture makes it difficult for us to tell the kinds of stories about ourselves that make sense of our lives. The ideal of a self united over time provides a standard for revealing the harm that is being done to us by this culture, but this standard is itself disputable. If Parfit is right, then what matters to us is not identity but certain psychological continuities. It is not necessarily the case that grand unifying biographies are needed to give life meaning. In short, the diachronically fragmenting features of modern life will be troubling only to those who want to tell larger stories about their lives. Phrasing the claim this way weakens significantly the communitarian case for political responsibility to respond to liberal selfcraft.

3

The Well-Ordered, Reason-Governed Soul

THE THEMES OF disorder and impoverishment in modern times are conspicuous in the writings of classical political rationalists. According to Strauss and many of his students, liberal democracy stunts human beings and fails to foster a well-ordered soul. They believe that the prevailing intellectual milieu is indifferent if not openly hostile to the idea of a truth-seeking soul that possesses a given hierarchical nature. For the classical political rationalists, the transition to modernity and postmodernity has harmed prospects for the best souls. Supporting this understanding of harm is the standard of an individual who is both reason-governed and engaged in the erotic pursuit of truth.

A full assessment of classical political rationalism would require replaying much of the history of Western thought, beginning with certain Platonic and Aristotelian teachings. Questions concerning truth, knowledge, reality, nature, speech, language, interpretation, religion, philosophy, and science would all have to be addressed in any comprehensive response to the classical political rationalists. Because such a project lies beyond the scope of this book, this chapter begins by touching on only a few of these themes and the questions that they raise. The second half of the chapter focuses on the problem of ranking the reason-governed soul against other kinds of souls, for it is this ranking that provides a criterion for criticizing the prevailing egalitarian milieu of liberal democracy.

Nature and Reason

The Straussian critical project turns on an understanding of the soul that is connected to a notion of nature as hierarchical. Moreover, knowing a particular soul requires placing it under a universal that is itself open to understanding. To call into question either the existence of a mind-independent nature, the idea of the soul, the hierarchy between and within souls, or the underlying epistemology would call into question much of that critical project. For there to be a political responsibility to engage in soulcraft, these questions must be adequately settled. If the coercive powers of the state are necessary to carry out the cultivation of our souls, natural right must be more than a possibility. In these first sections, I will consider a few problems associated with classical political rationalism's metaphysical and epistemological commitments. When we talk about nature, natural right, and souls, the ground may not be firm enough to support a political responsibility to engage in soulcraft.

To reject the idea of a mind-independent nature would strike at the root of the classical political rationalist critique of liberal democracy. In fact, the most direct and most radical challenge to that critique comes from what Strauss calls the third wave of modernity. This wave is characterized by a thoroughly historicized view of human nature and reason. On this view, what we are and how we think are functions of time and place. Nietzsche, one of the most thoroughgoing critics of rationalism, argues that human effort and will put into place the conventions and practices that govern our lives. Our political life is founded neither upon nature nor upon God. From a Nietzschean perspective, the classical political rationalists' rejection of the historicized view of human life is a form of nihilism. That is, by the Nietzschean accounting, Strauss and his students yearn for a certainty or a knowledge of the whole that is impossible to realize. Furthermore, they are constantly in danger of falling into a second form of nihilism by implying that the world is deprived of all value and meaning if certainty cannot be found in nature or if reason cannot establish the nature of good. In contrast, Nietzsche believes that it is possible to work through these forms of nihilism. Through human will and creation we can engage in the transvaluation of values. This transvaluation does not mean the abandonment of value; rather, it means that we are willing to live our lives with the knowledge that our values are human projects.[1]

In defense of the ideas of reason and natural right, the classical political rationalists deploy a number of arguments. The first is that reason must occupy a special place because we inevitably use reason to decide its place. Even if it is defeated, reason still has the last word. As Strauss suggests, "the successful quest for wisdom might lead to the result that wisdom is not the one thing needful. But this result would owe its relevance to the fact that it is the result of the quest for wisdom: the very disavowal of reason must be reasonable disavowal" (1953, 36). There

---

[1] Yet the kind of critique of reason offered by Nietzsche is not necessarily incompatible with the classical political rationalist position. This extremely abbreviated reading of Nietzsche's conception of nihilism opens up the possibility that the value attributed to nature and reason could be based upon an act of the will. Is a willful rationalism still rationalism? Admittedly, its yearning for a certainty would be severely shaken. Nevertheless, the possibility that reason must be grounded upon an initial act of will may not be that different from Strauss's suggestion that reason is ultimately based upon an act of faith. This reading of Strauss is also offered by Stanley Rosen (1987, 111) and is, to a certain extent, in accord with Shadia Drury's interpretation (1988).

can, of course, be disavowals that do not depend upon reason. Poets, romantics, mystics, and prophets may decide the place of reason without its use. It is not clear that those who seek wisdom necessarily offer a reasonable disavowal of reason. If this is the case, then perhaps Strauss is arguing that the disavowal of reason *should be* a reasonable disavowal. The question becomes whether this claim could ever be convincing to those who do not test their normative commitments before the bar of reason. In any case, even for those seeking a reasonable defense of reason, Strauss's argument is very cold comfort, for even a reasonable disavowal is still a disavowal. If, as Hobbes, Locke, and Hume argue (or reason), the passions should not (or cannot) be ruled by reason, then reason has abdicated its position.

A second argument in defense of reason and natural right expands upon this first claim by showing that those who subscribe to the third wave of modernity cannot demonstrate the impossibility of knowing nature or the whole without falling into self-refuting relativism. They cannot be absolutely sure there are no absolutes without subscribing to an absolute. Nor can they claim that truth as knowing a mind-independent reality is impossible without making a positive statement about the nature of truth. Without such proofs, an opening for nature and reason is always available.

Relativism and ethnocentrism can fall into self-refutation, but this is not the only possibility. Not all writers who refuse to subscribe to essentialism or natural right also offer a self-defeating relativism. Richard Rorty, for example, does not argue that the abandonment of realism is itself objectively required (Rorty 1991a, 23). His pragmatism is not meant to be one more theory about Truth. Rorty is not claiming that there are no absolutes. Instead, he argues that within our understandings and practices we use truth in certain ways and in certain situations. Truth is "a commendatory term for well-justified beliefs" (24). One can look at human life through a notion of solidarity that simply circumvents the self-refuting charge.

But does this strategy, in fact, circumvent appeals to absolutes? After all, Rorty's solidarity with his own cultural/social context or his belief that cruelty is the worst thing we can do appear to be absolutes. Indeed, when Rorty says such things as, "For all we share with all other humans is the same thing we share with all other animals—the ability to feel pain" (1989, 177), he seems to be positing things that would hold true regardless of time and place. Is the claim "that there is nothing to be said about truth save that each of us will commend as true those beliefs which he or she finds good to believe" (1991a, 24), not a positive theory about the nature of reality (Truth)? In effect, Rorty is either surreptitiously appealing to absolutes (truths) or he is asserting that there are absolutely no absolutes.

The pragmatic response to the first claim is that all of those appeals that look like absolute standards are actually warranted only given a larger set of social practices and beliefs. That is, presumably, what makes them well-justified and true. Rorty's response to the second claim is that his way of using the word *truth* has nothing to do with the nature of reality. It is not, he argues, an epistemological or metaphysical claim. Consequently, it cannot claim that there are absolutely no absolutes. That kind of claim makes sense only if one subscribes to a notion of truth that requires that propositions correspond to reality. Because Rorty does not use *truth* in that manner, he evades the categories of the classical political rationalists.

A classical political rationalist could argue that Rorty's avoidance of self-refutation is successful only if one accepts his definition of truth, a definition that blinds us to the pursuit of an external reality. Although this is correct, it doesn't show that Rorty is trapped by self-refutation. Moreover, it raises the question of how one could choose between these understandings of truth. Rorty argues that this matter cannot be settled by turning to notions of nature or natural right without already begging the issue in favor of seeing truth as that which corresponds to reality (24). On the other hand, classical rationalists could argue that this issue cannot be settled on purely pragmatic grounds without begging the issue in favor of Rorty.

But perhaps the classical political rationalists are not completely without resources on Rorty's turf. For the question of how to understand truth could be framed as "a straightforward empirical, sociological-historical one about the sort of glue that is required to hold a community together" (178). Classical political rationalists could argue that nature and natural right are necessary to sustain our political arrangements. Because liberal democracies are founded upon notions such as inalienable rights and self-evident truths, the Rortarian and Nietzschean positions undermine these political foundations. Once people believe that there are no self-evident truths they will come to see the law as merely an imposition of another's will on their own. They will lose any sense of responsibility to a common political life and they will be unwilling to defend the regime when the chips are down.

One problem with this response is that it is compatible with the claim that notions of reason and nature are necessary fictions. If the classical political rationalists were correct about the glue needed for liberal democracy, then Rorty's position would receive a serious blow. Nevertheless, such an empirical settlement could still be congruous with Rorty's ethnocentrism. A second problem is that this instrumentalist response can be circular: on the one hand, liberal democracy is a worthy regime because it lives up to the standards lodged in our existence as a certain sort of social, rational animal; on the other hand, we should subscribe to this conception of ourselves because it is ultimately necessary to support liberal democracy. In either its instrumentalist or circular formulations, this argument does not get the classical political rationalists where they want to go.

Perhaps the best case for knowing nature and natural right is connected to the notion of dialectic. This argument appeals to the actual experience of knowing. It suggests that the existence of universally valid principles can be demonstrated only by actually coming into contact with them. In a sense, the classical political rationalists argue that one cannot inductively or deductively prove nature or natural right. Only through a properly and seriously engaged conversation can one be open to its possibility. Pangle offers a particularly clear formulation of this Socratic position (1992, 184–94). His discussion suggests, however, that the soul must be prepared in a number of ways in order to engage in this pursuit.[2]

The first step in this preparation is to examine opinions seriously. The dialectic begins, as Strauss notes, with the common opinions one finds in and around oneself (Strauss 1953, 124). There is here no Cartesian stripping away of everything that one can doubt. Rather, the learner starts with those principles and beliefs that we rely upon every day to govern our actions. The dialectic begins when we notice that these opinions conflict with one another. In the face of this conflict we are forced to ask which principle or belief should guide our actions. For those who are not properly prepared, however, playing off one opinion against the other and ripping arguments apart will be seen as a game. According to Pangle, only after individuals acquire "a rich and compelling moral education in artistically and poetically inspired republican virtue" will they possess the requisite seriousness and moral maturity (1992, 188). Without this seriousness of purpose the examination of opinion can never progress beyond mere play.

A second form of required preparation comes through the experiences of learning mathematics and the natural sciences. A prepared individual must not only be morally mature, but also must already have

[2] Foucault, from a very different perspective, also recognizes the importance of preparation in Greek thought. He writes, "Even if it is true that Greek philosophy founded rationality, it always held that a subject could not have access to the truth if he did not first operate upon himself a certain work which would make him susceptible to knowing the truth—a work of purification, conversion of the soul by contemplation of the soul itself" (1984b, 371).

had the taste of an objective truth. Pangle claims that without some such educational background, the dialectic would become a purely destructive device. The point of the sciences is to "draw the eye of the soul up and out of the changing particularity of history and empirical experience, showing the intellect's capacity to see underlying principles that are invisible to the eye, but demonstrably at work always and everywhere in the manifold of temporal and spatial experience" (188). These sciences not only reassure us that our explorations will not be necessarily in vain, but they also help us recognize when we have encountered a truth.

These conditions, however necessary, are not sufficient. In this retelling of Plato's allegory of the cave, Pangle argues that the pursuit of science must itself become reflective. There are certain problems and questions that must be left unasked when engaging in science: we may study the stars and formulate principles that describe their regularity, but to ask why there is regularity in the first place poses a different sort of question. More troubling, Pangle says, are questions about the goodness of the pursuit of science itself. This practice entails a radical form of self-criticism: looking at and questioning one's deepest commitments. In this part of the dialectic one must scrutinize what has been most deeply inscribed into the soul. Pangle acknowledges the difficulty of this task. "The problem, as Socrates' metaphor [of the cave] makes abundantly clear, is indeed an immense one—possibly, in the final analysis, insoluble" (193).

Plato's allegory of the cave and the view of philosophy as the passionate exploration of the presumptions that govern human activity are undeniably attractive. Nevertheless, this view of philosophy does not itself demonstrate that a careful and serious exploration of those presumptions gets one out of a cave and into contact with what is truly real. Philosophy could be conceived in much the same way without the belief that it ultimately leads to an unmediated experience of reality. For example, Michael Oakeshott's conception of understanding may offer just such an alternative idea of philosophy. As in the allegory of the cave, Oakeshott argues that we must begin with practice, but he rejects Plato's tendency to write off the understandings within the cave as "nescience" (1975, 27). As with Plato's allegory, Oakeshott believes that philosophy entails the exploration of the deeper postulates and commitments that are used, but not fully understood, in everyday practice. Thinking about these postulates leads into a world of abstract concepts and ideas. Oakeshott argues, however, that these abstractions should not replace and cannot improve the conduct of everyday life. Oakeshott presents a Socratic dialectic without its realist optimism.

The classical political rationalists leave us with the claim that until you have experienced foundational, higher truths, they should not be disparaged or forsaken. But the project itself appears jeopardized by the influence of a Kuhnian view of science upon the personal experience of scientific certainty and by the absence of criteria establishing when we have directly experienced a mind-independent reality. In the former case, there are legitimate questions regarding whether science brings us into contact with universal truths or merely presents a coherent intersubjectively agreed-upon paradigm. If science does not give us a taste for truth, then how can such a taste be acquired? In the latter case the problem is to distinguish the criteria that establish a genuine experience of reality from a passion-induced charade. These kinds of questions, obviously, do not put an end to a realist metaphysics. They do, however, raise deep problems for appeals to a natural order of the soul.

Particular Souls and Knowing the Whole

In addition to these difficult metaphysical questions, the classical political rationalist position also draws on a disputable theory of knowledge. One of classical political rationalism's features is its holism. To know something, rationalists argue, requires placing it under some universal. Particulars, as such, cannot be known unless and until they are placed under the appropriate universal category. In rendering his understanding of Plato, Strauss writes that "all understanding presupposes a fundamental awareness of the whole: prior to any perception of particular things, the human soul must have had a vision of the ideas, a vision of the articulated whole" (1953, 125). A somewhat less Platonic and more Aristotelian epistemology can be found in Salkever's definition of rationality as a "name given in the first instance to the activity of scientific inquiry itself, that of placing particulars relative to relevant universals" (1990, 21).[3] At least in its Platonic formulation, holistic epistemology has an acknowledged limit built into it. If something cannot be brought under a universal category, then it cannot be understood. Harry Jaffa brings this argument to bear on the debate between reason and revelation. Jaffa writes, "The God of the Bible not only is One, but is unknowable precisely because He is One: What is unique is, from Plato's own point of view, unknowable" (1984, 18). Being singular and falling under no universal, God's essential nature cannot be understood. It remains veiled in mystery and is glimpsed at only when it reveals itself through its actions, but even then we can conclude only that God works in strange and mysterious ways.

[3] Pangle sees this as an essential part of the Socratic dialectic. It entails "accurately distinguishing the kinds or classes into which all particulars fall" (1992, 184).

For the most part, this epistemology is underdefended and sketchy in classical political rationalist writings. It raises, however, intriguing and difficult questions regarding whether Plato's view of universals is superior to Aristotle's, how individuation occurs, whether universals exist, and why direct cognition of individuals is impossible. If we put aside these larger questions, this epistemology is interesting because it not only purports to tell us how we know what we know, but also what we cannot know. What is less clear is how we know whether something is unique or part of a universal category. In order to engage in soultalk, souls must not be particulars in the way that God is in Jaffa's view. If every soul is unique in the sense of not being an instantiation of some universal, essential characteristics, then it lies on the other side of what can be known. In this one respect, the soul would be godlike. Rousseau expresses this position in his *Confessions.* "I am made unlike anyone I have ever met; I will even venture to say that I am like no one in the whole world. I may be no better, but at least I am different" (Lukes 1973, 67). Although this emphasis upon difference and uniqueness came into full bloom with nineteenth-century Romanticism, its roots reach back to medieval nominalism.[4] The twelfth-century theologian Peter Abelard observed that "although people say that Socrates and Plato are one in their humanity, how can that be accepted, when it is obvious that all men are different from each other both in matter and in form?" (Morris 1972, 65).[5] This celebration of uniqueness and difference supports a form of individualism that a classical epistemology cannot account for. Each soul becomes a mysterious, unique thing that, like God, can be known and judged only by its actions. Even on those occasions of its acting, no one knows its heart of hearts, not even the actor.

The soultalk of the classical political rationalists depends upon its ability to defeat the idea of the unique soul. Bloom, I think, is aware of this problem, but instead of talking about a unique soul he uses the term *self.*[6] Bloom wrote that in our search for the self "we go back and back, ever farther, hunting the self as it retreats into the forest, just a step ahead of us. Although disquieting, this may, from the point of view of its

---

[4] According to George Simmel, the new German individualism of the nineteenth century was "the individualism of difference, with the deepening of individuality to the point of the individual's incomparability, to which he is 'called' both in his nature and in his achievement" (Lukes 1973, 18).

[5] Colin Morris, however, notes that Abelard backed away from this extreme individualism and assigned "some partial reality to universals" (1972, 65).

[6] Bloom and other classical political rationalists have also taken the self as a concept that is opposed to the possibility of a nature (Strauss 1968, 261; Mansfield 1991, 32). While Strauss is sensitive to uses of the idea of the self that may resemble uses of the soul, Bloom is certain that the terms are mutually exclusive (Bloom 1975, 660). For Bloom, the soul is our nature, whereas the self is a fabrication, a mere social construction.

latest interpretation, be the essence of the self: mysterious, ineffable, indefinable, unlimited, creative, known only by its deeds; in short, like God, of whom it is the impious mirror image (1987, 173). If we see the self as a surrogate for the notion of a unique soul, what is classical political rationalism's response to this possibility? For the moment, it appears, there is no response, except for Bloom's (ironic?) claim that the mysterious soul (self) is blasphemous. Without such a response, the soul could be shrouded in mystery. If this is possible, then its opaque character cannot provide the kind of leverage classical political rationalists need to assess the quality of our politics.

The Rule of Reason

Even if the possibility of knowing nature and the nature of the soul could be established firmly, the classical political rationalist ordering of the soul would still have to be established. As noted in chapter 1, Strauss argues that the psychic rule of reason or of the higher over the lower is despotic.[7] He argues that an individual cannot

> rule his body by persuasion. This fact alone shows that even despotic rule is not per se against nature. What is true of self-restraint, self-coercion, and power over one's self applies in principle to the restraint and coercion of others and to power over others. To take the extreme case, despotic rule is unjust only if it is applied to beings who can be ruled by persuasion or whose understanding is sufficient: Prospero's rule over Caliban is by nature just. Justice and coercion are not mutually exclusive. (1953, 133)

Here, Strauss makes a number of important claims. First, he is suggesting that psychic rule is directly parallel to political rule. The lessons learned in governing ourselves bear upon how we govern others. Conversely, the whole notion of governing others is applicable to governing ourselves. Although this internal politics is not very complex or developed, it is still part of Strauss's position. Second, its presence means that Strauss does not abandon all hope for a fruitful analogy between politics and psyche. This last point becomes important to understanding Strauss's and Bloom's interpretations of the key metaphor for an internal politics of identity—that found in Plato's *Republic*.

For the classical political rationalists there is a natural hierarchy within the soul. Sometimes they express this hierarchy in terms of the soul's rule over the body, sometimes in terms of reason's rule over passion. In

---

[7] For an alternative view that argues that reason rules on the basis of consent, see Reeve (1988, 142–43).

either case, this hierarchy is a matter of achievement; it is not an automatic state of affairs. Liberal democratic culture has disorganized our souls to the extent that "people no longer believe in a natural hierarchy of the soul's varied and conflicting inclinations, the traditions that provided a substitute for nature have crumbled. The soul becomes a stage for a repertory company that changes plays regularly" (Bloom 1987, 155–56).[8] The idea of restoring the rule of reason, however, rests upon the presumption that reason has a right to govern.

Classical political rationalists portray the pursuit of wisdom as the highest expression of a well-ordered, reason-governed soul. According to them, to demonstrate the superiority of philosophy is also to demonstrate the superiority of the rule of reason. Such a demonstration would mean that the philosophic life is superior, for example, to a life of accumulating wealth, or a military life, or a life devoted to the obedience of God's laws. The superiority of the rule of reason also provides classical political rationalists with a standard for judging the effects of liberal democracy. By fostering a radical egalitarianism and relativism, this regime not only undermines the possibility for the healthiest of souls, it also sours the possibilities for the rule of reason in intellectuals or that class of public-spirited individuals Strauss referred to as gentlemen. This judgment of harm by the classical political rationalists extends beyond a prudential concern for sustaining the regime and ultimately rests upon an understanding of what is the best way of life. It is the problematic status of this standard that the rest of this chapter explores.

Reason and Pleasure

According to Shadia Drury, Strauss never clearly set out his defense of the philosophic way of life: "Why is contemplation the highest end which politics must serve? Is it not conceivable that there is a plurality of equal and incommensurable goods that politics must serve? ... Strauss provides few, if any, answers to these questions in his writings. One must suppose that ideas that are covertly held and transmitted need no argument" (1988, 132). Drury, however, concludes that Strauss is actually a philosophical hedonist or, to use Strauss's language, a philosophical conventionalist. Drury attempts to show a distinction between Strauss's public teachings (his exoteric doctrine) and his real beliefs (his esoteric doctrine). According to Drury, Strauss's esoteric doctrine was meant for a few followers and was conveyed only in private. She argues that al-

---

[8] Deutsch and Soffer put it this way: "Gone is the conception of the soul as a natural hierarchy of parts" (1987, 8).

though Strauss taught publicly that the pursuit of wisdom and truth for their own sakes was most important, he really believed that pleasure is the highest good. Thus, as a philosophical conventionalist, Strauss would have believed that reason should rule because it yields the highest pleasures. The life of the philosopher is superior to all other forms of life because it is the most pleasant (94).

The importance of eros to the philosophic life bolsters Drury's interpretation to a certain extent. Philosophy is the love of wisdom, and that love is erotic. Eros is a kind of intellectual itch that cries out to be scratched. Bloom understands eros as a desire for completion that expresses itself both through our sexuality and through our intellectual pursuits. Insofar as we want to know the truth of the matter, or to know the whole story, eros drives us. Eros is clearly a want or desire. When manifested in sexuality it is compatible with a vulgar form of hedonism. Drury's argument is that philosophy is accompanied by its own form of hedonism (see also Holmes 1993, 71–73).

As mentioned in chapter 1, Bloom believes that we have lost a sense of the erotic. Our desire for completion has been played out through our infatuation with rock music, the equation of sexuality with pornography, and the culture of drugs. Bloom predicts that those students who have lost the sense of the erotic "will assiduously study economics or the professions and the Michael Jackson costume will slip off to reveal a Brooks Brothers suit beneath. They will want to get ahead and live comfortably. But this life is as empty and false as the one they left behind" (1987, 81).[9] On Drury's interpretation, Bloom is trying to turn his students away from a vulgar hedonism and towards a philosophical hedonism. In either case, however, pleasure is still the highest pursuit.

If we accept for a moment Drury's interpretation of Strauss, does it offer a convincing case for the superiority of philosophy over other ways of life? Is the rule of reason justified by the pleasure it brings? The implication of this position is that anybody who experienced the pleasures of pushpin and poetry would prefer poetry. Anyone who experienced the pleasures of poetry and philosophy would choose philosophy. The problem with this, of course, is that most people do not find the pleasures associated with careful, intense thought particularly enjoyable. What is and is not pleasurable seems to be something over which there is a great

---

[9] Bloom elaborates this theme in his last book, *Love and Friendship*. "The de-eroticization of the world, a companion of its disenchantment, is a complex phenomenon. It seems to result from a combination of causes—our democratic regime and its tendencies toward leveling and self-protection, a reductionist-materialist science that inevitably interprets eros as sex, and the atmosphere generated by 'the death of God' and of the subordinate god, Eros" (1993, 15).

deal of disagreement. If Strauss's preference for philosophy were based upon pleasure, then its basis would be fairly subjective. Holding everything else equal, is there reason enough why liberal democracy should be concerned with providing the conditions for satisfying the pleasures of philosophy rather than the pleasures for poetry or pushpin?

Yet there are reasons for doubting Drury's interpretation. Insofar as Strauss and other classical political rationalists are disposed favorably to the classical idea that nature provides a standard for right and wrong, then it is unlikely that they would use hedonism to defend the superiority of the philosophic way of life. Strauss makes this quite clear by first conceding that "the thesis that the life according to nature is the life of human excellence can be defended on hedonistic grounds," and then observing that instead of taking this way out,

> the classics protested against this manner of understanding the good life. For, from the point of view of hedonism, nobility of character is good because it is conducive to a life of pleasure or even indispensable for it: nobility of character is the handmaid of pleasure; it is not good for its own sake. According to the classics, this interpretation distorts the phenomena as they are known from experience to every unbiased and competent, i.e., not morally obtuse, man. We admire excellence without any regard to our pleasures or to our benefits. (Strauss 1953, 128)

Whether we actually do admire excellence for its own sake or are simply obtuse, the important point is that Strauss did not see the classics as moving in the direction that Drury suggests, and to the extent that he followed the classics in this matter, he himself did not go in that direction.

This response leaves open the role of eros in the pursuit of wisdom. Why doesn't the emphasis upon eros lead to hedonism? Strauss avoids this association by distinguishing between wants and pleasures. He argues that although pleasures are indeed connected with wants, "the wants precede the pleasures" (126). This opens the possibility that not only are the wants not themselves pleasures, but also that their satisfaction may be something other than pleasant—i.e., it may be noble. The idea that wants can be noble is consistent with Strauss's further claim that these wants have a natural order (126). The argument would be that eros is a want high in that order, expressed as a desire for completion. Its fulfillment may be pleasurable when associated with sexuality or noble when associated with the intellect. Eros entices and drives the life of the mind even through the pains of thought and crises of confidence that accompany it.

Distinguishing wants from pleasures allows Strauss to distinguish the love of wisdom from physical pleasures. But can we sustain a distinction between wants and pleasures, particularly with regard to eros? Eros is so tightly connected to pleasure, that it is difficult to see what a pleasure-free eros would mean. In contrast, Bloom writes that, "it is generally agreed that Eros is connected with pleasure, a very powerful pleasure" (1993, 432). At the very least, it is unlikely that the classical political rationalists would justify reason's rule on the basis of its production of pleasure.

Reason and Revelation

The central problem with ranking a reason-governed life above all others is that there are competing ways of life that see things differently. Classical political rationalists are, in fact, well aware of these alternatives. Sorting through some of these alternatives will help clarify the issues and problems in justifying the rule of reason. For Strauss and many of his students the most serious challenge to the philosophic way of life comes from a life governed by revelation and faith. Strauss frames the choice between reason and faith as a choice between "a life of obedient love versus a life of free insight" (Strauss 1953, 74).

Why should unaided reason and not the word of God govern one's soul? For Strauss, these two ways of life cannot be reconciled without sacrificing the purity of one or the other. The dispute between what Strauss called "Jerusalem and Athens" appears to be deadlocked: "All arguments in favor of revelation seem to be valid only if belief in revelation is presupposed; and all arguments against revelation seem to be valid only if unbelief is presupposed" (75). Nevertheless, Strauss admits that Athens is at a decided disadvantage. According to him, unaided reason cannot deny the possibility of revelation—reason simply is not powerful enough to rule out the possibility of divine intervention. Strauss suggests that if revelation cannot be ruled out then it is possible that the "philosophic life is not necessarily, not evidently, *the* right life. . . . The mere fact that philosophy and revelation cannot refute each other would constitute the refutation of philosophy by revelation" (75).[10]

[10] Pangle notes that reason could defeat revelation only if the philosopher could show that he had in principle "a clear and exhaustive explanation of how and why everything in the entire cosmos is as it is and behaves as it does. . . . The mature Socrates seems to have been the first philosopher who realized not merely that such a comprehensive account of things eludes men, but how dire are the consequences of this fact for the claims of philosophy" (1983, 22).

Although in *Natural Right and History*, Strauss backs off from "these awful depths" (76), it appears that he takes the plunge in other writings. In his essay, "Progress or Return?" Strauss asks what the consequences are of admitting the possibility of revelation. The answer, Strauss argues, is quite clear. It implies that choosing philosophy over revelation cannot ultimately be grounded in reason, and this admits that the "choice of philosophy is based on faith. In other words, the quest for evident knowledge rests itself on an unevident premise" (Strauss 1989, 269). This conclusion appears to directly parallel Strauss's interpretation of Max Weber, for whom science or philosophy rested "not on evident premises that are at the disposal of man as man but on faith" (Strauss 1953, 71).[11]

Once again, Drury provides an alternative interpretation of Strauss's position. According to Drury, "Strauss believes that philosophy *has* refuted faith and *has* an absolute right to rule unhampered by law, even if these are 'truths' that must be kept hidden" (Drury 1988, 187; Holmes 1993, 63–66). In other words, the position that the dispute between reason and revelation is intractable or that philosophy rests upon a faith in reason are part of Strauss's exoteric doctrine. Drury argues that Strauss actually subscribes to the position that unlike philosophy, society rests upon the myths and laws that faith and revelation provide. Yet because abandoning faith and revelation would harm society irreparably, Strauss hid his esoteric beliefs. What Nietzsche said in the light of day, Strauss was willing to say only behind closed doors. Strauss's real doctrine is fundamentally incompatible with the demands of religion in general and unfriendly to Christianity in particular. On Drury's interpretation, Strauss sees religion as nothing more than a pious swindle needed to preserve the race (Drury 1988, 20).

As provocative as Drury's interpretation is, it must simply dismiss any of Strauss's statements that contradict it as part of the swindle. A more pedestrian but straightforward reading is that the classical political rationalists appear to present two possible relationships between reason

---

[11] Although philosophy rests upon a faith in reason, philosophy is not the same as religion. Pangle makes this distinction by arguing that

The choice to live as a philosopher ceases to be simply an act of faith or of will if and only if it is a choice to live as a philosopher preoccupied with the serious examination of the phenomena and the arguments of faith: if and only if, that is, the philosopher never completely ceases engaging in conversational scrutiny of those who articulate most authoritatively and compellingly the claims of the faithful and if and only if through that perscrutation he repeatedly shows to his own satisfaction and to that of others that he has . . . a fuller account of the moral experiences to which the pious point as their most significant experiences. (Pangle 1983, 22)

and revelation.[12] Either reason ultimately rests on faith, or these two ways of life exist in an unresolvable tension.[13] In neither case is revelation understood as subservient to philosophy. The classical political rationalists do not demonstrate that a way of life directed by revelation is inferior to one directed by reason. The failure of the liberal democratic regime to foster or encourage the rule of reason, then, cannot be synonymous with a failure to encourage the best way of life that is humanly possible. Now one could also argue that this regime is not only secular but actually hostile to religion. If the classical political rationalists adopted this strategy and argued that the rule of reason is not necessarily what is most important, then their deeper claims regarding what constitutes a well-ordered soul would be transformed significantly. Perhaps they could argue that there are two kinds of equally well-ordered souls and that this regime stunts them both. The effect of this stunting is that it further encourages the relativism and conformism of liberal democracy that classical political rationalists disparage.

Intellectual versus Moral Virtue

Before proceeding, it may be useful to rehearse the argument up to now. The point of looking at the justification for the rule of reason is to assess the standards that the classical political rationalists use to judge the effects of liberal democracy. For classical political rationalists, at least part of the problem is that a "bloodless and philistine relativism" (Pangle 1992, 213) has displaced reason and impoverished philosophy. This displacement has not affected merely philosophers, it has also allegedly affected the moral, civic, and intellectual integrity of great numbers of thinking, democratic citizens (212). According to the classical political rationalists, the harm done is not only to the stability of the regime but the possibility of human excellence. On this analysis, the recovery of a natural hierarchy of virtue, talent, and wisdom may also improve the character of the regime by improving the character of our souls.

It is only by understanding what constitutes the healthiest souls that

[12] With regard to this problem, David Lowenthal notes that "Strauss's overall position hardly seems consistent" (1985, 314–15) and that "the overall impression . . . [Strauss] leaves is that classical philosophy wins out over moderns—Plato over Machiavelli . . . —but then itself succumbs to revelation" (318).

[13] Harry Jaffa argues that within Strauss's work there is indeed a presumption that favors revelation over reason. Jaffa claims that if there is no serious argument for the Bible, there is no serious argument for classical political philosophy (1984, 15–17). In contrast, Gordon Wood claims that Strauss once said that "a philosophy based on faith is no longer philosophy" (Wood 1988, 33; see also Rosen 1987, 112).

classical political rationalists can judge the effects of liberal democracy. If the well-ordered, reason-governed soul is not the highest or at least a higher expression of human excellence, then the displacement of reason becomes less of an issue. This kind of critique of contemporary soulcraft thus relies upon ranking the reason-governed soul above souls that are merely courageous, trustworthy, honest, liberal, patient, modest, and so on. For the classical political rationalists, the problem raised by the displacement of reason is felt most seriously in our intellectual life because our intellectual life expresses what is best about ourselves as human beings. The problematic relationship between reason and faith begins to raise certain questions regarding the standard provided by the reason-governed soul. Exploring that standard also requires addressing the ranking of that soul in relation to more mundane but moral ways of life.

In his reading of Plato, Strauss bluntly asserts that "the man who is merely just or moral without being a philosopher appears as a mutilated human being" (Strauss 1953, 151). *Mutilation* emphasizes just how different the life of the philosopher is from the life of the ordinary person. Classical political rationalists can draw upon at least three arguments to support the superiority of the philosophic life to the purely moral life. The first is that the philosophic life entails a perfection of all the other virtues. This is part of the unity of the virtues argument and can be found in the writings of Plato, Aristotle, and Aquinas. For example, when Glaucon implies that philosophers "would be the best rulers *if* they possessed ... [all the relevant] virtues," Bloom writes, "Socrates responds to the doubt implied in Glaucon's condition by attempting to show that all the virtues are involved in the philosophers' very vocation and that thus they are good citizens. As a result of their love of wisdom, all the lovers of wisdom possess all the virtues, and more reliably than anyone else because they have a sufficient reason for being virtuous" (1968, 395). In other words, the wise person must also be temperate, just, and courageous. On this view, the philosopher has what the merely moral individual has and more. There is no tradeoff between pursuing philosophy and possessing the other virtues.

A second argument is that a philosophic life is superior because it pursues enduring questions, unlike a life lived under the standards of ordinary morality. This difference is based upon a belief that philosophy is in search of something that "is absolutely higher in dignity than any human things" (Strauss 1953, 151). The attempt to understand what is eternal, no matter how fleeting that understanding may be, is superior to what is merely contingent and passing (apparent features of all human relationships).

A third and related argument supporting the superiority of the philosophic life is that humans find their bliss in thinking (Pangle 1992, 120) and that the soul realizes all its possible excellences through reason. In contrast, the exercise of moral virtue does not place the same demands upon our abilities to reason. Rather, moral virtue requires the acquisition of a disposition or the right kinds of training. One could be morally virtuous without the desire to know the whole. In fact, moral virtue seems to require that we postpone or bracket our critical abilities and accept the virtues as they are taught to us. Thus from the philosopher's perspective, the merely moral human being appears crippled.

The Unity of the Virtues, the Pursuit of the Eternal, and Human Potential

The thesis that the philosopher has what the merely moral individual has plus more is subject to the same objection that plagues the unity of virtues argument, namely that wise individuals do not possess the other virtues necessarily. For example, even the classical political rationalists would consider Heidegger a philosopher, even though it is difficult to argue that his behavior regarding Nazism demonstrated courage. The possibility that lovers of wisdom may not possess all the virtues renders the proposition that philosophy implies moral conduct deeply problematic.

The trouble may not be merely that philosophers can be thugs or depraved. Classical political rationalists imply paradoxically that the pursuit of the philosophic life is incompatible with sustaining moral virtue. This kind of incompatibility is suggested in the way classical political rationalists view the philosopher's relationship to the city. On their view, there will inevitably be, at the very least, an unresolvable tension between philosophy and the practices that sustain society. At worst, the pursuit of philosophy can rend the social fabric. Strauss illustrates this conflict by arguing that "philosophy or science, the highest activity of man, is the attempt to replace opinion about 'all things' by knowledge of 'all things'; but opinion is the element of society; philosophy or science is therefore the attempt to dissolve the element in which society breathes, and thus it endangers society" (Strauss 1959, 221). One implication of this relationship is that the pursuit of philosophy does not sustain society. For the most part our moral training is provided by the community and the culture in which we are raised. We do not and could not learn to keep our promises, or act respectfully, or do courageous things only after we had engaged in a higher philosophical education. We need to know how to behave towards one another long before we engage in critical rational thought.

Just because philosophy finds itself in opposition to the opinions of the city, however, does not mean that it will also find itself in opposition to moral virtue. From the classical political rationalist perspective, the common opinions about what constitutes courage, moderation, justice, and so on may be mistaken. What a society thinks is morally virtuous action may in fact turn out to be something quite different. Philosophers may sometimes act against what is merely thought to be and is not morally virtuous conduct.

It is also possible that even though society is based upon opinion, it could have the good fortune of possessing the right opinions. Paradoxically, the uneasy relationship between philosophy and moral virtue may be more evident in the case of a virtuous society. According to the classical political rationalists, philosophy attempts to move beyond opinion to knowledge. As Pangle's discussion of the dialectic demonstrates, philosophers call even the deeply held, "appropriate" opinions and virtues before the bar of reason. But pursuing knowledge is not the same as possessing it. Calling moral virtue before the bar of reason would not necessarily result in affirming those virtues. As the aporetic Platonic dialogues seem to attest, the result can depend upon the competence of the interlocutors. On many occasions, the discussion of a particular virtue brings the participants into Socratic ignorance. Without a guarantee of reaching the truth of the matter, questioning moral virtues could still dissolve the "element of society." Philosophy could leave people in a worse situation than when they possessed right opinions. It is an open question whether philosophy can supply a convincing replacement for the traditional foundations of moral virtue.

The life of philosophical inquiry will inevitably lead one to question the standards, values, and moral training that a given community provides. Even those moral virtues that are appropriate must withstand the acid of reason. For the classical political rationalists, philosophers must be willing to entertain any thought, no matter how impious and depraved it may be. Insofar as philosophers want to continue to think freely, however, they will be careful of what they say; out of necessity they will create the appearance of being virtuous. But this is not the same thing as saying that the philosopher is actually morally virtuous. The unresolvable tension between the demands of philosophy and the demands of the city implies that philosophy need not be consistent with fostering moral virtue in oneself or in others. The existence of this tension drives a wedge in the unity of the intellectual and moral virtues.

The second argument supporting the highest ranking of philosophy is that attempting to understand eternal things is preferable to merely trying to live properly in the stream of life. Does this preference lead one to the conclusion that a philosophical life is best? One problem with this argument is that the desire to understand what is eternal does not necessarily lead one to the life of the philosopher as the classical political rationalists set it out. This preference could also lead to a life of religious devotion. Now, a religious life is not necessarily a life directed towards understanding the eternal, but rather a life directed by pious respect for the eternal. Granting a distinction between respect and understanding, the classical political rationalists have to argue that it is better to try to understand the eternal than to respect its mystery. The distinction, however, raises once again the problematic dispute between reason and revelation. It is not clear that philosophy can rest its superiority on the pursuit of the eternal without subsuming itself under faith.

The third argument is that the philosophical way of life expresses our essential character as humans better than any other way of life. Thus to pursue philosophy is to realize a human potential that goes beyond the ability to interact properly with other human beings. From this perspective, any soul other than one governed by reason is maimed or mutilated. Of the three arguments defending the superiority of intellectual over moral virtue, this may be the most important.

The claim that a nonphilosophic life is a kind of mutilation appears to be an attempt to reverse a charge that was leveled against the first philosophers. For example, Pangle interprets Aristophanes' *Clouds* as portraying the philosopher Socrates as "laughably ignorant of the human soul and its remarkable heterogeneity. Above all, the philosopher is ignorant of his own soul and its needs. . . . Insofar as his soul is truly dead to love— love of pleasure, as well as love of beauty or nobility—the philosopher lacks a crucial awareness, or else has so suppressed and sublimated part of his awareness that he has mutilated himself without realizing it" (Pangle 1983, 12; see also West 1984, 34; Bloom 1993, 432). In contrast, Pangle argues, the later portrayals of Socrates by Plato and Xenophon were responses to Aristophanes' attack. At the very least Pangle suggests that the "new" Socrates is one who is more sensitive than the old to the demands and importance of the city. In a sense, the mature Socrates was beginning to learn that one has to cloak philosophy in the local virtues and pieties if one is to live to practice philosophy another day. In addition, by showing eros to be in the pursuit of truth, Plato portrayed Socrates as no longer "dead to love."

In spite of these changes, Pangle claims, "the closer one looks the more difficult it becomes to spell out precisely in what the newness consists" (1983, 13). If Pangle is correct, then Aristophanes' challenge requires a stronger response to show that philosophers do not have maimed souls. For if the soul of the philosopher is mutilated, then it would be unjustifiable to rank the philosophic life over a moral but non-philosophic life.[14]

It is not clear, however, whether the classical political rationalists do respond adequately to this challenge. This deficiency may be especially evident in Strauss's and Bloom's reading of Plato's *Republic*. Bloom reports that by the end of the dialogue "Socrates admits that we know nothing about the soul, which denies the value of the argument, calling into question the teaching of the whole dialogue which was based on an understanding of the soul" (Bloom 1968, 435; Strauss 1964, 138). Their reading suggests that what Plato says in the *Republic* would be largely useless in responding to Aristophanes' criticism. In contrast, I will argue that far from being useless, the Strauss/Bloom reading ultimately calls into question the possibility and desirability of the best soul.

The City and the Soul

The theme of the *Republic* is justice and the nature of the just human being. To get a better idea of what justice is like in the individual, Socrates suggests that he and his interlocutors consider justice writ large. Thus arises Plato's famous analogy between the city and the soul. By understanding a just politics, the analogy implies, we will have a better sense of the just soul. The discussion of politics appears to be a vehicle for understanding the soul. In highly controversial interpretations, Strauss and Bloom argue that Plato intended to portray the best regime as unworkable and undesirable. Nevertheless, they do not see this portrayal as affecting the possibility of the best soul. In other words, they argue that the analogy of the city and the soul does not hold. Conversely, I argue that the analogy holds, and hence the philosophic soul may not be the best soul in practice. If Strauss and Bloom are correct about the defects of the best regime in theory, then the existence of a parallel between the best soul and the best regime suggests that it is the best soul and not the moral individual who is mutilated.

As is well known, Strauss and Bloom contend that a central lesson of Plato's *Republic* is that while the rule of philosopher-kings is the best regime in theory, it is a disaster in practice. Bloom sums up this argument by claiming that "Socrates constructs his utopia to point up the dangers of what we would call utopianism: as such it is the greatest critique of political idealism ever written" (1968, 410). The city in speech is not a

---

[14] Pangle, however, is ambiguous. He writes that "the mature, Platonic Socrates did not abandon a dedication to a life of inquiry so consuming as to make him appear very, very strange—even inhuman" (1983, 14).

blueprint for practice, but an example of Socratic irony. This interpretation of the *Republic* has inspired heated and continuing debate.[15] Instead of contesting this part of their interpretation, however, I will focus upon what it entails for the analogy between the city and the soul.

Strauss argues that the parallel between the city and the individual is "surreptitiously established" and "defective" (1964, 101, 109). Bloom uses similar language, calling the identification of the city and the soul "spurious" and "most questionable" (1968, 379, 412). An important effect of denying this parallel is that the critique of utopianism does not infect Plato's understanding of the best soul. The breakdown of the metaphor preserves the possibility and hence the desirability of the aristocratic soul. Bloom is aware of the significance of the metaphor's failure: "Unlike the aristocratic city, the aristocratic man exists; he is a philosopher. Moreover, he is exactly like Socrates. He devotes himself to learning; he is totally indifferent to his body and other men's opinions of him; he is utterly dedicated and single-minded" (420). The question that naturally arises is why and how does the parallel fail? Moreover, why do Strauss and Bloom believe that the conclusions regarding the ideal city do not apply to the individual?

For both writers the central metaphor of Plato's *Republic* fails because there are qualitative differences between the city and the individual. These differences are so great that conclusions regarding the city cannot be transferred onto the individual. The combined arguments of Strauss and Bloom point to four hurdles that the analogy fails to leap: the place of spiritedness in the soul, the lack of eros in the city, the association of calculation (*logismos*) with reason, and the absence of the body. I will argue that Plato's analogy does leap these hurdles and does so in a way that extends their ironic reading of the *Republic*.[16] If Platonic irony extends to the best soul, then it jeopardizes the ranking of the philosophic over the ordinarily just life.

The Role of Spiritedness

Strauss argues that if the best soul were strictly parallel to the best city, then the soul would not only have the same parts as the city, but it would order those parts in the same way. Socrates argues that in the best regime philosophers should rule, warriors should defend the city, and the artisans and farmers should practice their crafts. These classes of people are

[15] See, for example Hall 1977; Bloom 1977; Burnyeat 1985; Cropsey et al. 1985; Klosko 1986; and Nussbaum 1987.

[16] It is important to note that the *Republic* is not the only place where Plato uses the parallel between city and soul. It also makes a brief appearance in *The Laws* (1980, 689b–c).

ranked rigidly. In turn, Strauss responds that "the parallel between the city and the soul requires that just as in the city the warriors occupy a higher rank than the moneymakers, in the soul spiritedness occupy [*sic*] a higher rank than desires. . . . But it is much less plausible that spiritedness as such should be higher in rank than desire as such" (1964, 110). Bloom makes the same point by suggesting that the place of "spiritedness is ambiguous" in the soul (Bloom 1968, 375). Although Socrates ranks spiritedness over desire, Bloom argues that Socrates does not intend that ranking to be taken seriously. According to Bloom, this ranking is not for our sake, but for Glaucon's: "Socrates, because he is trying to persuade Glaucon to be a good citizen of the good city, gives him an inadequate account of spiritedness in the soul—one which gives spiritedness the same role in the soul as it performed in the city, while forgetting the differences between a soul and a city" (376). For Bloom, Glaucon's problem is that he too readily associates spiritedness with desire. Glaucon's "form of spiritedness leads him off to war in pursuit of satisfaction of desire for pleasure and victory" (375). According to Bloom, Socrates portrays spiritedness as an ally of reason in order to steer Glaucon towards reason. Bloom argues that in reality spiritedness could ally itself with either desire or reason.

But why should the ambiguous character of spiritedness render the parallel problematic? If Socrates is trying to set out the well-ordered soul, as he is trying to set out the well-ordered city, he is not showing us what is usually the case. Spiritedness may very well be ambiguous, at times allying with reason and at times allying with desire, but this does not mean that in the well-ordered soul spiritedness will not be allied with reason. In order for Strauss and Bloom to make their case they have to show that within the best soul spiritedness would consistently and successfully oppose the rule of reason in its attempt to keep down the passions.

In one sense, Strauss and Bloom argue just this. They see spiritedness as ranked below an alliance between reason and desire in the aristocratic soul. This possibility brings us to role of eros and the second failure of the analogy between city and soul. Strauss argues that "in the thematic discussion of the respective rank of spiritedness and desire, Socrates is silent about eros" (1964, 111). The metaphor fails because in the best city there can be no place for eros, even though it appears to be an essential component of the philosophic life. Bloom concurs. He argues that "a city, like a man, desires wealth, needs food, and deliberates. But a city cannot reproduce or philosophize; all forms of eros are cut off from it. In this sense a city cannot be properly compared to a man" (Bloom 1968, 376). The philosophic soul cannot be compared to an organization without eros. What Socrates says about the city cannot be applied to the soul because the city cannot be erotic.

To improve the discussion of the aristocratic soul, Strauss and Bloom argue that Socrates should have included a discussion of eros. This would have meant considering desires that are more important than courage—for example the desire of curiosity or the desire to learn and know. Bloom carries the association between eros and philosophy one step farther when he claims that "in some sense reason in the soul is a desire, and . . . spiritedness, to the extent that it opposes desire, opposes reason also" (376). Thus, a simple ranking of spiritedness above desire does not make sense once eros is included in the equation.

To support this interpretation Bloom examines Socrates' story of Leontius. In this story, Leontius came across some corpses lying by the public executioner. Initially, he resisted the desire to look, but ultimately his desiring eyes won out. The idea of spiritedness comes into play when Leontius got angry at his eyes for driving him to gawk at the corpses. For Socrates, this example shows spiritedness in opposition (albeit unsuccessful) to a desire that Leontius thinks is bad. He is angry at his inappropriate desire to look at the dead. In contrast, Bloom interprets this story as showing that spiritedness is "fighting curiosity, a close kin of the desire to know" (376). Instead of proving that spiritedness should govern desire, Bloom argues that this example shows why spiritedness should not be ranked above desire. He suggests that "the soul in which reason is most developed will—like Leontius's eyes—desire to see all kinds of things which the citizen is forbidden to see; it will abound with thoughts usually connected with selfishness, lust, and vice. . . . Spiritedness, in the form of anger and shame, will oppose reason's desiring" (377). In other words, spiritedness will find itself in opposition to the philosophical desire of curiosity. Given this opposition, spiritedness is not superior to desire.

Working backward through these arguments, first consider Bloom's interpretation of Leontius. It is not clear what the case of Leontius demonstrates. One problem is that there is nothing to indicate that Leontius was driven by the desire of curiosity. Any number of motives, aside from curiosity, could have compelled him to look at the corpses.[17] Second, even if Leontius was driven by curiosity, that does not mean that spiritedness mistakenly sanctioned his eyes. Curiosity may be a close kin to the

---

[17] For example, Leontius could have been a necrophiliac, but one whose reason told him that there was something ignoble about this practice. C.D.C. Reeve notes that "Leontius was notorious for his love for boys as pale as corpses" (1988, 129). If this is true, then the victory of his eyes and his anger at his weakness would have been an example of the alliance of spirit with reason. This explanation for why Leontius wants to look at the corpses also creates problems for Mary P. Nichols's interpretation. According to Nichols, the corpses offend spiritedness because they impart "a sense of impermanence, an understanding that can justify inactivity and support human weakness" and reveal the depth of conflict between humans and their city (1988, 54–55).

desire to know, but not all curiosity is philosophical. Leontius may have been engaging in an ancient form of rubbernecking. If idle forms of curiosity are seen as irrational or unreasonable, then a spiritedness that was governed by reason would be ranked ahead of the desire of curiosity. Third, even if Leontius's curiosity is philosophical, Bloom presumes that spiritedness will be opposed to matters profane. In order for this interpretation to make sense, Leontius's anger must be dependent upon what appears to be merely a conception of good and evil. The way Bloom puts this is that his spiritedness is driven not only by anger but by shame. Because shame is largely a result of conventional training and upbringing, it unduly restricts the pursuit of knowledge by chaining the philosopher to the prevailing religious mores and social practices, one of which may be to not stare at dead bodies. Philosophers must overcome a spiritedness driven by shame if they are to allow their curiosity free play.

The problem with this reading is that at most it shows that anger can get out of line. It does not, however, preclude spiritedness from being allied with reason in the best soul. If reason leads us to examine all sorts of things profane and profound, then it would seem that the appropriate role for spiritedness would entail getting angry at whatever tries to prohibit such philosophical examinations, including contrary desires. For from the point of view of reason, such a prohibition would be seen as unjust. Indeed, Socrates does provide just such a role for spiritedness. In the case where an individual has suffered injustice, Socrates asks, "Doesn't his spirit in this case boil and become harsh and form an alliance for battle with what seems just; and, even if it suffers in hunger, cold, and everything of the sort, doesn't it stand firm and conquer, and not cease from its noble efforts before it has succeeded, or death intervenes, or before it becomes gentle, having been called in by the speech within him like a dog by a herdsman?" (*Republic*, 440c–d). At best, Bloom offers a reading of a soul that is "corrupted by bad rearing" (441a). It does not show that spiritedness should be subservient to all desire. Indeed, assuming that Leontius is driven by a philosophical curiosity, the appropriate role of Leontius's spirit is to get angry at anything that would have opposed his philosophic endeavors. A properly governed spirit should properly govern desire.

What Bloom's interpretation of Leontius's curiosity does show is that when a desire to know is philosophical the ranking between reason-governed spiritedness and that particular desire is problematic. Does this not show the breakdown of the parallel between the best soul and best city? In response, one could say that this troublesome relationship does not address the ordering of reason-governed spiritedness vis à vis all the other possible desires humans possess. In the well-ordered soul it may still be the case that all other desires are ranked below spiritedness. A stronger response is that in Socrates' portrayal of the best soul the expression of that desire of curiosity in the form of eros disappears. This, of course, raises the larger issue of the relationship between reason and desire.

Reason and Desire

The problem we are faced with is whether the polity of the well-ordered soul requires that desire (in the form of eros) trump a reason-governed spiritedness. The answer can be found only in Socrates' portrayal of the well-ordered soul, but here the argument takes a strange twist, for Socrates' portrayal of the aristocratic soul is wholly unerotic. This suggests that in the best soul the rule of spirit in relation to eros does not arise. Strauss's and Bloom's response to the absence of eros is that this is precisely what is wrong with the metaphor. They contend that eros is inseparable from our understanding of the best soul. By omitting eros from his discussion of the best soul, Socrates renders the city/soul metaphor spurious. In other words, eros is a necessary component of the best soul.

There are two ways to respond to the argument that eros plays a necessary role in reason. The first posits that by omitting eros from his discussion of reason Socrates implies that in the best soul all desires, including eros, must be mastered. It is not that Socrates' metaphor shows that eros disappears; rather it shows that even eros should be subject to rational discipline. Reason should even be able to ask whether the desires of curiosity and for knowing the whole are worthy of pursuit.[18]

The problem with this first response is that this disciplining of eros could still be driven by eros. Indeed, there is nothing inconsistent about the idea of loving to love, or desiring to find out whether one should have desires. Perhaps even in questioning eros we must be driven by eros. The implication here is that reason cannot do anything unless it is motivated by a desire. This way of formulating the issue, however, turns Plato into a kind of Humean for whom reason itself cannot be a source of motivation. To take this route is to suggest that we cannot pursue excellence for the sake of excellence, but must pursue it because of whatever pleasure it may bring. In other words, we want to know the whole because of the erotic buzz that accompanies the pursuit of wisdom. If Bloom is correct that reason is a desire, then the classical political rationalist position begins to resemble that of the philosophical conventionalists that, as we saw earlier, Strauss rejects (Strauss 1953, 128).

Bloom himself hesitates to assert that reason and desire are coextensive when he states that reason is "in some sense" a desire. This hedge, of

---

[18] For example, Bloom suggests that we should be able to articulate our reasons for loving (1993, 434).

course, implies that reason is in some sense not a desire. To get a clearer view of the aristocratic soul perhaps Socrates has to emphasize the sense in which reason is not completely assimilable to eros. Perhaps in the best soul the nobility of the engagement in philosophy can be assured only by diminishing the significance of eros. If arguing that reason cannot do anything without desire turns Plato into a Humean, then arguing that reason must be fully disengaged from desire paints him as a Kantian, but this seems just as peculiar and one-sided as the Humean interpretation. The problem here is foisting the position that either reason must master eros or vice versa onto Plato's complex psychology. Is there a better explanation for Socrates' omission of eros?

The Absence of Eros

On the Strauss/Bloom reading, Plato either offers a mistaken analogy between city and soul that he cannot support, or he wants to point to the problematic nature of such an analogy and so excludes eros explicitly. An alternative reading is that Plato not only left eros out intentionally, but he also wanted to sustain the city/soul metaphor. To see what he is up to, we must turn to the relationship between eros and the best soul. Nowhere is this relationship more fully set out than in Diotima's speech in Plato's *Symposium*. According to Socrates, Diotima once told him that "wisdom is surely among the most beautiful of things, but Eros is love of the beautiful, so Eros is necessarily a philosopher, a lover of wisdom, and, being a philosopher, intermediate between wisdom and ignorance" (1991, 204b). Notice here the intermediate character of eros: eros desires something, and hence does not have it. In fact, this aspect of eros is one of the first lessons that Diotima teaches Socrates. But Diotima also tells Socrates the simple logical implication of this understanding of eros: namely, "no god loves wisdom or desires to become wise—for he is so; nor, if anyone else is wise, does he love wisdom" (203e–204a). Because the wise already have wisdom, they do not desire it. The wise, in the case of gods and men, lack eros.[19]

Socrates appears to accept this position when he says that

> it is the nature of the real lover of learning to strive for what *is*; and he does not tarry by each of the many things opined to *be* but goes forward and does not lose the keenness of his passionate love nor cease from it before he grasps the

---

[19] R. A. Markus suggests that in the *Symposium* Socrates appears to want to desire his cake and eat it too. On his reading, Socrates argues that it is possible to love even when one has possession of love's object. Presumably the desire that continues even after possession is a desire for continued possession based upon a fear of losing the object (Markus 1971, 136). However, Markus notes that this may not be so satisfying a solution. Socrates' position still places him in a logical dilemma: "for either perfect happiness (which consists in perfect

nature itself of each thing which *is* with the part of the soul fit to grasp a thing of that sort; and it is the part akin to it that is fit. And once near it and coupled with what really is, having begotten intelligence and truth, he knows and lives truly, is nourished and so ceases from his labor pains, but not before. (*Republic,* 490a–b)[20]

The idea that one does not lose one's passionate love before grasping the nature of the thing suggests that this love disappears after discovering that nature. Moreover, if we follow out this metaphor of birth, after one has begotten intelligence and truth, and undergone the pains of labor, there is no more desire to possess what is already possessed. The truly wise individual, thus, is not erotic.[21]

This conclusion may be useful in deciphering Plato's view of the best soul that corresponds to the best regime. Is this best soul a lover of wisdom, or is this soul wise? The absence of eros suggests the latter. Consider Bloom's translation of the following rhetorical questions that arise immediately after the discussion of the best soul:

"Isn't it by now necessary that the private man be wise in the same way and because of the same thing as the city was wise? . . . Isn't it proper for the calculating part to rule, since it is wise and has forethought about all the soul, and for the spirited part to be obedient to it and its ally?" (*Republic,* 441c, e)

The fact (which Strauss and Bloom make so much of) that the aristocratic soul is not a lover of wisdom may be because Socrates wants to show us a soul that is already wise. If we trust Bloom's translation, this is borne out by Socrates' description of this soul as being wise. Consequently, Plato is presenting us with an ideal soul, just as the city in speech is the ideal city. In the ideal soul, the problem of spirit governing eros disappears because eros has no role to play.[22]

---

possession of the good and fulfillment of all desire—cf. 204E) is impossible of attainment; or love must cease, since it must, by definition, involve unsatisfied desire, on the attainment of perfect happiness" (136). On Bloom's interpretation, "Eros is the impossible desire for eternity" (Bloom 1993, 498). In a sense, he takes hold of the first horn of Markus's dilemma.

[20] If Plato's irony runs through his discussion of the ideal soul, then when he says that such a person would have a "healthy and just disposition, which is also accompanied by moderation" (*Republic,* 490c), we should not take him at his word. See the discussion on the body below.

[21] A further, paradoxical implication of this position is that the more certain one becomes, the less one will resemble a philosopher.

[22] This, of course, disagrees with Bloom's conclusion that "if the radically incomplete discussion of the soul in the *Republic* were to be made comprehensive, it would have to be enlarged to provide an adequate account of eros" (Bloom 1968, 423). I do not think Plato saw his discussion of the wise soul as radically incomplete.

One objection that could be raised against this reading is that it suggests that not only eros but spiritedness also disappears. Why would the wise soul experience anger? If the wise soul is completely cool, then the metaphor between city and soul once again breaks down. Presumably the wise soul would not be moved to anger against desires that violated the demands of reason, since they would be under control. Moreover, the wise person would not get angry at someone whom he or she believed was acting justly, but as long as the wise are treated *unjustly*, there will be a role for spiritedness (*Republic*, 440c–d). Unjust treatment in this case could consist of forcibly preventing the wise from contemplating whatever they know. If anything, bringing them into the world, so to speak, would make their spirit boil.

I am suggesting that the parallel between the city and the soul is actually strengthened once we get a clearer sense of the kind of soul that Socrates is trying to describe. Does this mean that the Socratic irony that Strauss and Bloom believe attends the city in speech also attends the ideal soul? It may, but before answering this question, the other alleged failures of the metaphor must be addressed.

Reason and Calculation

Bloom argues that when Plato discusses the parallel between the city and the soul, reason is not only unerotic, it is solely associated with calculation.[23] As such, he suggests, it is "akin to that of rulers who deliberate about public affairs" (1977, 323). Bloom suggests, however, that in book 5

> a totally different account of the rational part of the soul is given, one which shows that the parallel between city and soul breaks down. . . . Deliberation or calculation (*logismos*), which was the only attribute of the rational part of the soul given in Book IV, is no longer even mentioned. The opposition between desire and calculation which was the defining characteristic of calculation in the earlier passage is overcome and philosophy is described as a form of eros (485c; 499b). (322)

---

[23] In contrast, Terence Irwin argues that even in book 4 the reasoning part of the soul is not in opposition to a desiring part. For Irwin, Plato's division of the soul concerns three kinds of desires: the appetitive part of the soul is composed of desires that are wholly independent of the good and nonrational; the emotive part is constituted by desires that are driven partially by beliefs regarding an overall good of the soul; and finally, the rational part is composed of beliefs about and desires for that overall good (Irwin 1977, 193–95). Irwin's interpretation raises the question of what happens to those desires when the rational part obtains or understands the good.

The movement from book 4 to book 6 is meant to suggest that what Plato first says about reason and the soul is not to be taken seriously. But does this conclusion follow from Bloom's evidence?

Bloom correctly points out that by book 5, Plato portrays philosophy as an erotic enterprise. Nevertheless, remember where we are in the metaphor. Socrates' discussion of philosophy in books 5 and 6 is meant to fill in what he means by philosopher-kings. As philosophers, they are taken to be lovers of wisdom and not wise per se. As I read the metaphor, the best soul corresponds not to philosopher-kings, who are merely a part of the best regime, but to the best regime itself. It corresponds to a whole, complete, idea. The problem with this reading is that if the ruling part of the soul is an unerotic conception of reason, why is the ruling part in the best regime occupied by philosopher-kings? Why did Socrates not portray the highest class in the best regime as possessing an unerotic form of reason? Moreover, why is deliberation the only aspect of reason in the best soul?

If the ruling class in the best regime were truly wise, it would deprive Plato's project of all plausibility. If philosophers are rare, then truly wise individuals must be even rarer (if not impossible). Having those who desire and love wisdom rule makes the best regime more attractive by being initially conceivable. The ironic reading of the republic will not work unless there is some element of plausibility to the blueprint. Another possibility is that although one can force philosophers to rule, one could not force the wise to govern. Not only does the best soul possess what it desires but, as we shall see below, it has little concern with the body. The combination of these factors suggests that forcing the wise to rule would inspire merely anger and not compliance.

The more interesting question is why deliberation or calculation is the only attribute of the best soul. One answer is that Socrates could not set out fully the characteristics of the wise soul without setting out a conception of wisdom. Doing so would have made things a great deal easier for us, but it would have conflicted with what Plato took to be the difficult task entailed in understanding it. But why is reason associated with calculation and not, for example, with contemplation? In this part of the *Republic*, Plato is concerned with the organization of the best soul and the role of reason in that internal governance. His concern here is with justice. This does not rule out contemplation. It means merely that justice and contemplation are two different things. For such a soul reason need not be desiring or erotically striving to find how to organize itself. It already knows and possesses its ends. Given this knowledge, the role of reason in relation to the other parts of the soul will be nothing more than to provide commands or algorithms for protecting and sustaining those ends. The very thin description of the best soul may be a function of what Plato took to be his audience's ignorance of what wisdom actually entails and his focus upon justice and internal governance.

The Body and Soul

The final argument addressing the failure of the analogy between the state and the individual concerns the absence of the body in Socrates' discussion of the soul. Strauss notes that "the parallel between the city and the individual by which the good city stands or falls, demands the abstraction from the body" (Strauss 1964, 109). Bloom suggests that "by treating the soul as the whole man, Socrates tacitly assumes the irrelevance of the body to the question of what justice in a man is" (Bloom 1968, 375). Not only the discussion of the soul, however, forgets the body. Bloom also raises this point in justifying the ironic reading of the best city. He argues that the demands of the body are forgotten in Socrates' discussion of naked men and women wrestling. For Bloom, this forgetting of the body is a "precondition of the equality of women" (382). Because Bloom sees the public association of naked men and women as preposterous, he uses it to count as one more piece of evidence that the best regime is a regime only in speech.[24]

Because the city cannot overcome the embodied character of human beings, Bloom argues that this ideal could never be actualized. Yet the notion of forgetting the body appears to be a greater possibility for the philosopher. For Bloom "the problem is that the body's demands lead to the establishment of an entire way of life and a set of beliefs contrary to those which would be most conducive to the perfection of a man's soul or the pursuit of truth. The way of life based on the body is directed to acquisition of the means of preserving and gratifying the body" (386). Later, Bloom argues that "from the example of the city in speech, a man would learn what he must overcome in himself in order to become a philosopher. Socrates forgets the body in order to make clear its importance" (387). These quotations suggest that unlike the city in speech, it is possible for individuals to adopt an ascetic way of life. Moreover, by forgetting the body, one loses connections to fellow human beings. Forgetting the body, then, suggests that the life of the wise is private

[24] A similar problem emerges, according to Bloom, in Plato's metaphor of the city as one body that shares pleasures and pains. Once again, Bloom argues that the unity of the city depends upon the forgetting of individual bodies (1968, 386).

(435).[25] But as Bloom himself reasons with regard to the city and the body, "The body cannot be forgotten" (419). We may fast, but we will die without food. We may be indifferent to cold, but we will die of exposure without shelter. We may live a life of contemplation, but we will have nothing to think about unless we have learned a language. Because of the embodied character of all human beings, the ideal soul would be a dead human being. Thus, one could not be the best soul, at least on earth.[26] Forgetting the body points to the impossibility of Socrates' conception of the best soul.

The Limits of Philosophy

If we accept the Strauss/Bloom reading of Plato's *Republic*, how far does Socratic irony go? Does it stop with the construction of the city in speech? Bloom argues that it does. He writes that "the most important point made in this section is that while the best city exists only in myth, the best man exists actually" (415). But perhaps the best soul is also a myth, one whose actualization would require that we lose eros, dismiss our contact with other human beings, and do whatever we can to forget our embodied character. Just as approximation to the best regime in theory requires enormous sacrifices, the closer we come to approximating the ideal soul, the more we have to twist and cripple our humanity. From the standard of what is humanly possible, the ideal soul is a mutilated human being.[27] The ideal soul, like the ideal city, may be worthy of celebration in theory, but it is a disaster in practice. And just as the ideal city is a utopia we could say that the wise soul is *utis* or nobody.[28]

On this reading, the *Republic* is a lesson in both political and philo-

[25] It may be a further implication of this ironic reading that there is even less likely a connection between Platonic justice and doing ordinarily just things. If the best soul is best only in theory, then the issue of how such a character would act is as problematic as how the just regime would act in international relations. For a contrasting position that sees the aristocratic soul as possible and as ordinarily just, see Vlastos 1971.

[26] Cornford is correct in pointing out that a sharp contrast between a thinking part of the soul and an irrational desiring part leads towards an extreme form of asceticism (1971, 121). I am suggesting here that Plato had this perspective in mind and brought it out to show its dangers.

[27] In his review of Bloom's *The Closing of the American Mind*, Norman Podhoretz raises a further threat of reason: "Dostoyevsky's ultimate message is that untrammeled reason leads you to murder not only a shopkeeper you've never known, but your father as well, or even (in the case of the Grand Inquisitor) Jesus Christ" (Podhoretz 1987, 37). The argument offered here is that untrammeled reason ultimately leads to self-annihilation.

[28] This neologism is derived from the name Odysseus gives himself when questioned by Polyphemos the Cyclops: "Nobody (*outis*) is my name" (Homer *The Odyssey*, 9.366). Spelling it *utis* is meant to convey a combination of good (*eu*) and no (*ou*).

sophical moderation. If this text is meant to cool off political idealism, it also cools off the pursuit of wisdom. In a sense, philosophers who want to become truly wise souls stand in a position analogous to those who want the absolutely just regime. By following this parallel, perhaps we can apply the distinction between theory and practice to souls. Strauss and others suggest that the best regime in theory is rule by the wise; the best regime in practice, however, is a mixed regime in which gentlemen execute and care for the law. One problem with the rule of the wise is that they can neither persuade nor force the unwise to accept their rule. The difficulty here is that philosophers are few and the unwise are many. Another problem with striving for the best regime is that it may lead to the worst possible regime. For in the pursuit of the best regime "what is more likely to happen is that an unwise man, appealing to the natural right of wisdom and catering to the lowest desires of the many, will persuade the multitude of his right: the prospects for tyranny are brighter than those for rule of the wise" (Strauss 1953, 141). These possibilities mean that consent must have some role in the practically best regime. For the classical thinkers, Strauss argues, such a regime is one in which ordinary people have some say in their own governance by consenting to a code of conduct written up by a wise legislator (141–42).

If the analogy between the city and soul does hold, then the best soul in theory is one in which reason rules. But does reason have the force necessary to keep down the other parts of the soul? If it does have the requisite force to rule spirit and desire, then the parallel in theory between the best regime and the best soul begins to break down.[29] On the other hand, perhaps reason would not have the necessary force to rule. If reason is primarily characterized by calculation, then perhaps it is in the same position as our philosopher-kings: unable to control the body by force and incapable of persuading the nonrational parts of the soul through reason. Moreover, perhaps the other parts of the soul are constantly in danger of accepting as rational what is merely a trumped-up desire or spirited act. Perhaps those who see themselves as philosophers run the greatest risk of governing their souls like tyrants. As with the practically best regime, the solution here may be for reason to draw up a code of conduct that is acceptable to the other parts of the soul—a kind of mixed regime.[30] Such a code could set out when it was appropri-

---

[29] It may not, however, break down completely because the problems associated with the demands of reason discussed earlier would remain.

[30] This implies, as Reeve argues, that the other parts of the soul are not brutish. Each part not only has desire but intelligence. Indeed, Reeve goes farther and argues that "Reason does not force appetite and aspiration into pursing its peculiar good (which is also their own). It is not an enlightened despot governing through *force majeure*. Instead, reason 'persuades' them to consent to its rule through a process of training and education begin-

ate to be angry, or passionate, and when to pursue wisdom. The best soul in practice appears to be governed by a set of rules. In contrast to Strauss's claim, the best soul in practice would not be one that rules the body despotically (133), nor would it be one in which the passions ruled without any guidance from reason. In any case, it would not be a soul that is single-mindedly devoted to the pursuit of wisdom (Bloom 1968, 420).

But for the best soul in practice, what plays the role of the impartial administrator of the law?[31] What plays the part of what Strauss calls the gentleman, the urban patrician? Because there is nothing within Plato's conception of the soul to guarantee a fair administration of the law, perhaps this code of conduct would be enforced by other souls similarly situated. One could imagine a code that was not only acceptable to one's own reason, spiritedness, and desire, but to others as well. At this juncture the best regime in practice may intersect with the best soul in practice.

If the parallel between city and soul does hold up, and the best soul in practice is governed by an ethic of rules, then what happens to the erotic life of the philosopher? If all of these arguments work (admittedly a big if), then the philosopher must also conclude that the best way of life is a radically bounded pursuit of wisdom. Much of the action in philosophy would lie in discerning those rules of conduct that would best fit the whole soul. After arriving at and consenting to those rules, reason, like spiritedness and desire, should live by them. What is left of philosophy after that would depend upon the accepted code of conduct.

Perhaps this argument goes too far. Indeed, perhaps it went wrong at the beginning. An alternative possibility is that the best soul for the classical political rationalists is not one that is wise, but one that loves wisdom. In other words, their ideal is someone who does not possess wisdom. The highest soul is one that loves the game or the chase. In his interpretation of the *Symposium*, Bloom writes that Socrates would not

---

ning in childhood and designed by the philosopher-kings, who are themselves ruled by reason, to have this very effect" (1988, 142). The problem here is in reconciling the idea of consent to training in such a way that his argument does not fall back upon a reliance upon force.

On Nichols's interpretation, the root of the danger is a spiritedness that, if not moderated, will destroy the complexity of the city and the soul (1988, 63). And although she sees the political solution as lying in a model of limited rule, it is not clear whether she would see such a solution extending to the order of the self (64).

[31] See also Irwin (1977, 244) for a brief discussion of this problem. Perhaps the best practical soul is possessed by someone who "looks fixedly at the regime within him . . . and guards against upsetting anything in it by the possession of too much or too little substance. In this way, insofar as possible, he governs his additions to, and expenditures of, his substance" (*Republic* 591e; see also 571e).

want to be a god because "a god would have to be wise and therefore would not pursue wisdom" (1993, 505). The implication of this position, which Bloom does not draw, is that Socrates does not want to be wise, period. To the extent that Socrates is representative of their aspirations, the classical political rationalists are not lovers of wisdom, they are lovers of philosophy. The problems that attend the possession of wisdom have little to do with the kind of person they want to cultivate—someone who loves the love of wisdom. Possessing no desire to be wise (because that would mean the end of eros) the classical political rationalists are thrilled to retrace repeatedly the attempts of others who have attempted to obtain wisdom. They are in love with eros.

I am not sure that this is an accurate interpretation, let alone a coherent position (although one could be in love with love). Could Socrates love wisdom and yet desire never to be wise? Moreover, this interpretation pushes the classical political rationalist position back into the philosophical conventionalists' camp. A second, less daring interpretation is that Strauss, at least, recognized the extremes of philosophy and the importance of moderation. This comes out most clearly when he talks about why the philosopher, in Plato's allegory of the cave, goes back down into the cave. According to Strauss, "In descending into the cave, the philosopher admits that what is intrinsically or by nature the highest is not the most urgent for man, who is essentially an 'in-between' being—between the brutes and the gods" (1953, 152). On the other hand, Strauss also argues that "moderation is not a virtue of thought: Plato likens philosophy to madness, the very opposite of sobriety or moderation; thought must not be moderate, but fearless, not to say shameless. But moderation is a virtue controlling the philosopher's speech" (1959, 32). This quote suggests madness in thought, moderation in speech. Moderation is a virtue in talk, presumably given the dangers that philosophy poses to society. It is not a virtue in thought. The interpretation of the *Republic* offered here reinforces the first position: it attempts to bring moderation into the project of philosophy, into the philosopher's soul. Moderation is needed not only for the health of society, but also as part of the best practical soul. Only in the case of a philosopher who could stay up all night, drink endless quantities of wine without getting drunk, and remain able to engage in philosophy the next day would the need for moderation be lessened.[32] We should remember that for us, Socrates at his best remains a man "in speech."

[32] All of this, of course, is part of the action of Plato's *Symposium*. Alcibiades' speech in the *Symposium* also mentions other extraordinary feats of Socrates. For example, during a military campaign, Socrates purportedly stood thinking in one place for twenty-four hours (220c–d). Moreover, the *Republic* is itself an act of incredible endurance as Socrates talks without break or food from the afternoon into the next morning (Strauss 1964, 64).

In their ironic reading of Plato's *Republic*, the classical political rationalists argue that the discussion of the ideal city is not to be taken as a blueprint for practice. If this ironic reading extends through the analogy between the city and the soul, then Plato may also be offering a critique of the reason-governed soul. The argument here is that if the classical political rationalists see Plato as criticizing utopianism and they accept that critique, then very little prevents this ironic reading from infecting Plato's view of the best soul. The classical political rationalist commitment to the critique of political idealism should, in fact, lead them to accept the problematic status of the best life.

The standard that intellectual virtue and the philosophic life set, therefore, may not be the relevant one to apply against any regime, including democracy. Judging the production of modern identity against the ideally best soul not only ignores the limits of politics, but the limits of philosophy as well. The question then becomes whether liberal democracy is obliged to foster the practically best soul. Once again, an answer to this question requires knowing what that standard entails. As suggested above, that standard may vary depending upon what is found agreeable to the various parts of the soul. This variation suggests that there is not one practically best soul. To apply a universal conception of what is best would be to ride roughshod over these differences.

The best practical solution may be to encourage people to reflect on their own lives, to think about the standards and norms that they have learned, and ask themselves if those norms are appropriate for who they are. Perhaps the most that should be asked of government is whether it fosters autonomous individuals. As we shall see, even this rather minimal demand presents large problems.

There are good reasons for doubting the usefulness of the well-ordered, reason-governed soul as a standard for judging the effects of liberal democracy. Some of these reasons are connected to very general problems associated with knowing natural right and individual souls. Other problems are raised by the hierarchical character of souls and the ranking of ways of life. The problematic relationship between reason and revelation, the questionable justification of the rule of reason, and the ironic reading of the best soul all point to the conclusion that liberal democracy should not be judged by the standard of the well-ordered, reason-governed soul.

4

The Complex, Performative Subject

MY CRITICISMS of the communitarian and classical political rationalist positions seem to lead to an endorsement of the genealogical position. I took issue with the communitarians by questioning the value they attribute to the role of unity in the conception of the self. I challenged the classical political rationalist position by calling into question the rule of reason in the well-ordered soul. The thrust of these criticisms accords well with important themes of the genealogical perspective. A critique of unity coincides with the genealogical criticism of a normalized, coherent identity. Questioning the rule of reason comports with the genealogical rejection of logocentrism.

More strongly, the genealogical perspective appears superior to the other positions because its conception of the self fits more easily into the pluralistic presumptions of liberalism. Both the classical political rationalists and the communitarians want to settle ontological questions before they engage in politics. In contrast, the genealogists present a more open-ended view of the self that does not require the same kind of settlement before participating in politics. Indeed, devising a politics to sustain the paradox of difference is Connolly's attempt to express this open-ended character of life. Similarly, Butler's notion of the performative self and her criticism of coherence eschews the static ontologies that these other schools of thought advance. The politics of difference and the performative self are both able to accommodate self-understandings that go beyond the other two schools of thought. To the extent that we possess differing understandings of the self, the genealogical position can better reflect this difference.

Reinforcing the openness of genealogy to competing conceptions of the self are themes in Butler's work that question the very use of the self as a basis for theorizing about politics. For example, she argues that

> the critique of the subject means more than the rehabilitation of a multiple subject whose various "parts" are interrelated within an overriding unity, a coalition subject, or an internal polity of pluralistically related points of view. Indeed, the political critique of the subject questions whether making a conception of identity into the ground of politics, however internally complicated, prematurely forecloses the possible cultural articulations of the subject-positions that a new politics might well generate. (1990b, 327)

The interesting claim here is that even an internally complex, coalition-ist, or pluralistic view of the self may suffer from the same problems as the communitarian or classical political rationalist positions. There is no way to guarantee that such a view will not be ultimately exclusive, if not repressive.[1] Elsewhere, Butler argues that "there is no ontology of gen-der on which we might construct a politics, for gender ontologies always operate within established political contexts as normative injunc-tions. . . . Ontology is, thus, not a foundation, but a normative injunction that operates insidiously by installing itself into political discourse as its necessary ground" (1990c, 148).

These claims clearly express Butler's distrust of a politics based upon a particular ordering or number of parts of the self. Nevertheless, there are other themes within her work that do point to a preferred self-con-ception. For example, her attacks on nature and coherence rest upon a set of judgments and generalizations regarding the character of our identity. She rejects theories that appeal to a naturally given self, sexual-ity, or body, basing this rejection on her belief that the actor is entirely constructed through a set of repeated deeds. She warns against a desire to establish a coherent identity. The justification for this warning stems from the harmful consequences that she believes follow from realizing such desires. Her preferred view of identity appears to be that of a com-plex performative self. Its performative character is derived from the claim that our identities are largely the effect of practices whose conven-tions and norms we are repeatedly forced to enact. Indeed, she argues that whatever grounds these practices ultimately is itself performative. The complexity of identity refers to the inability of its various aspects to mesh. Because the demand for coherence attempts to clear away this complexity, Butler considers it to be a form of cruelty (1993, 115).

As with the other schools of thought, the genealogical position criti-cizes the production of modern identity in part by appealing to pre-ferred views of the self. If Butler could be said to offer a complex per-formative view of the self, both Foucault and Connolly turn to the idea of a self that exceeds whatever identity is imposed upon it: the recog-nition of the contingent, fragmented, multiple character of our identi-ties is an important element in their judgments of and responses to the pressures of disciplinary power. Are these conceptions of the self pow-erful enough to warrant endorsing the genealogical criticisms of the dis-ciplined, naturalized self? Can genealogical criticisms succeed where communitarian and classical political rationalist criticisms failed? Gene-alogists' conceptions of the self are not powerful enough to provide a

---

[1] A recent, spirited defense of the multiple conception of the self and its importance to democratic politics is Bonnie Honig's *Political Theory and the Displacement of Politics* (1993).

general standard by which to judge the production of modern identity. To address their arguments, I will focus on the central ideas of discipline, naturalization, and coherence.

Two Approaches

Should contemporary liberal democratic culture be assessed on the basis of its involvement in the production of the naturalized, disciplinary subject? Moreover, is such a self an unfortunate or troubling production? The genealogical perspective has developed at least two responses to these problems. One is suggested by Connolly's idea that life always exceeds whatever identity is impressed upon it (1991; 1993a, 371): the "fugitive difference between my identity and that in me which slips though its conceptual net is to be prized; it forms a pool from which creativity can flow and attentiveness to the claims of other identities might be drawn" (Connolly 1991, 120). Disciplinary power is disturbing because it marginalizes and excludes that excess or difference. Does this appeal to excess or difference afford the necessary normative leverage against the production of the disciplinary subject? In other words, why does this internal difference matter?

Butler's writings express a second approach by emphasizing the theme that there are no points outside the social context, no moments that are free of the effects of power. For Butler, the notion that the subject or self is entirely constructed by its social context means that there is no standard external to that production by which to judge its quality. On this view, we could not say, for example, that the constructed self is cramped or narrowed, our true selves being richer and more expansive. The only subject is that produced by the repetition of certain performances of a socially mandated script. The problem with a disciplinary society is that it naturalizes, freezes, or reifies categories and distinctions that are purely performative. Butler's perspective raises questions regarding the character of the harm that the terms *naturalization* and *performativity* indicate.

To a certain extent, these two approaches are compatible. Connolly is not only concerned with difference, but also the naturalization of difference. Butler is not just concerned with naturalization, but also with the effects of that naturalization upon marginalized groups. Furthermore, both themes occur in Foucault's writing. There is, however, some dispute about whether Foucault believed that a normative fulcrum could lie outside the effects of power and social practice. On the one hand, he does say that power is everywhere and that there is no escaping it: "there are no 'margins' for those who break with the system to gambol in"; and "power is co-extensive with the social body; there are no spaces of primal liberty between the meshes of its network" (Foucault 1980c, 141, 142). On the other hand, in the first volume to his *History of Sexuality*, Foucault asks, "Should it be said that one is always 'inside' power, there is no 'escaping' it . . .? This would be to misunderstand the strictly relational character of power relationships" (1980a, 95). In his essay "Two Lectures," Foucault describes individuals circulating "between . . . [power's] threads" (1980b, 98), and in "Power and Strategies" he argues that "there is indeed always something in the social body, in classes, groups, and individuals themselves which in some sense escapes relations of power, something which is by no means a more or less docile or reactive primal matter, but rather a centrifugal movement, an inverse energy, a discharge" (1980c, 138). Butler notes other inconsistencies in this aspect of Foucault's analysis. She argues that at certain places in his work there are "pleasures that clearly transcend the regulation imposed upon them, and here we see Foucault's sentimental indulgence in the very emancipatory discourse his analysis in *The History of Sexuality* was meant to displace" (Butler 1990c, 96).[2] Finally, Butler sees Foucault as positing a body prior to power in his essay on "Nietzsche, Genealogy, History," and in his introduction to *Herculine Barbin*. These essays suggest that certain forces and pleasures exist prior to social conventions and regulations.

Similarly, in Connolly's work there are occasions in which that excess or difference seems to possess a prediscursive status. His appeals to "life" and to "fugitive differences" appear to reach for a point that lies outside power. On the other hand, all of these ontological (or ont*a*logical) appeals are highly self-conscious and provisional (Connolly 1991). Although Connolly finds it necessary to set out an ontology, he denies that it must exclude other foundations (220–21), but this view is meant to be

[2] According to Butler, in those places where Foucault suggests the existence of a body that is prior to power, he is backsliding into the very language his notion of power was meant to counteract. This backsliding also opens the possibility that Foucault's "own theory maintains an unacknowledged emancipatory ideal that proves increasingly difficult to maintain even with the structures of his own critical apparatus" (Butler 1990c, 94). The larger question, of course, is whether this is indeed backsliding. Foucault's later writing implies especially that the subject is not created solely out of forces of repression (Hacking 1986, 235). Foucault's notions of care for and knowledge of the self suggest that the constitution of the subject is even more complex.

Butler argues that Foucault's mistake is rooted in his reliance upon Nietzsche's conception of genealogy "which conceives the body as a surface and a set of subterranean 'forces' that are, indeed, repressed and transmuted by a mechanism of cultural construction external to that body" (Butler 1989, 602). There is something about the body that stands outside relations of power: "By maintaining a body prior to its cultural inscription, Foucault appears to assume a materiality prior to signification and form. Because this distinction operates as essential to the task of genealogy as he defines it, the distinction itself is precluded as an object of genealogical investigation" (Butler 1990c, 130).

no less shaky than more specific ontologies promising a natural purpose or ordering to the self.

Of the three writers, Butler seems to offer the most thoroughgoing rejection of a normative standpoint outside a given social script. For Butler, the social script also includes its own resistance. Drawing upon Foucault, she argues that the "culturally contradictory enterprise of the mechanism of repression is prohibitive and generative at once and makes the problematic of 'liberation' especially acute" (1990c, 93).[3] The significance of this claim cannot be underestimated. To the extent that there is a mismatch between what one is and what society demands, that slippage is also produced through the demands of society. Butler warns that "the female body that is freed from the shackles of the paternal law may well prove to be yet another incarnation of that law, posing as subversive but operating in the service of that law's self-amplification and proliferation" (93). If subjects are produced through exclusion, then the identities of those who are excluded radically depend upon the original production.[4] Although Butler rejects the possibility of a full-scale escape, she does leave open the possibility of parodic subversion as well as a coalition politics that draws together complex identities. But if the prevailing identities and that which resists those identities are not distinct productions, can normative value be attributed to either one of these terms?

Discipline

The normalizing and naturalizing features of modern soulcraft are portrayed by Foucault and Connolly as disturbing largely because of the violence such features enact against that which exceeds our identities.[5]

---

[3] Butler supports this claim by arguing that "if drives must first be repressed for language to exist, and if we can attribute meaning only to that which is representable in language, then to attribute meaning to drives prior to their emergence into language is impossible" (Butler 1990c, 88).

[4] Butler contends that "whereas Wittig clearly envisions lesbianism to be a full-scale refusal of heterosexuality, I would argue that even that refusal constitutes an engagement and, ultimately, a radical dependence on the very terms that lesbianism purports to transcend" (1990c, 124).

[5] Jane Flax pushes this claim even farther. She writes that although

Foucault stresses the existence and importance of "suppressed discourses" and local and particular forms of knowledge. . . . It is incomprehensible that such discourses could persist despite the "disciplinary and surveillance" aspects of power without the existence of some form of "self." Something must exist within and among persons that is not merely an effect of the dominating discourse. Otherwise how could conflict and struggle against dominance continue even in the most totalistic discursive formations? (1990, 231)

Why does this internal difference matter? Before addressing this question, we must consider the possibility that it may be inappropriate. Connolly has recently argued that we should refuse the legitimacy of such "why questions" because this kind of question automatically constructs a particular metaphysical framework. He argues that "the why question presupposes either a transcendental agent in the last instance or an intrinsic purpose in being that draws one toward it" (Connolly 1993c, 192). "Why?" presupposes such things because these appeals are the only way to stop its constant reappearance. Unless one comes to rest upon a transcendental agent (e.g., God) or an intrinsic purpose (e.g., nature), "it will always seem arbitrary to stop before the next stage of the question has been posed and answered" (192).

From a classical political rationalist perspective, this refusal is precisely what is wrong with the genealogical approach: in order to sustain itself, it must stifle and stunt our deepest desires to know why. The genealogists are asking us to restrain the erotic curiosity that the classical political rationalists celebrate. Surely, the latter would argue, something has gone wrong when philosophers argue that philosophy should be precluded from asking certain kinds of questions.

But one does not need to leave the genealogical perspective to call Connolly's argument into question. There is something about his position that suggests he is playing on both sides of the net. Why questions can be answered satisfactorily only by appealing to some deep metaphysical foundation, and it seems better to refuse the question than to be drawn into those murky and dangerous depths. This presupposes that the only satisfactory answer to the why question depends on a *finis ultimus*, while the point of genealogy is to accustom us to the unavailability of such a secure grounding. Indeed, if we can learn to live with a deepgoing contingency, it may be that on occasion a good enough answer to the why question can be found at or near the surface. In other words, Connolly's argument is itself grounded in the very metaphysical tradition that he is trying to warn us against. If we have little nostalgia for these deeper metaphysical "solutions" or we believe that one can answer a why question quite adequately without making these deeper appeals, then Connolly's refusal is less convincing.

Consider, for example, that Connolly's argument against entertaining why questions is itself an answer to the question, "Why should why questions be refused." Part of his answer is based on a desire not to be drawn into a particular metaphysics. Another part of his answer is based on the claim that these questions can produce aggressive and passive forms of nihilism (192). A final aspect of his answer appears to be that such concerns are redundant, for he argues that why questions should be converted into how questions. For example, we should ask not "Why be moral?" but "*How* can cultural forms and personal dispositions be worked upon to foster greater forbearance and generosity in the strife and interdependence of social relations?" (192). If we already have "footholds" for this question, "the why question proves to be either redundant or a mechanism through which the available footholds are made even more slippery" (192). By footholds, I think he means that we already believe that it is good to foster forbearance and generosity. We do not need to ask why.[6]

Perhaps the exploration of the notion of difference and harm could itself be reframed. Instead of asking why internal difference matters, we could ask, "How does the contingent view of identity and the importance of difference allow us to appreciate the harm embedded in the normal individual, the transcendental subject, natural gender duality, and normal sexuality?" Here we assume that we have a foothold in the harm of normalization and naturalization. But I do not think this is the case, particularly given the level of dispute over what an unharmed self is. To be convinced by its critique, the genealogical position should be able to offer fairly substantial footholds into the character of harm. We should not defer the question of what harm is embedded in modern forms of soulcraft.[7]

There are a number of possible ways of understanding the character of this harm, each of which appeals to a very different normative standard: the value of contingency, freedom of movement, respect for others, authenticity, style, and autonomy. The problem with these standards is that they ultimately do not jibe with other features of the genealogical understanding of the subject. Consequently, all encounter problems when used as a critical fulcrum against the identities produced by liberal culture.

Contingency

The first possibility rests upon the sheer contingency of the excess or pool that Foucault and Connolly see as excluded or marginalized. Perhaps the harm lodged within the disciplinary subject is simply the stifling of that excess. This argument begins by claiming that there is no ontological difference between what is subjugated into an identity and what composes this creative pool or difference. It is largely a matter of happenstance that we come to celebrate certain characteristics and margin-

---

[6] Once again, this appeal to redundancy is itself an answer to a why question.

[7] Connolly intends to "extend 'the harm principle' as it were, into the structures of identity and responsibility, while recognizing that no clean or uncontestable line can be drawn between effects that are indifferent and those that are harmful" (1991, 120). The question is whether one can draw even a blurry line that will be good enough to identify harm.

alize others within ourselves. The support for this claim is found in the genealogical project itself, which Foucault saw as exploding the pretensions to a coherent, essentialist self or soul (Foucault 1984a, 81). Connolly argues that an identity is the result of a variety of contingencies: genes, family, education, and culture that together yield an identity that both meshes and conflicts with itself. Because of these contingencies, who you are and how your identity hooks up with larger social values regarding race, sex, gender, age, and so on, is more a matter of fortune than virtue. The flip side of this argument is that who you are not (the part of your life that exceeds your identity and is shunted aside or repressed) and how your identity fails to fit with the given cultural norms is also a matter of fortune, and hence cannot bear a very heavy load of responsibility and blame (Connolly 1991, 171–81).

Connolly is not arguing that every element contained in our subjectivity should be viewed as completely dispensable or changeable: "Some elements will be crucial to the constitution of your identity, while others will be more like dispensable attributes you can maintain or drop" (174). Some aspects of identity are branded upon oneself. Connolly is arguing, however, that if the role of contingency is combined with the idea that there is always something to our lives that exceeds our role as subjects, then we should be less insistent upon the truth of our subjectivity and more respectful of the differences that are also part of us. Those who construe their identities as laced with contingencies are "in a better position to question and resist the drive to convert difference into otherness to be defeated, converted, or marginalized" (180). Excess and difference should be respected because they have no less claim upon our self-conception than those characteristics with which we are more comfortable.

What complicates this argument's normative thrust is that the genealogical position does not simply invert the hierarchy and value difference over identity. More significantly, it does not place identity and difference on par with one another. To do so would be to destroy the possibility of possessing an identity and Connolly's assumption that we cannot live without identity excludes such a possibility.[8] If this is true, then the contingent character of identity and difference does not level the internal playing field. On top of this is Connolly's further claim that even if there is no ontological necessity for our identities, there can be ethical reasons for valuing certain forms of identity and not others. For example, the contingent character of our identities does not redeem racist or misogynist interests, desires, or projects. Connolly argues that "identities that must define what deviates from them as intrinsically evil

[8] Identity provides some level of order or coherence to the self. For Nietzsche this is necessary because the "unordered soul is spiteful and dangerous, like 'a knot of savage serpents that are seldom at peace among themselves—thus they go forth alone to seek prey in the world' " (Thiele 1990, 75).

. . . in order to establish their own self-certainty are here defined as paradigm instances to counter and contest" (15). By itself, the sheer contingency of the components of our subjectivity does not carry much normative weight.

The contingency argument, however, is not freestanding. Connolly connects it to a claim that identity and difference have an interdependent relationship. Perhaps it is the combination of these claims that accounts for the value of difference within ourselves. The logic of interdependence is that in order to establish and affirm our identity, we need to establish what we are not: we need to establish difference. Connolly writes that "an identity is established in relation to a series of differences that have become socially recognized" (64). The maintenance of an identity requires that even internal differences must be kept at the margins. For to value those alternative desires and perspectives above one's endorsed desires and perspectives is to threaten one's identity. Our identities are intertwined with difference: on the one hand, difference is an essential part of defining identity; on the other hand, being true to difference softens and threatens the distinctions that support identity.

Does the combined weight of contingency and the interdependence of identity and difference provide a convincing account of why internal differences should be respected? Should we respect difference because it plays an essential part in defining who we are (a respect that will also be tempered by the threat that difference presents)? The logic of the identity/difference relationship is compelling. There are, however, whole universes of socially recognized things that we are not. The logic of this relationship suggests that the world provides a kind of "space" for identity. Although something can be identified by all of the things it is not, does this mean that we should respect all those things that we are socially recognized not to be? Existence versus nonexistence, life versus death, animal versus plant, human versus animal are all categorical distinctions that reveal differences that are essential to bounding our identities. It is certainly true that we may respect the second items in these oppositions, but is their role in sustaining identity sufficient for this respect? On this reading, there would be literally nothing that we should not respect because things would either be part of our identity and celebrated or part of what we are not and hence part of what defines what we are. The obvious problem with this kind of universal respect is that the notion of respect (its identity) loses any contrastive power and becomes meaningless.

Perhaps we need to reaffirm the element of contingency. What is important about difference is not merely that it defines identity, but that there are some differences with which we could have been identified, if it were not for happenstance. The large-scale oppositions mentioned above do not have this quality. For example, while it is true that part of my identity is defined by the fact that I am not a trout, I could not be a trout and still be me, unless I believed there was some further fact about my identity that was not exhausted by my various characteristics (e.g., if the core of my identity was a Cartesian ego or an immortal soul). In contrast, the value of our internal differences (that which exceeds my identity) is that if it were not for happenstance, a different set of characteristics could have identified me. Those differences not only help define who I am, but they remain as so many other possibilities and potentialities with which I could have been identified.

The combination of contingency with the interdependence of identity and difference provides an answer to why internal difference matters: not only is my identity dependent upon difference, but those internal differences could have been part of my identity, thus making less insistent the truth and necessity of my identity. But Connolly's claim that difference threatens identity appears to imply that these internal differences are not part of one's identity. To adopt these different attitudes or attributes would mean a transformation of my identity (one that would also generate a new set of differences). If they do not mean a transformation of my identity, then these internal differences do not necessarily threaten it. If all of this is true, then it is a mistake to claim that internal difference represents something that I could have been because those attributes would give me a different identity. In other words, internal differences do not represent other things that I could have been, they represent other identities, other people. I would not be different if I adopted what is found in that excess or pool, rather I (defined as a particular set of attributes) would no longer exist. On this reading, internal difference (if it truly threatens identity) does not represent a creative pool, but radical transformation or extinction.[9] Contingency and the logic of identity, far from engendering respect, may drive us to devalue and recoil from internal difference.

Freedom of Movement

A second standard that may provide leverage against the production of the disciplinary subject by the liberal democratic regime is freedom of movement. Perhaps the normalizing and totalizing aspects of discipli-

[9] Connolly's idea of branded contingencies that have become indispensable components to one's identity appears to diminish further the normative importance of contingency. From the perspective of one's branded contingencies, it is unlikely that conflicting internal difference is a matter of "there but for the grace of fortune am I." They would not be seen as things that one could have been.

nary power are troubling because they prevent us from doing what we want. This could mean that disciplinary power is expressed in practices and institutions that push people around: preventing them from living as they want to live, silencing their speech in public debate, marginalizing their interests, and depriving them of the freedom to pursue their own goals. To the extent that the totalizing and individualizing features of disciplinary power restrict people unjustifiably from doing what they want to do, the harm is familiar to liberal theorists. To the extent that liberal democratic politics sanctions or encourages these harms, it is failing to live up to its own standards and ideals, but the genealogical criticism goes beyond these concerns. The problem is not human conduct, but the kinds of humans we have become: there is something harmful or harmed about the disciplinary subject itself.

Perhaps the way to capture this deeper concern is through a second understanding of freedom. Here, the idea of *want* that is at the core of freedom includes whatever is found in Foucault's notion of an "inverse energy" or Connolly's "pool." Moreover, freedom can be abridged not only by obstacles put into place by other agents, but also by internal obstacles. Perhaps constant punishment and penalization of difference leads people ultimately to govern themselves more closely and to fortify their own resolve against acting on desires that exceed their identities. Disciplinary power restricts bodily movements, but these movements have their origins in the differences contained within ourselves, and the restrictions themselves are found in the subject. The subject serves as an oppressive gatekeeper over marginalized and excluded desires, wants, and feelings. The notion that one cannot ultimately control the internal presence of these wants just makes the nature of self-discipline even crueler. In a sense, the gatekeeper is the ultimate internalization of disciplinary power. At this level, freedom entails overthrowing the gatekeeper and allowing those different desires some control over the body. As Fraser puts it, "the internalized other is still other . . . . self-surveillance is still surveillance" (Fraser 1985, 179). Perhaps Foucault and Connolly are theorists of free movement. In this argument, it is the control over the movement of bodies that is ultimately troubling. Docility, normalization, and individualization are all problematic because they restrict even a very minimal notion of freedom.[10] Its minimal character

[10] In *The Philosophy and Politics of Freedom*, Richard Flathman sets out the different uses of the term freedom in the philosophical literature. The form of freedom discussed here is what Flathman calls freedom$_1$, which he defines as "self-activated movement plus the possibility of impediments to the movement in question" (Flathman 1987, 322). For Flathman, the presence of simple freedom of movement is not sufficient to establish whether one is free in a political or social sense. One must also possess agency and hence a degree of discipline or control of one's desires and instincts to be freedom evaluable.

comes from the fact that the source or object of those movements is irrelevant: if a desire is curbed, either externally or internally, then freedom has been abridged.

One problem with an argument based upon free movement is that there are occasions when the body is quite active, but it is difficult to see why those movements should be validated or celebrated. To validate any and all such movements would require validating psychosis and seizures. Is the problem with disciplinary power that we do not praise and applaud the movements of epileptics and psychotics? If freedom of movement is the linchpin to the argument, then it would seem that we must. To support this position, the Foucauldian would reply that it is only because of the prevailing norms regarding mental health and rationality that we refuse to respect these movements. After all, there was a time when people saw epileptic seizures as a gift from the gods. The real harm comes from those who, through various techniques and operations, try to "cure" these maladies. But Foucault and those associated with the antipsychiatry movement may underestimate the pain and hardship of losing a sense of a core self. For example, Jane Flax argues that "those who celebrate or call for a 'decentered' self seem self-deceptively naive and unaware of the basic cohesion within themselves that makes the fragmentation of experiences something other than a terrifying slide into psychosis" (1990, 218–19).

Fortunately, one need not venture into this dispute to uncover internal difficulties with this celebration of bodily movement. For Connolly, the value accorded to identity itself rules out a willingness to see any and all possible sources of movement as free human actions. If all impulses and wants had equal claim to our body's movements, identity would be impossible. Freedom of movement by itself cannot supply much critical leverage against the effects of liberal democracy upon the subject.

There are also interpretive problems in associating unfreedom with the presence of internal obstacles. This association implies that by coercing people to act upon desires that they have repressed, they are actually being freed. Instead of opening the space for freedom, a rejection of internal forms of discipline may simply license further forms of external coercion. Richard Flathman goes further than this and argues that self-discipline is a necessary precondition for freedom (1987, 25–51). The lack of all control impairs an individual's ability to fulfill any desire other than the most simple and most immediate. If all desires had an equal claim upon our time, it is likely that none (or very few) would ever be met. Discipline may not only be necessary for identity, it may also forge freedom.

But is this not precisely the point? Doesn't Flathman's argument reveal the importance of discipline in sustaining freedom? Even if internal discipline is necessary for freedom, that does not mean that this kind of discipline is a form of harm—quite the contrary. If the notion of discipline is meant to make us think twice about the value we attribute to freedom, then we still need a sense of why discipline should be seen as troublesome.

Respect for Others

A third argument for respecting difference within oneself is that a failure to do so could generate resentment towards others who are different. If we do not provide space within ourselves for what falls outside the norm, then we are unlikely to tolerate differences in others. Thus the harm associated with the disciplinary subject is found in its effects upon our conduct, not within the subject as such. These effects ultimately mean the establishment of social institutions and practices that preclude people from pursuing what they see as good in life. The disciplinary subject leads to a disciplinary society that violates the more robust conception of freedom mentioned above. Alternatively, an interior agonistic respect is linked to a more widely held form of social tolerance and external agonistic respect.

This argument appears to hold greater promise than the first two for providing normative leverage against the disciplinary subject. By reasoning that this form of subjectivity leads to the totalization and individualization of differences in others, this contention appeals to the standard political conceptions of harm that revolve around conduct and treatment of others. Nevertheless, do we necessarily come to tolerate (or fail to tolerate) difference without if we respect (or fail to respect) difference within? There are enormous problems in trying to untangle the relationship between how we treat ourselves and how we treat others. The assumption here is that the disciplinary subject results in the discipline of others. In contrast, Foucault's example of the panopticon suggests that the disciplinary subject is the result of social discipline. The prison's architecture does not result from an original desire of prisoners to discipline themselves. This difference in causal direction, of course, does not mean that those social disciplines cannot be reinforced or intensified as a result of self-discipline. It does suggest, however, that self-discipline proceeds only by reacting to prevailing social norms and standards.

There is a more immediate problem with the connection between the disciplinary subject and harming others. This connection assumes that lessening the disciplinary pressures within oneself lessens the desire to discipline difference elsewhere, but perhaps lessening these internal pressures has the opposite effect. If Connolly is correct, lessening internal disciplinary pressures could diminish the security of one's own identity, and one might attempt to compensate by increasing the pressure to discipline others. Furthermore, it is also possible that intensive self-discipline could have little effect upon external disciplinary pressures. A highly self-disciplined, contemplative way of life, for example, may add very little to the individualizing and totalizing pressures of modern life. These possibilities (and they are only possibilities) suggest that the disciplinary subject is not linked necessarily to a drive to discipline others. Given the complexity of these connections, we cannot conclude that the disciplinary subject is the primary cause of a disciplinary society.

Authenticity

A fourth possibility is that the disciplinary subject stifles what J. S. Mill calls *individuality* or *character* and what Charles Taylor calls *authenticity*. According to Mill, "A person whose desires and impulses are his own— are the expression of his own nature, as it has been developed and modified by his own culture—is said to have a character" (Mill 1975, 57). The governing assumption here is that "each of us has an original way of being human" (Taylor 1991a, 28). The best way of life is to discover and nurture that core of authenticity or individuality. To do this, we must listen closely to our own original inner voices. The best form of government is one that allows the full development and expression of individual character.

If the problem with the disciplinary subject is that it is a repressed individuality, then the harm is lodged in the social pressures to conform. A disciplinary society, like an enormous cookie cutter, excludes and attempts to reform what does not fit initially in the mold. On this reading, that excess is our authenticity and individuality. Because we value these attributes, disciplinary power appears harmful. This, of course, is a very familiar claim. Were the genealogists to invoke it, they would be joining the ranks not only of Herder and Mill, but Tocqueville, Thoreau, Emerson, Whitman, and many nineteenth-century Romantics.

Clearly, there are significant parallels between Foucault's account of the totalizing and individualizing aspects of power and nineteenth-century descriptions of political and social pressures to conform. Furthermore, as we saw earlier, Connolly argues that the part of life that exceeds identity is something to be "prized" (1991, 120). Like Mill's notion of individuality and Taylor's conception of authenticity, this difference is a source of creativity within oneself and tolerance of difference in others. The idea of the disciplinary subject, however, should not be assimilated to these earlier arguments. The most important difference between them is the genealogists' rejection of the idea that there is some original, creative, core attribute that is waiting to be discovered in each of us— that there is a true way of being that stands apart from the effects of power. More troublesome to the genealogists, authenticity would be privileged over whatever identity is imposed upon us. As we have seen, Connolly argues that there is no ontological superiority to what emerges as difference. Unlike an argument based upon authenticity or individuality, his position asserts that it is largely a matter of happenstance if our identities are one thing and not another. The genealogical conception of difference is not a repressed authenticity.

Style

If the notion of authenticity does not provide critical leverage, perhaps the idea of style can be more successful. Under this possibility, the production of the disciplined self inhibits or dries up the desire to give style to one's life. Unlike the claims surrounding authenticity, this argument does not rest upon a prediscursive, original core in the subject—one does not *discover* style. Rather, the problem is that discipline forecloses the creation of an aesthetic individualism.

The problem of appealing to the notion of style is that discipline is also part of the process of giving style to life. The notion of stylizing one's life does not entail simply letting internal differences exist. Rather, it entails a deliberate and disciplined forging of one's life into a work of art. This is particularly evident in Nietzsche's formulation of this ideal: giving style to one's life is not a matter of creating a democratic soul in which all instincts and desires have a rough equality. As Leslie Paul Thiele argues, "Nietzsche's contempt for a democratic politics applied both to the world without and within the self. The politics of the soul is laudatory, not because it gives equal voice to every drive, but because all of one's drives are exploited in the creation of a powerful regime embodying beauty and order" (1990, 66). Giving style to one's life entails the formulation of an internal order. Discipline is an unavoidable element of this process (171, 209): internal campaigns must encourage certain desires and refuse others in order to forge order, beauty, and nobility. Education, for example, plays an important role in providing a "protracted discipline" as the student learns to "internalize the force of education, coming to discipline himself" (171). In addition, whatever order is created is only temporary. Thiele argues that "the 'well-ordered' soul is in this sense a misnomer: There are only souls being put into order and souls falling into disorder" (91).

Foucault appeared to endorse Nietzsche's idea of giving style to one's existence (Foucault 1984c, 351). He asked, for example, "couldn't everyone's life become a work of art? Why should the lamp or the house be an art object, but not our life?" (350). Similarly, Connolly writes that "to accept the contingency of identity, is not to oppose every effort to work on the self. Far from it. Such acceptance requires considerable work on the self" (1991, 178). Foucault's notion of life as a work of art and Connolly's idea of working on the self are possible points of opposition to the totalizing and individualizing aspects of disciplinary power. As Nietzsche had, they too appear to endorse a variety of internal restrictions and rigors. According to Foucault, practices in antiquity, such as Stoicism, that sought to "reproduce certain examples, leave behind them an exalted reputation, give maximum possible brilliance to their lives" could not be accomplished without a variety of regimes and rigors (Foucault 1984b, 362). Connolly's notion of working on the self also requires a degree of self-discipline that is far removed from a simple celebration of difference.[11]

But why is the self-discipline associated with giving style to one's life more acceptable than what is applied to the disciplinary subject? If the disciplinary subject is being harmed, why isn't the self-disciplined aesthete also being harmed? This question is especially puzzling given the similarities between the two disciplines: both entail the establishment of order and the exclusion of difference. Life cannot be stylized without the creation of difference and order. Moreover, the idea of seeing one's life as a work of art and the notion of disciplinary power do not celebrate an egalitarian arrangement within the soul. Both forms of discipline reject the norm of acting on immediate thoughts and desires. If the difference does not lie here, where is it?

The striking contrast between these forms of discipline is that in Nietzsche's idea of style there is a thoroughgoing rejection of the social norms that drive disciplinary power. The "counternorm" that accompanies style is that one should create one's own norms. According to Connolly, "Nietzsche examines some of the most pervasive assumptions and self-understandings of the modern era as if they were the hallucinations of an alien tribe" (1988, 168). It is from this perspective that Nietzsche's individual is able to refuse the standards of the community and strike out on his or her own: "The revocation of the individual's membership in the community of mankind is accompanied by the constitution of the

---

[11] For example, according to Connolly, "if you are drawn to sex with members of one gender but averse to affectional relations with them, the destructive effects such a combination has on you and others might encourage you to try to reconstitute elements in this combination, even while you do not hold yourself thoroughly responsible for the combination presently installed in you" (1991, 178).

individual himself as a community. Perspectivism, then, provides a remedy for its own philosophical ills. The self-enclosure of the individual is counteracted by the multiple perspectives each individual is capable of maintaining" (Thiele 1990, 37).

Should we be troubled by the disciplinary subject because it precludes individual style? To answer that question requires that the accompanying counternorm is conceivable. As the discussion of normative standpoints outside of power showed, Foucault's own beliefs are ambiguous. He does occasionally speak of being "at the frontiers" (Foucault 1984a, 45), of pushing past the boundaries of modern discourse. Far from relying on the limits or possibilities of human practices and norms, this presents the "possibility of no longer being, doing, or thinking what we are, do, or think" (46). Similarly, Connolly's notion of a creative reservoir that exceeds identity does open the possibility of transcending a given set of social practices and standards. On the other hand, one could argue that this Nietzschean ideal of style is impossible and that the attempt to think outside the practices and conventions of society is indeed "'unthinkable,' 'self-contradictory,' 'self-defeating,' 'perverse,' or 'mad'" (Connolly 1988, 4). From a genealogical perspective, the ideal of style would have to entail the ability to break free of the limitations of disciplinary power.

But even if Nietzsche's extreme antinomianism is conceivable, it is still problematic to use style to judge the identities that liberal democratic culture produces. First, if taken seriously, this standard could generate an enormous amount of resentment against those unchangeable aspects of one's self—we may come to resent what we cannot stylize. And that part of our lives that we can stylize would be constantly under scrutiny. Turning oneself into a work of art does not mean turning oneself into kitsch. To give style to one's life suggests an unending concern with whether one's life is art and not just a cheap imitation. Second, if style became yet another norm, it could establish demands that were even crueler than what are seen as the effects of disciplinary power. Given the difficulty of becoming a work of art, it is unclear why those who succeeded would have any respect for those who failed. Finally, Nietzsche's notion of style appears to devalue any ongoing practice that could entail the cultivation and care for one's life. It rejects the idea that an aesthetic individualism could be built upon practices that are already available. But Foucault may not go this far, for he accepts the possibility that an ongoing, established social practice could encourage an aesthetics of existence. According to Foucault, Stoicism may have been just such a social practice. However, the possibility that one could style one's life according to external norms and standards erodes the distinction between the self-discipline of style and the results of disciplinary power. This brings

us back to our original question: what is the difference between disciplinary power and the self-discipline accompanying a social practice capable of forging an aesthetics of existence?

Foucault's view of Stoicism may help here. According to him, an important feature of Stoicism is that it was not normalizing because

> the principle target of this kind of ethics was an aesthetic one. First, this kind
> of ethics was only a problem of personal choice. Second, it was reserved for a
> few people in the population, it was not a question of giving a pattern of
> behavior for everybody. It was a personal choice for a small elite. The reason
> for making this choice was the will to live a beautiful life, and to leave to others
> memories of a beautiful existence. I don't think that we can say that this kind
> of ethics was an attempt to normalize the population. (Foucault 1984c, 341)

If the combination of personal choice and exclusivity is what renders
Stoicism's social practices and disciplines less troublesome than those
accompanying disciplinary power, then the problem with the production of modern identity is that it stigmatizes and punishes rarefied pursuits of beauty. Disciplinary power precludes an aesthetic aristocracy.
One problem with this interpretation is that it is not clear why Stoicism's
exclusivity is relevant. Suppose, for example, that more and more people
were attracted to Stoicism, although it was not intended originally to
serve as a pattern of behavior for the general population. Moreover, assume that this continued to be a matter of an uncoerced, reflective
choice on the part of each individual. Does the sheer number of people
participating transform this from a disciplining of the self to the creating
of a disciplinary subject? It does not seem as though it would, unless
there was a kind of bandwagon effect that came to influence individual
choices (e.g., if it became more and more difficult not to be a Stoic). But
this would shift the issue to whether people were choosing to do something reflectively or being simply swept along with the crowd. The relevant difference between an acceptable form of self-discipline and a disciplinary subject now appears to depend upon the autonomy of the
chooser. Does the genealogical critique of liberal democracy rest upon
the value of autonomy?

Autonomy

As defined by S. I. Benn, autonomy is not so much a matter of creating
a law of one's own, but reflecting consciously upon and then choosing
between a given set of norms and practices, whatever their source (Benn
1975–1976). On this version of autonomy, the relevant contrast is to
someone who habitually, automatically, or routinely follows a set of practices and norms. One is autonomous when one makes a conscious,

reflective judgment to accept one set of norms over another. Autonomy differs from authenticity. Unlike authenticity, autonomy does not depend upon harmony with an inner creative core of being. Choosing autonomously tells us very little about the nature of the choice that is made.

If autonomy is the relevant standard, then the problem with disciplinary power is that it mobilizes enormous pressures against reflectively considering the rules that govern life. Disciplinary power discourages, remonstrates, and punishes those who would judge, amend, or abandon the normal practices of society. The disciplined self is heteronomous: it is a subject who refuses to question the profuse pressures to normalize. Contemporary liberal democratic culture, then, harms us by making it harder and harder to be autonomous.

It is difficult, however, to see how the genealogical approach could sanction the criterion of autonomy. First, as some have suggested, there is a sense that, like the idea of authenticity, autonomy is just another, perhaps more insidious trap. Fraser argues that there is a reading of Foucault in which "humanism is intrinsically undesirable, that the conception of freedom as autonomy is a formula for domination *tout court*" (Fraser 1985, 177; Gruber 1989, 621). The self-reflection and self-discipline necessary to engage in autonomy may be part of a larger disciplinary practice. A second problem is that the capacity to reflect thoughtfully upon the norms governing one's life is not the same as the notion of difference that the genealogists are trying to advance. Difference is not autonomy, particularly when it makes its appearance as resistance. Foucault refers to resistance as "a centrifugal movement, an inverse energy, a discharge" (1980b, 138). Connolly appeals to a "fugitive difference" and a "pool" (1991, 120). This notion of resistance is reminiscent of the Nietzschean notion of drives and instincts that can never be mastered completely. The language of discharge, energy, and movement is antithetical to the intentional, reasoned character of autonomy. The disciplinary subject is not troublesome because it is heteronomous.

Even when the subject is understood as possessing an excess that could possibly provide normative leverage, it is unclear what harm is being done to the disciplinary subject. The problem is that the pieces composing the idea of the disciplinary subject do not yield a coherent sense of what is wrong when differences within ourselves are disciplined. Possible standards, such as contingency, respect for others, freedom of movement, authenticity, style, and autonomy do not seem to characterize properly why that pool or inverse energy should be celebrated. In some cases these standards themselves seem implicated in disciplinary power.

On the other hand, these standards do not exhaust the universe of possibilities. For there may be a standard or a set of criteria embedded within the notion of discipline that has yet to be articulated. Until that articulation is made, the harm associated with discipline appears, at most, to be agent relative. Some may see discipline as a harm, some may not, and some may even see it as a good. The absence of an intersubjective criterion establishing the harm associated with discipline does not preclude any of these claims. But it also suggests that none of these demands should possess special urgency within the realm of politics. Without that urgency, the argument that political institutions have a responsibility to respond to the effects of disciplinary power is weakened.

If the notions of excess and difference run into problems in carrying the normative weight of the genealogical argument, it would seem that Butler's approach would encounter even greater difficulties. For Butler the trap goes all the way down. Even these pools and excesses are products of prevailing social practices and norms. The question is not how resistance is produced or whether resistance is possible, but why resistance should be respected and valued.[12] Butler's answer is connected to ideas of performativity and citationality. If escape, as such, is impossible, then the most that we can hope for is a variety of traps or a trap that allows more variety. For Butler, the idea of the complex performative self opens up this possibility and allows a response to the pressures that seek to naturalize or coalesce our identities. Is Butler's conception of the self convincing? Does it offer a coherent account of the harm and cruelty lodged in the production of modern identity?

Performatives and Citationality

In response to the belief that the prevailing categories of gender or sex are timeless or necessarily coherent, Butler sees the subject as the result of gestures and actions that are performed repeatedly and that effectively cite a set of authoritative practices (1993, 227). This conception of identity provides her with critical leverage against our current self-understandings regarding sex and gender. If these understandings are not grounded in timeless universals, then the forms of exclusion and domination that our current categories justify are oppressive and cruel. This

---

[12] Nancy Fraser has raised the argument that Foucault cannot sustain a normative position against disciplinary power. For example, Fraser argues that Foucault could be read as offering a conception of a society in which the disciplinary norms are so totalistic and so thoroughly internalized, that it is effectively impossible to get any critical leverage on them (Fraser 1985, 179). But this interpretation sees disciplinary power as being so successful that it precludes the possibility for resistance. Foucault's argument is that disciplinary power could never be *that* effective—there is always something that will exceed even the most disciplined of selves. Whether that resistance exists independently of, or is produced by disciplinary power, Fraser's reading is problematic. Nevertheless, her general point that the genealogical position cannot provide critical leverage is compelling.

argument depends not only upon whether the ideas of citationality and performativity offer an adequate account of the subject, but also upon whether these ideas provide an adequate response to the kinds of harms with which Butler is concerned.

Butler depicts gender, sex, the body, and the self as performative acts. They are discursive constructions that we are forced to enact repeatedly and cite throughout our lives. In J. L. Austin's discussion of performative utterances, he originally distinguished performatives from what he called constatives. Performatives are words that do things in our language: promises, threats, warnings, bets, declarations, vows, oaths, and so on. The central attribute of a performative is that in the proper circumstances saying the words makes it so. Moreover, performative utterances are not themselves true or false, but rather successful or unsuccessful. In contrast, Austin portrays constatives as statements that can be judged true or false (e.g., *The cat is on the mat*). In the case of a constative, saying the words does not make it so. Eventually, however, Austin viewed the performative/constative distinction as problematic. He argued that all utterances have a performative and a constative dimension (1975, 148).[13] For example, in order for a promise to be successful, certain things have to be true: I must have a certain intention, I must be able to carry out the promised act, I must have said certain words and so on (45–46). Without these constative elements, a promise would never get off the ground.

Butler draws upon Austin's conception of the performative to illuminate our identities. Nevertheless, she modifies it in a number of ways. Instead of applying the concept to discrete, willful actions (e.g., commands, promises, warnings, etc.), Butler applies it to identity categories. Moreover, she interprets statements regarding gender and sex not as constatives (as Austin would have probably done), but as the effect of repetitive, forced behaviors that may or may not be done intentionally. As with Austin, Butler appears to find the distinction between performatives and constatives inadequate. Her approach, however, is to dissolve constatives into performatives. In other words, whatever we claim as lying at the bottom of our understandings of the self or gender is just another performative. Our current self-understandings are inadequate not only because they ignore the performative character of our identities but because they are grounded in thoroughly conventional claims regarding

---

[13] Ultimately, Austin settled on a distinction between locutionary, illocutionary, and perlocutionary acts. A locutionary act is the performance *of* the act of saying something; an illocutionary act is the performance of an act *in* saying something; a perlocutionary act is the effect that a locution may have upon the listener (Austin 1975, 99–101, 109). As with his argument that performatives and constatives are abstractions, Austin argues that every genuine speech act is both a locutionary and an illocutionary act (146).

the body or matter. For Butler, to understand how it is that performativity "runs all the way down" is also to understand how misguided our current self-understandings are. The consideration of this aspect of Butler's argument is important because it highlights certain difficulties in her position's ability to criticize and address the harms of our current self-conceptions.

The idea that performativity runs all the way down emerges most clearly in Butler's discussion of what makes a performative successful. Drawing upon Jacques Derrida's work, Butler suggests that success depends upon an appeal to a more encompassing set of conventions. This appeal is a citation. Butler writes, "If a performative provisionally succeeds (and I will suggest that 'success' is always and only provisional), then it is not because an intention successfully governs the action of speech, but only because that action echoes prior actions and *accumulates the force of authority through the repetition or citation of a prior, authoritative set of practices*" (1993, 226–27). Our practices are grounded ultimately in a foundation that we have constructed for the purposes of stopping the demand for justification. As discussed in chapter 1, Butler uses the idea of citationality to explain how this ruse works: in the drive to justify our practices we first presuppose and then endow with authority a grounding that lies beyond all our practices and conventions. This foundation, then, is itself a performative: it is something of our own creation, but one whose legitimacy requires that we forget or hide its character as artifice. Butler seeks to reveal the fictional authority of our practices in order to shake us from our naturalistic slumbers. Her hope is that without the clothing of authority the predominate gender and sexual practices may become less staid and more fluid.

If gender is a performative, however, it cites ultimately certain "facts" about our sexuality. If sexuality is seen as performative, it appeals ultimately to certain irresistible, undeniable "facts" about human bodies. These facts, in turn, may come to rest upon the "fact" of matter. It is Butler's contention that what we take to be irresistible, undeniable "facts" are actually performatives with a history. Instead of viewing these things as existing prior to cultural understanding and practice, Butler suggests that the body and matter may themselves be an effect. For Butler, the body is "productive, constitutive, one might even argue *performative*" (30). This does not mean that the body or matter is illusory or nonexistent. They are no more illusory than any of the practices and conventions that structure and enable our ways of living. More specifically, they are no more illusory than things like promises, warnings, marriage vows, commands, and so on.

As with Foucault and Connolly, a great deal of Butler's project depends upon genealogy shaking our view of the world. A central claim of her genealogy is that what we have come to see as prior to our social practices is actually weighed down with a set of conventions and norms. For example, she argues that a history of matter will reveal that sex and sexuality are integral to our understandings of matter. Although we appeal to the body or to matter to justify our claims regarding gender and sexual differences, these terms are already imbued with particular understandings of sexuality. In a sense, built into these understandings is already a lot of talk about sex. Butler argues that "we may seek to return to matter as prior to discourse to ground our claims about sexual difference only to discover that matter is fully sedimented with discourses on sex and sexuality that prefigure and constrain the uses to which that term can be put" (29). On her reading of Plato, for example, "sexual difference operates in the very formulation of matter" (52). Whether the same holds for later understandings of matter remains to be seen. Butler notes that "we have barely begun to discern the history of sexual difference encoded in the history of matter" (54).

It may be important here to remind ourselves of who Butler is targeting. In general, she is taking aim at all social and political conventions that appeal to a prediscursive body in order to justify certain facets of our identities and norms of behavior. Her concern is not merely with practices that make such appeals in order to discriminate against or oppress women. Butler also rejects starting from the body as a way to "authorize feminist epistemologies and ethics" (28). In her view, the concept of *woman* expresses nothing in particular about the world. She is attempting to confront and resist all positions that turn to a grounding in the body.

Limits to Genealogy

One challenge to this genealogical approach is that it can only give us a history of the *concept* of matter. It certainly cannot give us a history of matter as such. For matter is really what stands outside of language—it is what the concept of matter is meant to represent. Butler responds by arguing that even positing that matter stands outside of language is still to posit something within language. Butler claims that we do not have an understanding of matter beyond our understanding of matter. Indeed, Butler suggests that the belief that there is something outside our understanding that can judge the accuracy of our concepts serves the purpose of establishing and privileging certain understandings over others. The effect of this privileging is to secure a set of beliefs and to exclude other

beliefs from serious consideration. Once again, the purpose of genealogy appears to shake these beliefs.

But Butler does not merely want to disabuse us of such naturalistic
sensibilities. She also wants to convince us that these complex, diffuse
beginnings have significance for current use. This part of her argument
raises a second set of problems. By itself, the employment of genealogy
strikes at the idea of a stable, unchanging understanding of matter and
bodies. The metaphor of sedimented or layered meanings conveys the
sense that the past may be buried, but it is not dead and gone. In other
words, those sedimented layers haunt our current meanings. Whether
we are indeed haunted by past meanings is something that would have to
be demonstrated. It may be reasonable to assume that matter, for example, is no different than other concepts: some past meanings resonate
strongly today while others have become dulled or silent. By itself, genealogy can only recover the diffuse, contingent origins of words. We need
something more to show that those beginnings are relevant to our current understandings. More troubling is the possibility that the concept
itself may currently possess multiple conflicting meanings, each with its
own history. Once again, genealogy may not tell us how the understandings of matter and bodies presented, for example, in Lacanian psychoanalysis are related to other specialized and ordinary understandings of
these terms. These kinds of questions do not mean that our notions of
matter and body are free of sexual differentiations, but they raise serious
questions regarding the importance of historical sedimentation to the
prodigious diversity of current uses of these terms.

A third set of issues concerns how far down we can apply the notion of
performativity. To put this another way, is it possible to offer a comprehensive history about our beliefs regarding matter and bodies? For
those who hold that it is possible to have an unmediated understanding
of nature, Butler's project denies common sense and reality. But one
does not need to adopt such a perspective to find her project problematic. The key feature of her genealogy is that matter and bodies can be
revealed as entirely historical constructions. But there may be aspects of
our practices for which *we* cannot give histories. Some features of our
conventions may be so deeply part of our way of viewing the world that
they serve as "hinges" for our practices: they must remain in place in
order for our practices to function. If these hinges were to slip, many of
our practices and conventions would become inconceivable or simply
pointless. One example of this is Wittgenstein's discussion of weighing
cheese (1958, I:142). If cheese could change its weight while on the
scale, then the practice of weighing it would be, at best, a senseless ritual.
We count on this material character of cheese to engage in this practice,
just as we count on innumerable other mundane, general "facts of na-

ture" in building walls, buckling seat belts, and dodging objects.[14] From within our practices these attributes of materiality are irresistible. It may be impossible to tell a story of how we could possibly understand matter or bodies in any other way. Indeed, it may difficult, if not impossible, for us to comprehend someone who had an alternative understanding.[15]

Butler admits that materiality may be "something without which we cannot do anything," but she appears to argue that our understanding of matter is (potentially) fluid and historical (Butler 1993, 29), while I suggest that there are limits to our abilities to tell a complete history of matter from within our practices. This means that we could not give a history of how we came to believe that our hands were attached to our wrists, or how we arrived at the belief that it is better to walk around rather than through rocks and trees.

If there are limits to the fluidity of our understandings of matter and bodies, then Butler's paradigm of citationality needs adjustment. For example, the practice of weighing cheese appeals to (or cites) the "fact" that it does not expand and contract when placed on a scale. For Butler, the characterization of this feature of cheese is a ruse that could, with careful analysis, be revealed. Alternatively, this fact could be understood as a generalization about the world that we can count on regularly; if it is a ruse, it is one that we could not see as such without a drastic change in our overall worldview. If a citation can appeal to a Wittgensteinian fact of nature, then genealogy may have very little success in its disruption. Or, rather, it is not clear what *disruption* means.

Still, the difficulty that genealogists will have in telling a history of facts of nature (and with the notion of agency) does not mean that we must endorse necessarily the practices that rest upon such facts. It is unlikely that these facts ever serve as a sufficient condition for a set of rules or conventions. The fact that cheese fails to expand and contract when put on a scale does not mean that we should weigh cheese or that doing so is a good thing. Similarly, certain facts about bodies and matter may be necessary for explaining why we build walls and buckle seat belts, but whether we do these things as opposed to others is not given to us by these facts.

Butler, of course, is not offering a history of cheese weighing or explaining why we do not regularly doubt whether our limbs are still attached or why we are so certain about the futility of walking through

---

[14] Richard Flathman argues that Wittgenstein's facts of nature should not be assimilated to a set of natural laws or natural rights. These are nothing less and, more importantly, nothing more than regularities (Flathman 1973, 29–30; 1987, 139). To contest Butler's argument, then, does not push one back necessarily into essentialism.

[15] The notion of *we* here is meant to refer to everyone for whom these mundane "facts of nature" are unproblematic.

large rocks. She is concerned with the role that sexual terms have played in our understanding of matter and materiality. More generally, she is concerned with the historical character of the sexed body. But even here there may be hinges. Kathleen Jones, for example, argues that there are stubborn, if not persistent elements in our understanding of sex and body. She claims that one problem with Butler's position is its refusal to accept that we emerged "not from the head of Zeus, but from the body of a woman. What is refused is not only the 'fact' of our mortality but also the 'fact' of our natality: that we came out of the body of some woman in particular, that we have a past, that we are not self-made" (Jones 1993, 79).[16] Although I think that Jones is mistaken in attributing to Butler the claim that individuals create themselves, her uses of "fact" may be compatible with Wittgenstein's facts of nature. Namely, for us, the facts of natality and mortality of human bodies are irresistible. In other words, this grounding of our practices will be difficult, if not impossible to displace. But this does not mean that we could not abandon or displace certain practices that appealed to such groundings. Rather, these facts are compatible with a plethora of human practices and conventions, some of which will be worthy of endorsement and others of which will not be. At this point it is enough to note that to the extent that Butler's project requires the revelation of a ruse, it is not clear how far that project can go.

Harm and Ultimate Groundings

Even if Butler's genealogical project could work all the way down, it is not clear what effect it would have ultimately on our practices. For Butler, domination, oppression, and exclusion are connected to self-understandings that are either grounded in nature or excessively concerned with coherence. To the extent that politics naturalizes identities or cultivates the coherence of identities it has cruel, harmful results. She believes that by coming to see ourselves in a different way, our politics may be improved and the harms associated with these self understandings will be alleviated. This section will explore the connection between how we understand the grounding of our identities and certain harmful effects.

[16] Although the facts of mortality and natality appear to be facts of nature, this may not be true of the claim regarding the necessity of being born of some woman in particular. Given the possibility of surrogate motherhood and grandmothers bearing their grandchildren, a number of women could play a direct role in birth. Although we do not emerge from the head of Zeus, our natality in the future may be connected more closely to a petri dish.

The complex performative self that Butler advances is governed in no small part by the prevailing conventions of gender and sex. Butler believes that these conventions are, in turn, justified and supported by appeals to the nature of the human body and, ultimately, to the nature of matter. To the extent that these ultimate justifications are successful, it is because body and matter are understood as irresistible, undeniable facts. As we have seen, Butler believes that this justification is actually a dissimulation.[17] Although we believe that that ultimate authorization for our identities stands outside of our culture and conventions, it is merely the effect of a forgotten set of actions and beliefs. Butler claims that the realization of this ruse can eventually have a favorable effect on how we understand one another and conduct politics, but the path from seeing this ruse to a set of desired consequences is neither clear nor singular. What are some of the possible consequences of "seeing through" the justification of our practices? Is it possible that by revealing the pretense we actually disrupt and deauthorize the original source of authority? This approach may lead us to believe either that the project of authorizing our practices is itself hopeless or that we can establish an alternative authorization. If we believe that authorization is itself hopeless, we may either reject all that follows from that authorization (passive nihilism) or believe that we can get on with life without the demand that our practices possess an ultimate authority. On the other hand, if we believe that such an authority is necessary, we may either reaffirm our current understanding or replace it with something else. The problem is that it is not clear that either route will lead to Butler's desired outcome: an effective response to the exclusions and harms generated by our current practices and gendered identities.

As suggested above, one result of seeing the ruse could be passive nihilism. If the ultimate citations of our practices have the same status as our other conventions and norms, we may give up on finding any basis or justification for action. Clearly, Butler does not advocate this alternative (Butler 1993, 30). Although she wishes to shake our certainty about some matters, she remains hopeful that there are better ways to think about and conduct politics. Nevertheless, it is not clear what would prevent a slide into passive nihilism. Perhaps her answer is that the exposure

---

[17] There is, I believe, an additional problem in Butler's explanation of how citationality functions. As she has framed this process, there is a point at which we create the authority of that original source in a performative act. If the establishment of this ultimate authority is truly a performative act, then it cannot rest upon an appeal to any other conventions or practices, since the authority of those conventions and practices must come from this original source. To the extent that this performative is successful, it has a kind of purity to it that is deeply problematic (See Digeser 1994). On the other hand, if this performative is merely a ruse and its success illusory (as if we were given a check with a forged signature), then the question arises of whether Butler is offering an alternative conception of authorization.

of the ruse will be experienced as a liberation from harmful and oppressive identity categories, and that the nihilistic possibilities of revealing the ruse will be overshadowed by the eventual benefits of the revelation.

If we should not simply give up on the problem of justification, how should we take Butler's conclusions regarding the basis of our practices and identity? Perhaps we may come to realize that we have misunderstood the practice of justification if we believed that it was based necessarily upon an ultimate endpoint or grounding. In this case, what we initially thought of as a dissimulation is actually a misunderstanding of how we justify what we do. The practice of justification may itself be more complex than the citational paradigm initially implies, for on some occasions justification may stop with Wittgensteinian facts of nature. On other occasions, the potentially infinite practice of citation may itself be enough to authorize our practices. Authority is not found in an original, unreachable source. Rather, it is found when one has offered enough reasons and appealed to enough authoritative practices. Whether these reasons are compelling or inadequate will depend upon the case. From this perspective, Butler is making the same mistake as those who attempt to ground human practices in some unreachable source. Whereas they believe that citing this source is sufficient to justify a practice, Butler believes that calling that citation into question is sufficient to shake their authority. Both positions are sharply at odds with how we actually go about attempting to justify ourselves.

If the idea of an ultimate citation does not accord with our actual practices of justification, then revealing the ruse may have little effect on those practices. If those practices potentially appeal to other practices and conventions, then there is no ruse to reveal. If they are based upon Wittgensteinian facts of nature, then claiming that they are imposed by us is not to call them into question. The perceived regularities upon which these facts are based are nothing more than that. The only way to call them into question would be to demonstrate that the exceptions to the rule are more prevalent than the rule itself. Saying that, however, would be like saying that there is a good chance that cheese will expand or contract when put on a scale. As surprising as this would be, it would not be the same as uncovering a fraud.

On the other hand, what if Butler is correct about how we actually engage in the practice of justification? Would revealing the ruse in our ultimate citations change our practices?[18] Must the ultimate justification

[18] At the very least, revealing the ruse would change our practice of authorization. Unmasking the ruse would imply that the justification to our conventions could not be found in an original source outside our social practices. If Butler is correct about how our practice of justification works, revealing the ruse requires that we live with the "truth" that truth is installed by us. This may ultimately change nothing regarding the content of those practices and norms that were in operation before we realized the ruse.

for a set of practices affect the nature of those practices? The implication of Butler's explorations of citationality, performativity, materiality, and bodies is that by disturbing what ultimately authorizes these practices, one may ultimately disturb the practices themselves. Butler hopes that by understanding this origin as fictional we will be less insistent upon its maintenance and more willing to contest it in the light of whatever exclusion it happens to generate. She certainly believes that this disturbance will have favorable political results, particularly for feminism. In contrast, it is important to emphasize that there are a number of possible outcomes. The first and most optimistic is that revealing the ruse at the bottom of our gender and sexual practices would foster a kind of an understanding of human identity that is flexible, subject to compromise, tolerant of difference, and agonistic, but not hegemonic. Without an essentialist grounding, politics could achieve an openness and fluidity that is otherwise closed off. To the extent that there is "nothing about femaleness that is waiting to be expressed" (Butler 1990a, 281) different views of women would be accepted, if not prized.

But it is also possible that revealing the ruse would have no effect upon our gender practices and politics. We could, for example, come to understand that whatever conception of the body or matter serves as the foundation for our practices is simply placed there by us. This realization would denaturalize that foundation, but it would not displace it necessarily. As Butler herself argues, it is quite possible to see gender roles or sexuality as wholly conventional and still enforce them (Butler 1993, 125, 133). In other words, the process of authorization could remain the same even if the grounding of that authority has been thoroughly denaturalized. There is nothing about the realization of the ruse that, by itself, would lead us to alter it necessarily. More to the point, destructive, uncompromising, exclusionary, oppressive divisions and conventions can thrive without appealing to an ontological or metaphysical grounding. For example, factions based upon economic or social status can pull apart a political movement or polity even though the various parties do not appeal to an original authority to justify their position. Changing the ontological status of a claim may do little to moderate the character or quality of a faction.

Could revealing the ruse of citationality make things worse? Although Butler rejects passive nihilism, there is no guarantee that others would not embrace it. The more ephemeral their identities seem, the less they may care about the world. Alternatively, the more ephemeral their identities, the more insistent they may become in policing and maintaining them. Even on the view that there is nothing more to the legitimacy of our identities than their repetition, one may still be unwilling to accept those who attempt to vary or subvert a given set of roles. In other words, it is far from clear that revealing the ruse would have the kinds of effects

Butler desires. Preferring one ontological theory to another on the basis of its hoped-for effects is extremely shaky. Without evidence that the results of a performative conception of the self would be necessarily less dangerous than any other conception, looking to consequences may settle very little. These large-scale philosophical judgments regarding the self have a very tenuous connection to specific political effects.

Coherence and Harm

Finally, it may also be useful to take a closer look at the ends that Butler is attempting to achieve. In some of her work she believes that denaturalization will increase the number of self-understandings and forms of gendered identities. For example, she writes that "if feminism presupposes that 'women' designates an undesignatable field of differences, one that cannot be totalized or summarized by a descriptive identity category, then the very term becomes a site of permanent openness and resignifiability. I would argue that the rifts among women over the content of the term ought to be safeguarded and prized, indeed, that this constant rifting ought to be affirmed as the ungrounded ground of feminist theory" (1992a, 16). This celebration of rifts, however, sits uneasily with other aspects of her work that focus upon connections between differing groups or identity positions (1993, 112–19). At the very least, Butler appears less sure that constant rifting should, by itself, be "affirmed as the ungrounded ground" of political movements. The problem, Butler notes, is that factions tend to be locked into a logic in which the production of one identity is purchased at the expense of another (112). For example, the identities of whites, heterosexuals, and men are sustained and rendered coherent by rejecting and degrading people of color, gays, lesbians, and women. Butler argues that this logic also comes to infect the identities of those who are rejected and degraded. In order to sustain and render coherent their identities, people of color, gays, lesbians, and women may reject and degrade other identities (including white, heterosexual males).

We have seen this logic, of course, in Connolly's discussion of the relationship between identity and difference: identity both requires and is threatened by difference. In order to help mitigate the transformation of difference into excluded and oppressed "otherness," Connolly appeals to a culture of genealogy and an agonistic democracy. Butler's response is to cultivate connections by calling into question the value of a coherent identity. For it is not merely essentialism, but also the drive to establish coherent identities that generates exclusion and abjection. The desire for a coherent identity encourages us to ignore the role that difference plays and to deny the inherent complexity of our own identities. In contrast, the cultivation of connection entails understanding the importance of difference and drawing upon similarities between complex identities.

Questioning coherence, however, runs the risk of calling into question identity itself. The less coherent an identity becomes, the less it becomes an identity. Butler, however, is not advocating an abandonment of identity. Her position is not "meant to suggest that identity is to be denied, overcome, erased" (117). Whatever lessening the drive to establish a coherent identity means, it does not mean the attempt to jump out of the discourse of identity altogether. Moreover, like Connolly, Butler appears to see difference as both a necessity for and threat to identity. For example, she is doubtful that the pressures to create abject identities could ever be eliminated (115–16). Nevertheless, she is concerned that the drive to create a coherent, stable identity not only degrades and excludes others, but that it may also be self-defeating. The forms of exclusion that created the current rifts and factions within this culture can come to haunt those factions in their attempt to enforce a coherent identity. Those identities that have been produced through the "violence" of liberal humanism, should not "repeat that violence without a significant difference, reflexively and prescriptively, within the articulatory struggles of those specific identities forged from and through a state of siege" (118). If violence is inevitable, at least we can be more reflective about it. More strongly, Butler advocates that these forms of violence should be "perpetually in the process of being overcome" (53).

At least for Butler, the process of perpetually overcoming the violence of exclusion does not mean the simple multiplication of identities. She argues that such a proliferation falls into the hands of a liberal pluralism that separates and disempowers identities (116–17). The multiplication of identity categories, by itself, makes the realization of connections between identity positions difficult. To a certain extent, Butler understands all too well the Madisonian project of increasing factions as a form of regulation. She sees it, however, not as a way to divide and diminish the power of groups that would threaten the general welfare or the liberties of other individuals, but as a way to disempower identity positions that are opposed to those that currently dominate.

What Butler's position does not seem to acknowledge, however, is that the drive to coherence and factionalization need not be so bad, and the desire for connection and ease of coalition building need not be good. For those understandings that can facilitate connections between identities can also reinforce the strength of hegemonic identities. Similarly, the drive for coherence that has the effect of separating oppressed groups should also break apart dominant identities (or what Madison called majority factions). As Madison so clearly understood, all attempts at controlling power are double-edged. The significance of this logic is that it renders ambiguous the value Butler places upon connections as well as her criticism of coherence. For, clearly, certain connections between factions may reinforce a set of dominant identities while a reduced concern with coherence may further undermine the viability of marginalized groups.

Essentialism and Harm

Even if Butler's complex, performative conception of the self would not necessarily mitigate forms of discrimination or domination, perhaps it permits a clearer identification of the harms and risks of essentialist self-understandings. Indeed, there are at least two accounts of the harm of essentialism suggested by Butler's analysis. The first starts with the claim that the prevailing binary roles of gender inevitably exclude others. To reassure the dominant identities and justify the exclusion of others these roles are accorded the status of being natural or essential, thus making them extremely difficult to challenge. Moreover, the idea of natural categories of gender can be deployed to justify the domination of those who fail to live up to their "natures" or their essential characters. On this account of the harm of essentialism, the idea of performativity eliminates an important source of justification, and it opens up possibilities for disputing the prevailing gender roles. Without the ideas of nature or essence, those roles will be seen as merely conventional. With a performative conception of gender we will be less insistent upon enforcing whatever distinctions and regulations currently flow from our conceptions of gender.

In this first understanding, performativity does not play much of a role in identifying the harm itself. The abstract theoretical apparatus of performativity is not needed to understand the deprivation of political rights, the depreciation of interests, the differences of wages, or the lack of respect that women (along with other groups) have faced and continue to face. The notion of performativity does imply, however, that if we shift our self-understandings it would become more difficult to legitimize these forms of treatment.

The question then becomes whether we would, in fact, be better off with a complex, performative conception of ourselves. Perhaps the only way to answer this question is to consider and compare the possible consequences of a political strategy that relied upon essentialism with a strategy that rested upon Butler's notion of performativity. At the very least, this comparison would have to assess the political efficacy of each strategy while taking into account their respective drawbacks. A number of things would make this kind of comparison difficult. First, although it is true that essentialism has served the purposes of justifying oppression and domination, it has also been used to justify overthrowing oppression and domination. Second, the attribution of something being natural or essential is fairly flexible. Could it be the nature or essence of gender that it is pluralistic and multifaceted? Third, as Butler is aware in her citation of Gayatri Spivak, operational essentialism could provide a point of solidarity and resistance (Butler 1990a, 280). Fourth, it is possible that by depriving the notions of gender and sex of any essential or universal content, Butler removes an important source of unity for those who are marginalized. Finally, providing a meaningful assessment of an essentialist political movement would entail judging its effectiveness in eliminating forms of domination while generating other forms of exclusion through its essentialist claims. In the case of a movement that took Butler's idea of performativity seriously, one would have to evaluate the efficacy of a loosely organized coalition that itself did not generate its own exclusions (could it include women who held onto essences and natures?), but which required some (perhaps a great deal of) energy to sustain the coalition. Without some such comparison, Butler cannot show that the effects of a performative conception of identity are preferable to the effects of essentialist conceptions. These points are not meant so much as to defend essentialism as to show the serious difficulties involved in comparing the effects of a performative conception with an essentialist one. It is only on the basis of such an unwieldy comparison that the advantages of a performative self-understanding could be shown.

But the harm of our prevailing categories of gender may be more insidious. This brings us to the second understanding of harm implied by Butler's view of identity. She argues that "subjects are constituted through exclusion, that is, through the creation of a domain of deauthorized subjects, presubjects, figures of abjection, populations erased from view" (1992a, 13). More specifically, "the repression of the feminine does not require that the agency of repression and the object of repression be ontologically distinct. Indeed, repression may be understood to produce the object that it comes to deny" (1990c, 93). On her view, the social practices and discourses that produce the normal and natural also produce the abnormal and unnatural. Butler's idea extends beyond the claim that a desire can be produced by its prohibition (e.g., the fox and the grapes). It also goes beyond the situation in which the law explicitly generates its own violations (e.g., sting operations). For Butler, there is something to the logic of our social practices and discourses that produces those who are marginalized. Perhaps it is only through the production of what is forbidden or unacceptable that we can define clearly what is to be celebrated or deemed acceptable. However this logic works, it suggests that the social practices that sustain a given set of identities are also directly responsible for the prohibited ways of being.

If this logic holds, then there may be something doubly cruel about essentialist practices. On the one hand, essentialism would make it difficult to challenge the given, prevailing identities. On the other, if the prevailing identities are responsible for the production of marginalized identities, this production would be obscured by the claims of essentialism. This second claim is based upon the belief that essentialist categories of gender or sex would probably preclude recognizing Butler's connection between repression and production. To the extent that we see our categories of gender and sex as reflecting a given natural order, then those who fall outside those categories are subverting and twisting nature. On this view, it is unlikely in the extreme that the social practices that maintain and enforce those categories would also be seen as producing those who fail to live up to the demands of nature. Those who are marginalized under essentialist categories are much more likely to be seen as the results of either misfortune or choice.

In Butler's connection between repression and production, the central harm is the actual production and subsequent treatment of the marginalized by the dominant identities. And while the notion of performativity may unmask this connection, it does not appear to provide a form of subjectivity that would circumvent this logic. For this reason, Butler criticizes the drive towards coherence in our identities. By lessening this drive, she is trying to avoid an economy in which one identity is purchased at the expense of another. The hope is that understanding the contingent, complex character of identity would foster a sense of respect for and connection with those who are different. Without evidence to the contrary, however, it is also possible that the notions of complexity and performativity could have the opposite effect: knowing that identity was merely a matter of repeated performances could have the effect of reinforcing an insistence on ordering and regulating a given ephemeral identity.

These kinds of empirical problems raise questions regarding the status of a logic that links the production of identities with repression (or Connolly's connection between identity and difference). First, the universal, iron-clad character of this logic itself runs counter to the historical, sociological nature of the genealogical perspective. If this logic is simply a function of our circumstances and times, then an alternative set of circumstances could circumvent it entirely. The question then becomes whether this Hegelian logic of identity can itself be displaced.

Second, this logic stretches the notion of harm. If Able's identity would not even exist save for a set of repressive circumstances, is Able being harmed by those circumstances? Perhaps we can talk about being harmed in such circumstances because Able *could* have been defined by some other set of identity categories. But if these categories did not exist, then Able may not exist either. If the choice under this logic is between harm and nonexistence, then the notion of harm makes little sense. Third, under this logic, somebody is inevitably going to be harmed by a set of identity categories. If this is true, then do we need to consider how this harm should be distributed (assuming we have some control over our self-understandings)? Are those identities that can encompass the most and marginalize the least number of individuals necessarily the best? Is the connection between genealogy and democracy a utilitarian identity theory? Or are there degrees of marginalization? As an identity encompasses more individuals and groups, does it become more adverse to those who are left out? Is it possible to construct a set of dominant self-conceptions that is mildly opposed to a larger set of identities?

Neither Connolly's and Foucault's notions of excess and difference nor Butler's conception of the complex performative self provides a clear account of the harm lodged in the disciplinary, naturalized, coherent subject. Part of the problem is that it is not clear how to represent the value of internal differences or the harm of discipline given a socially constructed character of the self. In addition, not only does the complex performative self run into difficulties in applying the conception of performativity all the way down, but it is dependent upon conceptual and empirical assumptions that are tenuous and underdefended.

The totalizing and normalizing mechanisms of disciplinary power may lead to disturbing forms of treatment of those who act or behave differently, but the key to the genealogical critique goes far beyond a focus upon conduct. It is one thing to argue that liberal societies are treating their citizens inequitably or unfairly. It is quite another to argue that they are producing objectionable self-understandings. It is this second kind of argument that unites the communitarian, classical political rationalist, and genealogical criticisms of liberal democracy. I have attempted to show the difficulties with the standards these critics use to judge the effects of liberal politics. Without a clear sense of and justification for those standards the case that liberal politics should engage in a particular form of selfcraft is severely diminished. The next two chapters examine whether liberal democracy should be defended on the basis of the quality of its soulcraft.

5

Liberal Soulcraft: Autonomy, Authenticity, and Autarchy

UP TO THIS POINT I have been considering the problems associated with various criticisms of liberal democracy. The core of these criticisms is that regimes of this type practice an objectionable soulcraft or selfcraft. Assessing these objections has entailed examining the criteria these critics use to establish what constitutes harm. The contrastive nature of the word *harm* implies that we are able to judge when something is being harmed only because we have an understanding of what not being harmed entails. In the case of the critics I have considered, that understanding is found in a preferred conception of the self or soul that provides critical leverage on the cultivation of modern identity. Without a convincing account of these preferred conceptions, it is impossible to give a convincing account of harm. Without such an account, the case that liberal democratic regimes have an obligation or a responsibility to foster a particular kind or ordering of self or soul is significantly diminished.

Critics of liberal democracy, however, are not the only ones who turn to the idea of soulcraft to judge the quality of political life. This chapter considers arguments that tie liberal politics to its ability to foster autonomy, authenticity, or autarchy. Like the ideas of the unitary self, the reason-governed soul, and the complex subject, these terms have provided important standards for assessing the effects of liberal democracy. Liberals such as Kant, T. H. Green, John Rawls (on occasion), and Joseph Raz argue that the best political life is not only expressive of what we are as free and rational beings, but also has the salutary effect of encouraging our autonomy.[1] Mill and Taylor argue that the ability to foster individuality or authenticity is an essential component of good government. Finally, because of the value liberal democratic theorists and practitioners attribute to choice, liberal democracy must forge purposive, desiring, autarchic humans. At the very least liberals must engage in a soulcraft that fosters agents. Should liberal democracy be judged, as

---

[1] More generally, Brian Barry argues that the ability of a liberal society to produce admirable characters is an unavoidable part of political justification for a liberal politics (Barry 1973, 126; see also Galston 1991, 96). Raz makes the stronger case that the state has a duty to establish the conditions that enable persons to realize their autonomy (Raz 1986, 418).

some of its defenders have alleged, on the basis of its ability to foster autonomy, authenticity, or autarchy?[2]

The notion that politics should be, at least in part, about the cultivation of an ideal of character has been an important theme within the liberal tradition. As with the critics of liberalism, however, "perfectionist" liberals must be able to offer a convincing account of why a failure to obtain a particular ideal of character is a harm that can be remedied or mitigated through political action. Is autonomy or authenticity so important that the state has a responsibility to foster either one of them? I believe we have good reasons to distrust the use of autonomy and authenticity as central criteria by which to judge liberal politics. Nevertheless, because of the value that we attribute to authenticity and autonomy, the state does have a qualified permission to encourage these ideals. In other words, liberals should not find objectionable the use of state resources to foster autonomy or to protect authenticity as long as those encouragements and protections do not violate other obligations of the state. Here, my central concern is not with making space for the permission, but arguing against the case for an obligation.

In considering whether the liberal state has an obligation to foster our capacity for choice, I examine the value we attribute to agency and the harm we associate with its deprivation. It is clear that agency can be diminished or deprived in all sorts of ways. At the very least, the liberal democratic state has an obligation not to harm our capacity for agency. It is less clear, however, that the state has an affirmative obligation to foster it.

Formal Autonomy

In discussing the genealogists I brought up the ideal of autonomy in conjunction with Foucault's conception of the disciplinary subject. That discussion drew on Stanley Benn's conception of autonomy—conduct predicated on the critical, reflective consideration of the norms and practices that govern one's life. In this view, an individual is autonomous to the extent that he or she does not live in an unthoughtful, habitual manner, but rather actually and actively judges the standards and rules that govern behavior. In Benn's terms, "To be autonomous is to live (in Rousseau's phrase) 'according to a law that one prescribes to oneself' "

---

[2] My focus upon autonomy, authenticity, and autarchy is driven largely by the fact that these ideals set out particularly well-developed understandings of what the self is or how it should be ordered. Character- and virtue-based liberalisms abound (e.g., William Galston, Mary Ann Glendon, Stephen Macedo, and Nancy Rosenblum) but do not provide necessarily a full conception of the nature or ordering of the self.

(Benn 1988, 155). Gerald Dworkin concurs when he argues that this ideal entails the "capacity of a person critically to reflect upon, and then attempt to accept or change, his or her preferences, desires, values, and ideals" (1988, 48; Raz 1986, 369).

This is a fairly formal notion of autonomy that leaves open the conclusions that can be reached through reflection and careful thought. To be autonomous on this view is not to be good, virtuous, or right. It does not create necessarily one kind of life or another. "There is no reason," Benn argues, "why an autonomous man should not be deeply concerned about social justice and community—but I have said nothing to suggest he will be. If Cesare Borgia turned out to have been no less autonomous than Socrates, one would still be hard put to it to share Machiavelli's unqualified admiration" (Benn 1975–1976, 129–30). Dworkin echoes these sentiments by saying that an autonomous person can be "a tyrant or a slave, a saint or sinner, a rugged individualist or champion of fraternity, a leader or a follower" (1988, 29). In short, one can do evil autonomously (Raz 1986, 380).

It is important to note that the word autonomy has a prodigious variety of formal and informal uses. For example, in its formal use, the term can denote not only making a law one's own, but it can refer to someone who is not subject to the will of others (Young 1986, 19). In the latter case an autonomous person is like a sovereign state in control of its foreign affairs. To the extent that autonomy merely means the freedom to act without the interference of others, it is very close to, if not identical with, the negative conception of freedom and the notion of sovereignty in political theory and international law. But even this very simple use is somewhat ambiguous, for to describe individuals as autonomous could mean that they actually possess the capacity for self-government or that they possess the right to have those capacities realized or respected (Feinberg 1989, 28).

For our consideration of soulcraft, however, this use of autonomy is less important than those that suggest an organization of the self or an ideal of character. To continue the metaphor of the state, the self-government in which I am interested has less to do with free action in foreign affairs and more to do with the quality of internal governance. Consequently, I will use the view of autonomy set out by Benn, Dworkin, and Raz in lieu of autonomy understood as sovereignty or negative freedom.

Formal conceptions of autonomy, however, can be contrasted usefully to more substantive understandings. Here, a notion of autonomy is substantive if it leads to a specific end or objective. For example, in Kant's understanding, persons are autonomous when they govern themselves with valid moral principles. Moral principles, in turn, are valid if they pass the test of universalizability. Kant's notion of autonomy, then, is deeply connected to his understanding of what it means to be a fully rational agent (Hill 1989; 1991, 29–30; Lindley 1986, 16–20; Young 1986, 2).[3]

In contrast to a substantive conception, the advantage and disadvantage of the formal conception of autonomy is its very weakness. Because it does not dictate a set of ends it is compatible with the liberal belief that there is a plurality of conceptions of the good life. On the other hand, because of its openness, autonomy itself can serve both good and bad ends. As an example, Loren Lomasky asks us to consider as autonomous those individuals who wonder if "'Perhaps I ought to work to overcome my visceral repugnance toward the torture of innocent persons if I could thereby improve my score on the utilitarian calculus.' One who has come to entertain these reflections may be a person whose capacities for autonomous choice has expanded wonderfully; he may also have become morally corrupted" (Lomasky 1987, 44). Russell Hardin argues that we cannot view autonomy as "the core value of our moral theory unless we are content with a hollow core" (Hardin 1989, 198). This compatibility with almost any end raises the question of why autonomy is at all valuable. An obligation to foster autonomy must, at the very least, provide a convincing answer to this question. In sorting out whether the liberal state has a responsibility to cultivate formal autonomy, let us first turn to the argument that autonomy has instrumental value.

The Instrumental Value of Autonomy

Perhaps autonomy is important because it can lead to greater contentment, self-development, or truth (Young 1986, 22). The formal character of autonomy, however, suggests that there is no tight relationship between it and these other goods. In fact, autonomy is not even a necessary condition for the pursuit of some of these goods. After all, contentment for some people may involve a lack of reflection. Certain goods do not require the careful, reasoned thought that autonomy demands. We do, after all, occasionally enjoy the spontaneous, the sudden, and the surprising. More seriously, the possession of truth in some religious orders may be regarded as a result of contemplation and loving obedience than critical, rational reflection. Furthermore, it is possible to view per-

---

[3] The problems associated with Kant's conception of autonomy, reason, and the self have been well considered by others (Larmore 1987; Lindley 1986, 21–25; Sandel 1982). There are good reasons for avoiding Kant's notion of autonomy as a basis for liberal theory or as a criterion for judging liberal practice. Not only are his understanding of reason and his test of universalizability too abstract to yield the substantive results for which Kant hoped, but his conception of the self has also been subject to cogent criticisms.

sons as courageous, loving, loyal, just, and moderate without their being autonomous. The acquisition and exercise of moral virtues may not require deep critical thought. In short, the instrumental value of autonomy is probably limited to a fairly small set of goods. As Flathman argues, autonomy is "an ideal that some pursue avidly but that is little understood by or of little concern to many." (Flathman 1987, 297).[4]

Even if autonomy is important to only a small set of goods, these goods can still be of enormous significance. The classical political rationalists could, for example, attribute a high value to the Socratic way of life. Even though not everyone will pursue it, this way of life best expresses human excellence and consequently is superior to any other form of human existence. To the extent that autonomy is necessary for this way of life, and to the extent that liberal democracy should be judged by its ability to foster human excellence, then the ability of the regime to foster autonomy is an important standard.

The most direct response to this argument is to question the superiority of the way of life that autonomy encourages. If the pursuit of the intellectual virtues is not necessarily superior to other ways of life, then the fundamental value of autonomy is also challenged. This argument does not deny that intellectual virtues are goods or that autonomy is a necessary condition for their achievement. Rather, it denies that these goods and autonomy should be the ends of liberal democratic society.

A similar argument can be made by seeing autonomy as the basis for self-realization and individuality. Although Mill does not use the idea of autonomy, he clearly values the ability to choose our plans of life thoughtfully. For Mill, this capacity for critical judgment is important because it can lead to individuality and self-development. The goal is critical reflection that is in harmony with one's nature (Mill 1975, 57). Once again, the best response to this kind of argument is to look at the value of the end that autonomy is meant to serve. This examination will be taken up later in the discussion of authenticity.

The Intrinsic Value of Autonomy

The problems associated with the instrumental value of autonomy would not surprise those who see it formally. For example, Benn does not view autonomy as an "all-embracing excellence, redeeming all the rest"

---

[4] Galston sees this ideal as "unnecessarily partial and partisan" (1991, 153). The problem with Galston's position is that he seeks to use political philosophy to provide an ideal standard for judging political practice. Given that he wants to link liberalism to a set of virtues and truth claims, the value of autonomous reflection should be quite high within his system.

(Benn 1975–1976, 130).[5] What, then, is its "excellence"? To attribute intrinsic value to autonomy seems to generate a paradox in that autonomy requires justifying our values to ourselves and not accepting uncritically what we are taught. The paradox is whether the value we attribute to autonomy must be validated autonomously.[6] If not, then there are some values that hold our allegiance even if they are not justified reflectively. In other words, it is permissible to be heteronomously autonomous. If the value of autonomy can only be validated autonomously, then to be heteronomous cannot be seen as a failure, because to a heteronomous person, autonomy would not be valuable.

Benn resolves the paradox by arguing that the value we attribute to autonomy follows from our capacity to be autarchic or to have agency. By autarchy, Benn means a minimal capacity for human choice. Someone who cared about his or her ontological status as a chooser "must acknowledge that the autonomous person has realized the potentialities of his autarchic status to a higher degree than someone who merely falls in with the projects of others and assesses his performance by standards thrust on him by his environment" (129). The requirements for being autarchic include such things as: the existence of a single acting person over time; the ability to recognize evidence as a basis for changing beliefs; the capacity for choosing and acting upon options; the capability to adjust decisions and policies on the basis of changes in beliefs; and the potential to make decisions now for the sake of a preferred future state (Benn 1975–1976, 116; Raz 1986, 372–73).[7] As Benn notes, human beings can fall short of these requirements and hence be disqualified as choosers. When such disqualification occurs, Benn refers to the individual as being impelled (1975–1976, 113).

Benn argues that if you value the human capacity to choose, then you

[5] Dworkin also argues that there are other values (dignity, health, well-being, integrity, security, not to mention freedom) whose promotion may require the sacrifice of "some autonomy. It is also possible that promotion of autonomy in the long run requires sacrificing autonomy in the short run" (1988, 114).

[6] This is a reformulation of a paradox that Dworkin raises. His version begins with the statement that moral agents ought to be autonomous. Dworkin then argues that "either that statement is an objectively true statement or it is not. If it is, then there is at least one moral assertion whose claim to validity does not rest on its being accepted by a moral agent. If it is not, then no criticism can be made of an agent who refuses to accept it" (1988, 39).

[7] Michael Oakeshott expresses this minimal capacity for choice in terms of agency. On David Mapel's interpretation of Oakeshott, agency means the capacity to exhibit intelligence, the possession of no natural or nonoptional ends, and the capacity to interpret the world and choose particular contingent responses in light of that interpretation (Mapel 1990, 395). Although Benn's notion of autarchy is not exactly the same as Oakeshott's notion of agency, they do not contradict one another and are close enough to be used interchangeably.

will also value the human capacity to be autonomous. Although Benn captures the intrinsic value of autonomy, it is not valuable enough to serve as an elemental criterion in judging liberal democracy. Before setting out this argument, I want first to examine positions that add more weight to the intrinsic value of autonomy. For example, Dworkin argues that autonomy is valuable because it implies a kind of control over life. He suggests that autonomy plays "a fundamental role in our conception of what it is to respect other persons and to accept the moral point of view" (Dworkin 1988, 30). It plays this fundamental role, he argues, because "what makes an individual the particular person he is is his life-plan, his projects. In pursuing autonomy, one shapes one's life, one constructs its meaning. The autonomous person gives meaning to his life" (31). On this basis, Dworkin claims that we have a responsibility to develop and exercise our capacity to be autonomous (32).[8]

Autonomy and Second-Order Preferences

In contrast to Benn's position, Dworkin's obviously raises the stakes. For Dworkin, autonomy is valuable in itself because it expresses an important way in which the self is organized.[9] Autonomy expresses our capacity to judge and assess our immediate desires and wants. This capacity is distinctively human. As Dworkin suggests, "One may not just desire to smoke, but also desire that one not have that desire. I may not just be motivated by jealousy or anger, but may also desire that my motivations be different (or the same)" (15). In relying upon a similar schema, Harry

[8] One could agree that what must be respected are the life-plans and conceptions of the good of individuals, but from this one could not then conclude that these plans are valuable only if they are constructed autonomously. Clearly, we have many projects and plans that are not the result of careful, deliberate reflection. Many of our projects, as Lomasky suggests, may be "ingested with one's mother's milk, become by imperceptible degrees more firmly fixed over time within one's volitional makeup, and never be trotted out to be cross-examined at the bar of reason" (Lomasky 1987, 44). A conception of the good should be respected even if, as for most of us, it is taken up through upbringing and education. As careful as Dworkin is not to elevate autonomy to a higher status than it deserves (Dworkin 1988, 32), he may go too far in saying that autonomy plays a fundamental role in our conception of respect and the moral point of view. Perhaps it would be more appropriate to say that Benn's notion of autarchy—that is, our capacity to make choices—should play this role. As Lomasky notes, autonomy is not "a necessary condition for being a project pursuer" (1987, 183).

[9] Young argues that autonomy provides a hierarchical organization of the self. Unlike the classical political rationalist view that tests the quality of an ordering against the demands of natural right, Young asks whether it relieves us from "bitterness, frustration, and resentment" (1986, 57).

Frankfurt argues that the ability to judge one's first-order desires by one's second-order desires is what makes one a person and not a wanton (Frankfurt 1989, 67; see also Lindley 1986, 122–23). Persons, unlike lesser beings, can want an existing desire to move one to action. This is what Frankfurt calls a second-order volition (Frankfurt 1989, 67). Although Frankfurt does not use the language of autonomy to describe second-order volitions (as Dworkin does), he still provides a useful way for setting out the value of autonomy. For if our personhood is connected to the ability to judge lower-order desires, and autonomy is nothing less than this ability, then autonomy is intrinsically valuable to our personhood.

Perhaps the most troubling feature of associating autonomy with higher-order preferences is that it leaves open the nature of these preferences. Formally, higher-order preferences or desires are nothing more than preferences or desires about other preferences and desires. But why are second-order preferences so special? John Christman argues that a purely formal or structural analysis of autonomy is incomplete as long as it ignores the formation of these preferences (Christman 1989, 10). The problem with the structural analysis is that second-order preferences could themselves be the result of external forces or random generation. Given this possibility, it is not clear why they should have a superior status to first-order preferences or why they should express autonomy. In order to preserve the notion of autonomy, unchosen second-order preferences should be governed by autonomous third-order preferences. But this is not much of a solution. If our wantonness can infect our higher-order desires, then we begin to slide towards an infinite regress: in order to preserve our autonomy, we must then appeal to third- and fourth-order preferences and so on (Thalberg 1989, 130–35; Watson 1989, 118–19; Wolf 1989, 141–42).

In response, although Frankfurt and Dworkin agree that there is no theoretical limit to how far this metareflection may go, they suggest that as a matter of practice it cannot go very far (Dworkin 1988, 19; Frankfurt 1989, 71). More importantly, Frankfurt suggests that what is significant about these higher-ordered preferences is that they permit a decisive identification with one's lower-order desires. Frankfurt argues that "when a person identifies himself *decisively* with one of his first-order desires, this commitment 'resounds' throughout the potentially endless array of higher orders" (Frankfurt 1989, 71). This notion of decisive identification is meant to put an end to the possibility of regress and to show us why wantonness need not run very deep. Similarly, Dworkin also appeals to the notion of identification. These higher-order preferences are important if a person "identifies with the influences that motivate him, assimilates them to himself, views himself as the kind of person who wishes to be moved in particular ways, that these influences are to be identified as 'his'" (Dworkin 1989, 60).[10]

Decisiveness and Identification

When we consider each of these responses in turn, neither advances our understanding of the intrinsic value of autonomy very far. First, as Christman notes, Frankfurt's idea of decisiveness is still compatible with heteronomous manipulations. It is possible that the source of that decisive identification is an effect of an earlier form of control (Christman 1989, 10). Second, it is possible to be autonomous without the kind of resounding decisiveness suggested by Frankfurt. Autonomy requires reflection and careful thought, but it does not require that one be overwhelmingly enthusiastic about the conclusions at which one arrives. The notion of decisiveness has only oblique connections to autonomy.[11]

Does Dworkin's notion of identification better account for the character and value of autonomy? Like Frankfurt's idea of commitment, one's identifications may also be heteronomous. Dworkin admits this possibility and argues that "a person is autonomous if he identifies with his desires, goals, and values, and such identification is not itself influenced in ways which make the process of identification in some way alien to the individual" (Dworkin 1989, 61). This, of course, means merely that instead of talking about second-order desires, our autonomy requires that we talk about second-order identifications. Once again we are on the road towards an infinite regress. To put it in Dworkin's terms, how do we prevent the process of identification from being in some way alien to the individual?

The answer to this question is what Dworkin calls procedural independence (1988, 18). Identification becomes alien when reflective and critical faculties are subverted. Some examples of such subversions include "hypnotic suggestion, manipulation, coercive persuasion, subliminal influence" (18). In effect, these second-order identifications or wants must meet the minimal conditions of what Benn calls autarchy. The implication here is that Dworkin's first-order identifications and desires need not live up to the demands of procedural inde-

[10] One difference between Frankfurt's and Dworkin's ideas of identification is that Frankfurt's idea of commitment calls a halt to any further regress by as little as an ipse dixit. Dworkin, on the other hand, seems to be concerned that our identification is governed by certain standards of how we want to be identified, of what kind of person we want to be.

[11] In fairness to Frankfurt, he does not see himself as setting out an understanding of autonomy, even though his position is used for this purpose.

pendence or, in Benn's terms, need not be expressions of autarchy. The difference between lower- and higher-order wants, desires, preferences, and identifications is that only the latter must meet the demands of autarchy in order to satisfy the requirements of autonomy. To once again put it in Benn's language, autonomy equals autarchy plus second-order preferences.

But what happens when first-order preferences meet the demands of procedural independence? For first-order desires need not be the result of hypnosis or manipulation. Could satisfying the requirements of procedural independence at the first-order level render the discussion of higher-order desires superfluous for understanding autonomy? I think that higher-order language is still useful. Even if first-order desires and wants met the requirements of procedural independence, one could still ask whether to identify with those desires and wants. Simply being autarchic, in other words, is not enough for autonomy. What is important in autonomy is not decisiveness or simple identification, but autarchic identification with one's desires.

Autonomy and Revising Preferences

In ferreting out the intrinsic value of autonomy we are now left with two claims. The first is that autonomy is valuable, as Benn suggests, because it is an expression of our developed autarchic capacities. The second claim, which comes out when we use Dworkin's first-order/second-order language, is that autonomy is valuable because it expresses our ability to revise our preferences. Is this ability by itself important? Clearly it is not necessarily important. If a society existed in which there were no inconsistencies within its value system or conflicts between values, then the entire question of autonomous choice or revision would never arise.[12] A necessary precondition for autonomy is that people are drawn between competing values and systems that call for their allegiance. It is in this sense that Benn notes that "autonomy is an ideal for troubled times. When a rapidly changing and receptive culture invites inputs from strange sources which it admits faster than it can readily absorb, men and women feel the need either to discover what matters to them (or more objectively, what really matters), or to seek certainty by short cuts, submitting to some authority which will reinforce guilt and peer-group

---

[12] Benn notes that "a monolithic system, in which, for instance, social and environmental conditions had remained virtually unchanging for centuries, and in which ways of acting had been routinized by a kind of natural selection process for all the major eventualities, and which encountered no alien cultures, would simply lack the incoherences which leave space for autonomous development" (1988, 182).

opinion in the repression of disturbing ideas" (1988, 183). Societies that
permit plural norms and traditions will provide the necessary conditions
for autonomy. Autonomy, then, does not entail some kind of Nietzschean form of stylistic creation. The law by which we choose to govern
ourselves is not fabricated out of thin air, but from the presence of competing and conflicting norms. The ability to revise the norms and standards that govern one's life may be of value only under certain conditions that, for the most part, are present in and encouraged by large
liberal democratic societies.

Joseph Raz not only agrees with the claim that the value of autonomy
depends upon the character of one's society and culture, but he takes it
a step farther. He argues that "for those who live in an autonomy-supporting environment there is no choice but to be autonomous: there is
no other way to prosper in such a society" (Raz 1986, 391). Because we
live in a pluralistic culture with competing conceptions of the good life,
autonomy is the only way to flourish within that environment. More significantly, Raz argues that valuing autonomy does not affect merely the
manner in which we arrive at a conception of the good life, it also affects
the character of the opportunities themselves. It is not the case that autonomy-supporting cultures have everything that traditional cultures
have and more. Rather, autonomy-supporting cultures add new opportunities and thereby transform the traditional alternatives (392). Traditional conceptions of marriage, work, and parenting are themselves
changed when other opportunities become feasible. In effect, we no
longer have a choice of whether to be autonomous. We must be autonomous if we are to succeed in a pluralistic culture.

The implication of Raz's argument is that we should associate heteronomy with a kind of stunting or failure to flourish. People who drift
through life and accept unquestioningly whatever careers and practices
they fall into may be unfortunate, pitiful characters—especially if they
have simply muddled through those careers and practices. It is less clear,
however, why we should pity those who have excelled within a given practice but who have never deeply questioned the practice itself or its governing norms. Someone could have always wanted to spend her life in a
particular way and have actually lived that life without looking back.
Such a life could be described as single-minded, devoted, vocational,
and heteronomous. When we look at careers and lives that have flour-
ished, do our judgments depend upon whether the particular individuals entertained other options seriously and called into question the prevailing standards and norms? It is certainly possible to flourish by being
autonomous, but autonomy is also compatible with living a miserable
existence. The value that we associate with revising norms should not be
overestimated. Although it is clearly important, it is not a necessary condition for value in a pluralistic society.

To sum up, autonomy clearly has instrumental value for a set of important goods and ends of life. Furthermore, it has intrinsic value to the extent that it expresses autarchic capacities and allows us to reflect upon the challenges that pluralism brings. On the other hand, autonomy is not instrumental for all goods, heteronomy is not necessarily an evil, and autonomy is no guarantee against the adoption of mistaken or unacceptable norms.

Autonomy and Harm

The pursuit of autonomy by both individuals and the state can clearly have serious costs. Not only can one be autonomously cruel and evil, but autonomy can also conflict with other values. Dworkin argues that "these include dignity, health, well-being, integrity, security" (Dworkin 1988, 114). But our concern here is not so much the costs to individuals of their own pursuit of autonomy, but rather those costs imposed by a government that uses its authority and power to encourage this pursuit.

Autonomy differs from freedom in that freedom entails the capacity for autarchy, with no external impediment to action. Given the formal character of autonomy, securing it would also prevent political institutions from imposing "ends, values, and attitudes upon the citizens of a society" (10). But the pursuit of autonomy as itself an end could, and usually does, require that we sacrifice freedom. For example, requiring young adults to stay in school attempts to encourage autonomy at the expense of their freedom. The prohibition of certain drugs may also be an exchange of freedom for the hope of greater autonomy.[13] Similarly, the laws prohibiting prostitution and regulating gambling can be seen as attempts to foster autonomy. As these examples illustrate, the exchange of freedom for the possibility of greater autonomy is not necessarily an evil.

The relationship between freedom and autonomy reveals two very powerful but "inveterately conflicting impulses" within liberalism. Flathman frames this conflict as between the desire "to celebrate the freedom of human beings to be what they are and to do what (being what they are) they are disposed to do, and the desire to see human beings become

[13] The case of drug use is fairly complex, for the reason for restricting certain highly addictive drugs could be that they disable the basic capacity for agency. The reason for this, however, is not that the drugs are simply addictive, but that the addiction is of a certain sort. Cigarette smoking, for example, while highly addictive, does not destroy wholesale the capacity for choice. Similarly, alcohol does not necessarily destroy either autonomy or autarchy. On the other hand, any addiction tends to preclude autonomy vis à vis the addictive behavior.

more self-conscious and self-critical about what they are and do" (Flathman 1987, 220), the balance between which is extremely difficult to establish.[14] Indeed, it may be impossible to discern what principle, if any,
governs this tradeoff in practice. We are certainly willing to sacrifice
some freedoms in the name of autonomy. But what would society be like
if we allowed autonomy to trump our celebration of letting people do
what they want to do? How could the government foster careful reflection and deliberation in other areas of life? Perhaps the government
could establish a twenty-four-hour waiting/counseling/educational period for mundane activities.[15] One could conceive of a law that required
going back to school each time one wanted to buy a bottle of wine. (Do
you really know the risks of liver damage associated with each sip?) Indeed, one could conceive of a waiting/educational period before sales
or contracts went into effect. Sales clerks could be required to examine
customers on their purchases. (How many pairs of shoes do you really
need?) Restaurateurs could greet their customers by asking if they really
should be going out to eat instead of devoting that money to UNICEF.
The attempt to foster autonomy could go far beyond the marketplace.
With the computer it is possible for televisions to become interactive
machines. Before being able to tune into ESPN, the television could ask
viewers whether they wouldn't prefer reading some Proust. Or, even better, it could quiz the viewer on the day's events, testing whether he or she
had read the newspaper carefully. Refrigerators could be timed in such
a way that in order to snack between meals one would have to pass a test
regarding the caloric content of various foods. After all, what's wrong
with stopping to think about whether one really wants another piece of
clothing, or a drink of wine, or to watch television? Is it not the point of
government to make people the best they can be?

The intrusive and insulting character of these attempts to foster autonomy shows us why its pursuit is not without cost. Perhaps no one has
put this better than Isaiah Berlin. In his discussion of "true freedom,"
which looks much like the idea of autonomy, Berlin begins by quoting
T. H. Green: "The ideal of true freedom is the maximum of power for all

---

[14] "The sine qua non of all such strategies," Flathman notes, "is recognition that the
conflicts are genuine and difficult to resolve" (1987, 220).

[15] Some states have attempted to institute such a waiting/counseling period for abortions. It is possible, however, that a twenty-four-hour waiting period is actually a ruse to
discourage women from having abortions. By placing counseling centers only in large met-
ropolitan areas, the costs to some women in rural areas may become prohibitive. Putting to
the side this possibility, as well as the possibility of biased counseling, the twenty-four-hour
waiting period is an attempt to encourage women to be more reflective and critical about
their actions. But for those women who have already thoughtfully considered the issue, the
regulation could be taken as another bit of evidence that this society does not trust their
capacity to make serious decisions. The attempt to foster autonomy will itself be a patroniz-
ing violation of autonomy.

the members of human society alike to make the best of themselves."
Berlin then writes, "Apart from the confusion of freedom with equality,
this entails that if a man chose some immediate pleasure—which (in
whose view?) would not enable him to make the best of himself (what
self?)—what he was exercising was not 'true' freedom: and if deprived of
it, would not lose anything that mattered. Green was a genuine liberal:
but many a tyrant could use this formula to justify his worst acts of oppression" (1969, 133 n.1). The governmental pursuit of its subjects' autonomy can be oppressive. Indeed, a global pursuit of autonomy would
be expressive of a kind of collective neurosis, an overwhelming fear that
whatever we do spontaneously could be wrong, that whatever habits we
happened to acquire diminish our humanity. A government driven by
these concerns would be not only oppressive but destructive; it would
require the sacrifice of human spontaneity, habituation, and the free
circulation of goods and services.

If the direct pursuit of autonomy is troublesome, if not paradoxical,
perhaps the state has a minimal duty to provide the conditions for autonomy. Raz argues that by preventing coercion or manipulation, by developing the cognitive and emotional capacities for individuals to make
autonomous decisions, and by creating an adequate range of options,
the state can fulfill a duty of fostering autonomy (1986, 407–8). In effect,
the state can live up to an obligation to cultivate perfectionism with a
minimum of coercion. Moreover, this weak form of selfcraft is compatible with a number of educational, vocational, and political programs and
policies that are generally accepted by liberals. Why not accept the claim
that the state has a obligation to sustain the necessary conditions for
autonomy?

The answer to this question does not turn upon what is necessary to
fulfill such an obligation to cultivate autonomy, but upon whether such
an obligation exists. If the basis for the obligation cannot be sustained
then whether we call it weak or strong makes no difference. As we saw
earlier, Raz argues that the basis for his perfectionism is the claim that in
order to flourish within a liberal pluralistic culture one must be autonomous. I have argued, however, that this may not be the case. Because
becoming autonomous is not a necessary condition for pursuing conceptions of the good life, then the obligation cannot be sustained.

Community and Autonomy

The problems with a duty to foster autonomy become particularly severe
when considering communities and minority groups within a liberal culture that reject this ideal. The charge against autonomy is that it can be
incompatible with community. One form of this charge rests upon a

particular understanding of autonomy that, to use Sandel's terminology, sees the self as unencumbered. On this version of autonomy, the self must detach itself from every conceivable social influence and make a radical choice. While this kind of choice may be ultimately impossible, Lomasky has argued that the attempt to choose in this way results in anomie (1987, 249). In effect, this form of autonomy "simultaneously extols self-direction while systematically uprooting the homey markers that indicate to agents where the value that is accessible to them lies" (249). To see autonomy as a kind of self-rule that precludes all social connection would indeed make it incompatible with society and community (Flathman 1987, 299).

The problem with this view is that it associates autonomy with Nietzsche's conception of style. It is difficult to think of a serious defender of autonomy who would view it in this manner.[16] Neither Mill, Benn, Raz, nor Dworkin see autonomy as purely self-generated. Benn addresses this problem explicitly by arguing that "to be autonomous one must have reasons for acting, and be capable of second thoughts in the light of new reasons; it is not to have a capacity for conjuring criteria out of nowhere" (Benn 1975–1976, 126).[17] Autonomy, then, is not inconsistent with the social character of human life and language.

The second argument that sees autonomy as incongruous with community does not rely upon such a straw portrayal of autonomy. The problem with autonomy is not that it is incompatible with community per se, but that it is detrimental to certain forms of community. We celebrate autonomy, on this argument, only if we are also willing to endure the mishmash of a pluralistic society. But what if that larger liberal society contains within it smaller communities for which autonomy is not valued, as is true of the United States, Canada, and Australia? For such communities, the very idea of choosing autonomously between their own cultural life and the larger pluralistic one may be rejected.

This objection is not as easily parried as the previous one. It is true that the formal notion of autonomy does not prevent one from rejecting autonomy itself and reaffirming a tightly woven, highly integrated form of community. But the attribution of value to this kind of reflection may be foreign to the community itself. It is possible that in some communities "the individual might be expected to accept uncritically the long-standing practices of the cultural group. Critical reflection need play no part in their conceptions of the good life" (Kukathas 1992a, 120). In these cases, fostering autonomy deeply disrupts how these people understand themselves and their relationship to their community. To foster auton-

---

[16] Robert Paul Wolff's interpretation of Kant's conception of autonomy is one exception to this claim (Wolff 1970).

[17] Flathman notes that "one pursues autonomy not by extracting oneself from society and culture but by relating to them in a critically rational manner" (1987, 218).

omy in a culture that never valued it is, at the very least, to alter that culture in a significant way.

Chandran Kukathas (1992a) has argued that the right to freedom of association trumps the value of autonomy. Cultural communities should be left alone to govern their own affairs as long as the individuals within that community have a right to exit. The value that the larger liberal society attributes to autonomy does not provide a standing warrant for cracking the shell of a cultural community whenever autonomy is threatened or violated. That kind of interference, it appears, is only deemed appropriate when the right to exit is threatened.

Kukathas's position raises the problematic relationship between autonomy and freedom in another form. In the earlier discussion of that relationship I argued that freedom (in Kukathas's case it would be freedom of association) should not always trump autonomy. There may be good reasons for restricting freedom. For example, not to foster an awareness of the larger community may be a form of disempowerment. To insure that individuals really know they can exit their own community seems to require some autonomous capacity. Furthermore, those remaining ignorant of and yet living within a larger society in which a federal government handles matters of enforcement, welfare, administration, and taxation, are at a distinct disadvantage. Finally, not encouraging individual autonomy may balkanize the state. To attribute absolute value to freedom of association may be to prevent integration and foster mutual hostility and mistrust. As a practical necessity, fostering some level of autonomy would seem to be part of the value we attribute to the ability to exit, participate in democracy, and govern a large state. But how far should this go?

Once again, as with the earlier discussion of the relationship between freedom and autonomy, the appropriate balance between individual autonomy and community (or freedom of association) is difficult to discern.[18] The shells of these cultural communities have become increasingly porous and their attempts to keep out alien ideas and goods have only been partially successful. The problem is not one of meeting the prerequisites for exercising freedom of exit or integration, but one of sustaining the community itself. For our purposes we need note only that the unrestrained pursuit of autonomy violates other deeply held values of liberalism. In one case, this value is the simple freedom to do what one wants to do. In the other case, the freedom may be a freedom to associate with others. When we combine the argument for the value of autonomy with the arguments surrounding its costs, it is clear that it cannot be understood as liberal democracy's primary good. Although there may be

---

[18] To see how liberals have wrestled with this problem see Raz (1986, 423–24), Kymlicka (1989), and the Kymlicka/Kukathas exchange (1992; 1992a).

sound reasons for the state to foster autonomy and protect its exercise, it is going much too far to suggest either that people have a right to be autonomous or that a regime has a responsibility to cultivate it.

Authenticity and Individuality

Recently, Charles Taylor has argued that liberal governments, although not obliged to foster autonomy (or what he calls "self-determining freedom") do have a responsibility to foster authenticity.[19] The roots of Taylor's argument go deep into the liberal tradition—in, for example, Mill's discussion of individuality in *On Liberty*.[20] By authenticity, Taylor means the discovery of one's own unique capacities, talents, and abilities: "There is a certain way of being human that is *my* way. I am called upon to live my life in this way, and not in imitation of anyone else's. But this gives a new importance to being true to myself. If I am not, I miss the point of my life, I miss what being human is for *me*" (Taylor 1991a, 28–29). There is some original, singular voice that each of us possesses. It is only through the discovery of that voice that we realize our individuality or authenticity.

In clarifying what this ideal of character actually entails, there are two ways in which Taylor's notion of authenticity departs from Millian individuality. One important difference is that Taylor applies the notion of authenticity to groups and cultures. Although Mill associates progress with the ability of a society to encourage individuality, he does not attribute a unique voice to each society as a whole (Mill 1975, 66–67). Following Herder, Taylor argues that cultures should try to discover and preserve what is unique about their own way of life. This expanded view of authenticity entails more than a culture's control of its own laws and institutions: it also involves the expression and development of its perspective on the human condition.

A second difference can be found in how these writers defend the value of these ideals. Mill deploys a variety of arguments in support of individuality. One of these, which Benn also uses in his discussion of the value of a formal notion of autonomy, is that individuality allows us to develop our faculties. To the extent that we see things such as judgment, perception, and thought as good qualities, then their improvement is

[19] "Self-determining freedom demands that I break the hold of all such external impositions and decide for myself alone" (Taylor 1991a, 27).

[20] For a contemporary position that comes very close to Mill's see David Norton (1991). Norton associates autonomy with eudaimonism. "According to eudaimonism, a life-shaping choice is well made when it is founded in self-knowledge and serves to progressively actualize the ideal self that subsists in the individual initially *in potentia*" (62).

also good. As Mill argues, "The mental and moral, like the muscular powers, are improved only by being used" (55). A second argument in favor of individuality concerns our imperfect abilities to understand the truth. Individuality breeds difference, spontaneity, and experimentation. Without these things, we lose opportunities to know and test whether one way of life is truly better than another. Without individuality, Mill argues, we lose "the chief ingredient of individual and social progress" (54). A third argument is aesthetic and Nietzschean in flavor, as Mill claims that individuality allows humans to develop themselves into noble and beautiful objects (56, 59). This argument ties into a final claim made in favor of individuality, namely that it permits the development of genius. We cannot do without genius, Mill believes. Geniuses get us to open our eyes to our own originality, and they supply valuable counsel to popular governments (62–63).

In many respects, Taylor's defense of the good of authenticity is not as highly developed as Mill's defense of individuality. Taylor argues that "authenticity points us towards a more self-responsible form of life. It allows us to live (potentially) a fuller and more differentiated life, because more fully appropriated to our own. . . . But at its best authenticity allows a richer mode of existence" (Taylor 1991a, 74). Being inauthentic presumably means leading a thinner, less differentiated (perhaps more monotonous?) life. Why is authenticity so important to the fullness of life? Taylor argues that seeing one's inner life as a moral source is relatively new. Prior to the eighteenth century, fullness of life was connected to being in touch with God or ideas of the good. We now conceive of ourselves as beings whose inner depths contain not an awareness of God, or the good, but the self. Being in touch with our own feelings has acquired "crucial moral significance" (Taylor 1992, 28). Fullness of being requires contact with this new moral source, it requires "realizing a potentiality that is properly my own" (31).[21]

Fostering Authenticity and Individuality

If these are the goods of individuality and authenticity, how can they be connected to the actions of the state? In order to say that the state has a duty to foster authenticity it must, obviously, be able to foster it. As with autonomy, there is something paradoxical about a regime having a responsibility to foster individuality. The ever-present risk is that in a

[21] It is possible to see Taylor's argument as an attempt to walk a line between the classical political rationalists and the genealogists. On the one hand, Taylor sees the classical political rationalists as dismissing out of hand the ideal of authenticity. They refuse to acknowledge the claim that the self is a moral source. For Taylor, this refusal expresses a certain

clumsy attempt to cultivate self-realization the state could have the opposite effect of narrowing or normalizing diversity and experiments in living. As we shall see, Mill appears to be more sensitive to this risk than
Taylor. In any case, neither Mill nor Taylor argues that his ideal of character can be realized by persons in isolation. For both thinkers, individuality is a socially governed practice. More strongly, Taylor argues that
politics plays an essential role in fostering authenticity.

In Mill's case, the social character of individuality may be connected
to his distinction between higher and lower pleasures. On Wendy Donner's reading of Mill, this distinction not only differentiates pleasures,
but also expresses a belief that some forms of individuality are superior
to others. If it is better to be "Socrates dissatisfied than a fool satisfied" it
is because the latter "knows both sides" (Mill 1962, 260). According to
Donner, in saying that those who have pursued higher things know both
sides, Mill means that there are competent judges whose intellectual,
affective, and moral judgment allows them to make impersonal social
judgments on the worth of various projects. In other words, interpersonal standards govern our assessment of the quality of our pleasures
and there are competent judges who can help guide us in our self-development (Donner 1991, 93). Knowing those standards and learning from
these competent judges provides an important part of the environment
for self-development. Although Mill argues that we can be taught to be
critical of the standards that lead to our development, those standards
are themselves external to the individual. Our individuality is not simply
a matter of letting whatever potential we have flourish. Rather, this reading argues that there are some capacities that should flourish and some
that should not; interpersonal standards of self-development determine
which are which.

Taylor's notion of authenticity also rests upon interpersonal standards, what he calls the horizon of meaning. As with Mill, these standards govern our quest towards authenticity. What is potentially worthwhile to pursue—which voices we should listen to and which we should
not—is given to us by this horizon of meaning. Not only do we appeal to
an already-present horizon of meaning, but our understanding of our
selves becomes clearer as it is negotiated, defended, and considered with
others. The social character of Taylor's conception of authenticity is reinforced by his claim that we can only come to know who we are through
dialogue within a given a horizon of meaning.

---

blindness and contempt towards one's culture (Taylor 1991a, 15). On the other hand,
Taylor views the genealogists, given their Nietzschean commitments, as disregarding the
importance of a moral horizon to authenticity. At best, the Nietzschean position seems to
lead to a nihilistic celebration of self-determining freedom (60–61).

In light of their social character, can individuality or authenticity be fostered by the state? Of the two writers, Taylor expresses greater faith in the ability of the state to take an active and direct role in fostering authenticity. The basis for this activism stems from the connection he makes between authenticity and the need for recognition. To understand this connection it is first necessary to understand that Taylor distinguishes two forms of recognition, the first of which entails an acknowledgment based upon universal human characteristics (e.g., that our freedom deserves equal respect—we can call this the recognition of equal liberty). The second form of recognition entails the acknowledgment of difference or uniqueness—call this recognition of difference. Taylor implies that the recognition and protection of difference is a necessary condition for the cultivation of authenticity. This form of recognition goes beyond the protection of liberties and attempts to provide or preserve the conditions necessary for authenticity.

Given the connection between public recognition and authenticity, Taylor argues that liberal societies should adopt a politics of difference. In such a politics "what we are asked to recognize is the unique identity of this individual or group, their distinctness from everyone else" (Taylor 1992, 38). In practice, this may mean the establishment of special protections or group rights in order to allow the development and preservation of difference. Respect for these differences may require different forms of treatment. For example, Taylor points to the attempt by Quebecers to preserve their way of life through legislation that regulates the language of education, business, and public signs. Taylor advocates a liberal society that takes seriously the demands of cultural authenticity and protects collective goals and purposes (60–61). He believes that the state not only can foster authenticity, but that it should take a relatively active role in doing so.

It is less clear whether Mill believes that it is possible for the state to take a direct and active role in fostering individuality. On occasion Mill writes as if such cultivation were possible. For example, he argues that "the most important point of excellence which any form of government can possess is to promote the virtue and intelligence of the people themselves" (Mill 1948, 127). More directly, he claims that "it is not by wearing down into uniformity all that is individual in themselves, but by cultivating it, and calling it forth, within the limits imposed by the rights and interests of others, that human beings become a noble and beautiful object of contemplation" (Mill 1975, 59). Later in *On Liberty*, he says that "exceptional individuals" should be "encouraged in acting differently from the mass" (Mill 1972, 63). The question here is whether the notions of "calling forth" and encouragement refer to state actions.

Certainly, there are all sorts of things that social and private institutions could do to encourage or discourage the realization of individuality. Schools, religions, clubs, and friends could conceivably provide support for an individual in search of his or her own originality. Curricula could be devised, stories could be written, and honors could be bestowed in the attempt to advance a strong conception of individuality. Mill writes, "Nobody denies that people should be so taught and trained in youth as to know and benefit by the ascertained results of human experience" (1975, 55). But Mill sees the development of individuality as requiring two necessary conditions. Citing Wilhelm von Humboldt, Mill claims that "freedom, and variety of situations" are both necessary for individuality (68). Through the protection of equal liberty, the state creates enough space for people to challenge custom, act spontaneously, and be nonconformist. In other words, Mill would see Taylor's first form of recognition as essential. Whether the state can go farther and provide a heterogeneous social life is uncertain. Mill is not very optimistic. He sees politics as promoting mediocrity, education as encouraging homogeneity, improved communication as advancing conformity, commerce as leading to similarity, and the ascendancy of public opinion as reinforcing all of these tendencies. The problem with the state adopting a more active and direct role in cultivating individuality is that "the same things which are helps to one person towards the cultivation of higher nature are hindrances to another" (64). The best hope in his eyes is convincing "the intelligent part of the public" to understand the value of individuality (69).[22] Mill does not argue that the acknowledgment of difference is also essential.

A Right to Authenticity?

If an obligation to foster Millian individuality falters under the infeasibility of state action, such does not appear to be the case for Taylor's notion of authenticity. Should the state be responsible for fostering authenticity? Without question, individuality and authenticity are important ideals within liberalism, but they are not the only ideals, and they do not outweigh others necessarily. Taylor argues, for example, that there are fundamental rights that should never be infringed (Taylor 1992, 59). A politics of difference should be circumscribed by the "rights to life, liberty, due process, free speech, free practice of religion, and so on" (59). The arena within which a politics of difference should have free

[22] Donner argues that Mill advances a general right to self-development. In order to protect this right it is necessary to provide both "guarantees of noninterference with developmental attempts and also allocation of social resources, which requires positive action, to give all a decent opportunity to realize their unique potential" (Donner 1991, 183).

play would have to be defined by situations in which these fundamental rights do not apply.

Furthermore, in Taylor's own discussions, a politics of difference should be bounded by other moral sources that must be given their due (e.g., God and nature). Taylor does not defend a hierarchical ranking of these sources. What he does suggest is that to pursue God and nature without acknowledging the good of authenticity is as bad as pursuing authenticity without acknowledging the goods of God and nature. He does not believe that all of these moral sources necessarily fit into a harmonious whole (Taylor 1989a, 511). Choosing to pursue one conception of the good may divert our attention from other conceptions. Taylor's description of this dilemma suggests that authenticity may neither be the highest nor the only good.

The idea that individuality and authenticity must take their place alongside other goods is not enough to preclude them from being necessary (but neither the sole nor sufficient) objectives of a liberal society. Taylor's strongest argument in favor of the elemental character of authenticity is that a failure to *recognize* authenticity results in a grievous harm. He claims that people can "suffer real damage, real distortion," if they are misrecognized or not recognized at all (Taylor 1992, 25). Once again, this claim of harm may serve as the basis for a state responsibility to provide such recognition and foster authenticity. Is a failure to cultivate authenticity a harm?

One general problem with Taylor's conception of authenticity is that there is a tension between the demand for recognition of individuals and the application of the idea of authenticity to groups or cultures. Taylor's claim is that in a pluralistic society, recognition is essential for survival of cultures that find themselves in the minority. The difficulty is that in pluralistic societies the recognition of *individual* authenticity inevitably threatens the preservation of *cultural* authenticity. A good example of this problem is Taylor's case of the Quebec law that prohibits francophone and immigrant parents from sending their children to English-speaking schools. Securing individual pursuits of authenticity would require respecting the decision of individuals to send their children to whatever school they want or, if the children are old enough, to respect their decisions. But this is precisely what must be curtailed to preserve cultural authenticity. The problem with Taylor's use of authenticity and recognition is that he does not establish whether it is more important to apply these terms to individuals or to cultures. He does not show why we should sacrifice individual authenticity to the preservation of cultural authenticity. Indeed, once authenticity can apply to both individuals and groups, it does not necessarily lead to the support of group rights. More importantly, he does not justify the forms of coercion that would be required in making that tradeoff. Why would the right of an individual to be authentic not outweigh the right of a particular group?

A second problem emerges from a tension between the necessity of a moral horizon and the need for recognition. According to Taylor, a claim of mis- or nonrecognition must appeal to the shared horizon of meaning. It is possible that one's conception of authenticity could meet the larger, perhaps more amorphous demands of the moral horizon, but fail to be recognized by one's fellow citizens. Similarly, one could attempt to express a conception of authenticity that was not sanctioned by the shared moral horizon. In the latter case, one is simply out of luck. Taylor argues that for someone to say that these are his or her authentic desires and preferences simply because he or she chooses them would not be enough (1991a, 38). For example, it is not enough for choice to be the "crucial justifying reason" for sexual orientation: "It can't just be assumed a priori, on the grounds that anything we choose is all right" (38). The implication is that if the connection to the moral horizon is not good enough (Who decides this? Is this an opening for the tyranny of the majority?), then there really is nothing wrong with publicly belittling or demeaning the choices made.

Presumably, this would mean that unless or until homosexuals could appeal convincingly to our shared horizon of meaning there is no reason to respect or recognize their way of life. This example seems especially troublesome for Taylor. For, on the one hand, it is not clear why gays and lesbians should have to justify their conduct to the rest of society.[23] On the other hand, it is not clear that there is a shared horizon in this culture that respects homosexuality (or blacks or women).

This example raises a third problem. Because my desires and wants must meet the demands of a shared morality if they are to be recognized as authentic, it is possible that what I thought was an authentic desire or project was not. In other words, I can get my authenticity wrong. It is not clear that Taylor would take the additional step of arguing that someone else could know what my authentic desires are better than I, but his position does open the possibility of persons misconstruing their own authenticity. The prevailing moral horizon has a veto over conceptions of authenticity. I may believe that certain feelings or desires are authentic, but I may be mistaken. If they are not authentic, then they need not be recognized.

What is disturbing about this social veto over authenticity is that it could just as easily stifle the respect for difference as promote it. Thirty years ago a woman who believed that her authentic aptitudes and desires led her to a career in science or law or construction would not have had

---

[23] I owe this argument to Peter Diamond (1993).

those preferences confirmed by our shared social and moral beliefs. It was precisely because these authentic desires and preferences extended beyond our shared moral horizon that they required some level of respect and protection. Forms of authenticity that fall within the parameters of acceptability generally do not need what Taylor calls recognition.

The problem with authenticity is not merely that there is something paradoxical about it being produced by the state. Rather, the problem has to do with the role of recognition in its production. It is not clear what should be recognized to promote authenticity and it may be the case that recognition is as liable to stifle authenticity as promote it. A social veto over what is authentic may be another way to legitimate the belittling of those who are truly different. And yet, if there is no social veto, then the realization of a right to authenticity becomes entirely subjective. There is potentially no end to the claims that could be made on its behalf as individuals or groups engage in their quest for their true selves. In either case, there are good reasons to be suspicious of an obligation on the part of the state to foster authenticity as Taylor understands it.

Still, there is something compelling about the idea of being harmed if one does not have a chance to realize one's individuality or authenticity. After all, if Taylor is correct and I live an inauthentic life, then I have missed the whole point of my life. Given the purported stakes involved, is it unreasonable to think that the cultivation of authenticity should be a function of government? To make this obligation more acceptable, we could formulate it in such a way that it entailed more than the protection of equal liberty but less than the licensing of coercion. In other words, we could formulate an obligation to foster authenticity in the same way that Raz formulates an obligation to foster autonomy: by focusing upon the necessary conditions for the ideal of character. In the case of authenticity, this could mean the state would provide financial support or distribute honors and distinctions to encourage individuality. Or the state could (e.g., through federalism, extending the sphere or the recognition of group rights) actively bolster a more heterogeneous society. If these kinds of actions could foster authenticity, then why should the state not have an obligation to do so?

In this formulation, the obligation turns upon the harm that allegedly results when one fails to be an individual or authentic. Is this, in fact, a harm? Once again, in Mill's writings we get mixed signals. Influenced by Tocqueville, Mill is aware of the dangers of popular opinion in foreclosing individuality. At the very least this means that a society that does not protect the rights and liberties of its citizens to engage in experiments of living is permitting harm to occur. In other words, a failure to recognize and respect the equal liberty of others is a harm. What is not clear in

Mill's thought is whether a failure to recognize uniqueness is also harmful. Mill does argue that the prevailing ideal of conduct, which tends towards conformity and a suppression of strong feelings, "maim[s] by compression, like a Chinese lady's foot, every part of human nature which stands out prominently" (Mill 1975, 65). Combining these kinds of statements with his arguments in favor of individuality, it appears that a failure to cultivate individuality is indeed a kind of harm.[24]

As we saw earlier, even if a failure to secure individuality is a harm, Mill would appear to sanction very limited means for its prevention or remedy. On his view, the primary role of the state in cultivating individuality is in the protection of liberty. But perhaps Mill is wrong. If the failure to realize oneself is a harm, then the duty to cultivate individuality suggests a state that is more actively involved in selfcraft.

Part of the problem with even a minimal duty to foster authenticity concerns the meaning and value of the ideal itself. As discussed earlier, Taylor's vision of authenticity encounters a number of internal difficulties. The more general problem with such a duty is that it creates the presumption that alternative, incompatible conceptions of the self are mistaken. More strongly, it creates the presumption that self-realization is a good for everyone and that views of the self that reject authenticity should be discouraged and disparaged. For example, a duty to cultivate authenticity would supplant claims that the self should be subservient to universal reason or to the laws of God (what Mill calls the Calvinistic theory [58]) or that it is veiled in mystery or capable of changing over time or possessing multiple voices. In fact, these alternative self-conceptions could be seen as harmful to self-realization. These alternatives, it would seem, would have to be devalued publicly in a regime that saw itself as obligated to foster authenticity.

To a certain extent, Mill tries to show the inferiority of an ascetic or renunciatory conception of the self. He argues that if humans were made by a good Being, "it is more consistent with that faith to believe that this Being gave all human faculties that they might be cultivated and unfolded" (59). From a contestable view of the self, Mill is drawn to a contestable view of theology. Moreover, the problems of liberalism appealing to a particular theology are enormous. In order to support an obligation to foster authenticity a convincing case must be made for its superiority over alternative views of the self.

Does this mean that a failure to realize individuality or authenticity is not a harm? A failure to realize an authentic way of life may be a harm,

[24] Obviously, it is not a harm as Mill defines that term in *On Liberty*. There he defines a harm as a violation of a "distinct and assignable obligation" that one person has to another (Mill 1975, 75). Here we are using the notion of harm to determine whether an obligation on the part of the state even exists.

but so may a failure to obtain a form of life that requires the renunciation of the self. Without being able to establish definitively the character
of the harm, the case for an obligation to foster authenticity (or self-
renunciation for that matter) is significantly weakened.

Fostering Autarchy

Even accepting the foregoing arguments, one could claim that I have
been entirely too sanguine about disconnecting our judgments about
liberal democracy from its effects on our selves. After all, doesn't liberal
democracy have to cultivate people with the capacity to have desires,
formulate interests, and pursue projects? Would this regime be justified
if it precluded autarchy or agency?

Up to now, I have argued that neither the critics nor the defenders of
liberal democracy have demonstrated a state responsibility to engage in
soul- or selfcraft. Can this argument be extended to the cultivation of
autarchy? Is it possible that a failure to cultivate human beings with the
capacity for choice would not be seen as a harm? Or its production as an
elemental good?

As with autonomy and authenticity, first we have to turn to the problem of whether government can cultivate autarchy. If we are autarchic
regardless of what the regime does, then the issue is moot. Let us begin
where the ice is thick before venturing farther. We know that our capacity for choice can be diminished or destroyed in various ways. Compul-
sive or psychopathic behavior in which action is unaffected by changes in
belief, paranoid beliefs in which choices are made from fantasy-options,
and schizophrenic states in which one conceives of oneself as nothing
more than an object or process are all indicative of persons who have
diminished or lost their capacity as choosers (Benn 1975–1976, 113–16).
Although many of the causes of being inner impelled are related to
chemical imbalances or genetic defects, these disabilities can also be
brought on by environmental factors—abusive parents, drugs, and physical trauma. Autarchy may be lost not only if one is inner impelled but
also if one is heterarchic. According to Benn's definition, heterarchy,
unlike being inner impelled, is wholly caused by others. Examples of
heterarchic behavior include subjects "acting under hypnosis, or brainwashed, or unable to contemplate disobeying an authoritarian parent"
(116). Given the various ways in which autarchy can be diminished and
disabled, it is possible for it to be compromised through the actions of
others. This possibility implies that the government could instigate such
actions.

Let us then accept the claim that the actions of others can disable autarchy. Would a loss of autarchy ever be seen as an improvement? Could a movement from a state of autarchy to inner impulsion or heterarchy ever be taken as a good thing? Frontal lobotomies, behavior modification therapies, tranquilizers, and hypnotic suggestion all reduce one's capacity as an agent. They have, of course, all been justified as treatments to improve the autarchy of those who are suffering from various maladies. They have also been abused, and this tells us something about what is valued. To the extent that frontal lobotomies and tranquilizers are used to pacify and reduce the capacity for choice and are not used in the hope of improving autarchy, they are seen as abuses.[25] It would take a fairly convoluted scenario in order for somebody to look forward to being brainwashed or placed permanently in a catatonic state. In other words, to deprive someone of their autarchy is to harm them.

Why do we see inner-impulsion and heterarchy as defects and disabilities? In other words, why do we value autarchy? Benn argues that autarchy is a precondition for seeing the actions we perform and the things we do as valuable. He claims that if we woke up one day and came to believe that all of our projects and desires had been programmed into us by someone else, we would see those projects and desires as alien. More strongly, we would come to resent them if we could not change them. In such a situation, although we would have a set of dispositions and inclinations, they would have little importance to us. Is this a convincing account of the value of autarchy?

Benn's argument is certainly not a sufficient condition for valuing our desires and choices. There are times when we regret the choices we make and the things we want. Is autarchy a necessary condition for value? Could we value impulses and instincts that are, in Connolly's language, branded into us? In certain circumstances, the quality of unchosen reactions to stimuli could be seen as highly valuable. Dodging a car, ducking a flying object, or recovering one's balance need not be chosen actions to be valuable. Similarly, forms of behavior modification that stop people from smoking or allow them to concentrate their attention can also be highly valued. Indeed, the very fact that autarchy may not be generated autarchically indicates that not all things of value are subject to choice. Autarchy is not a necessary condition for the value we attribute to certain unthinking behaviors.

But what about more complex values and principles? Is Benn correct in thinking that we would come to resent principles that we thought we

---

[25] If I were a heavy smoker who wanted to break my addiction, I could certainly look forward to being hypnotized to lose this craving for nicotine. In this example, the hypnotic suggestion is meant to counteract my addiction. The end result, presumably, is to regain my ability to choose what to do after a meal or how to spend my pocket change.

were brainwashed to accept? Perhaps it depends upon the principle. For example, suppose that the principle "turn the other cheek," was "ingested with one's mother's milk" (Lomasky 1987, 44) or behaviorally conditioned into us (as it was in *A Clockwork Orange*). Moreover, suppose that anytime violence is done to us we can only respond passively. Would we necessarily resent this principle? If the conditioning was subtle enough (unlike in *A Clockwork Orange*), we may never call it into question. In communitarian terms we may see this principle as a central but unchosen constituent of our identities. But even if we knew that we had been socialized or conditioned into believing that one should turn the other cheek, we would not necessarily feel resentment towards such a principle. We may, for example, also be convinced that pacifism is the highest ethic one could adopt. In such a situation we may not object to this "brainwashing."

On the basis of such an argument Larmore concludes that the capacity for choice is a controversial value (Larmore 1990, 343). Some communitarian writers consider this capacity as neither a necessary nor sufficient condition for the values, projects, and desires we possess. If the communitarians make the case that our values can be free from any autarchic capacity, then there is less reason for holding that the liberal regime has an obligation to foster agency.

As useful as the communitarian argument may be for present purposes, it is not clear that they have made that case. In its strongest formulation, the capacity for choice would be of little value if we celebrated the absence of all distance between who we are and what our attributes happen to be. But even Sandel backs off from this claim. In order to prevent our identities from drowning in a sea of circumstance, Sandel argues that we must maintain some distance from our attributes. He sees this distance as created through a form of cognitive agency that rests upon discovery and not choice. Nevertheless, I argued that elements of choice remain embedded within his conception of cognitive agency. Without considering how the notion of choice finds its way back into other communitarian projects, I accept the claim that even though autarchy may not be a precondition for all that we value, it is a necessary condition for much of it.[26] If Benn's claim is not entirely true, it is true for a wide range of activities and projects in which we engage.

So far I have argued that our autarchy can be diminished and dis-

[26] In fact, this capacity is built into many Western social and political practices. For example, our understandings of freedom, obligation, responsibility, power, and rights all accord an important place to the capacity for choice. As Flathman argues, the capacity for autarchy and choice "are among the deep conventions that make up (in Wittgenstein's terms) the language games and forms of life that partly constitute the situatedness of modern Western peoples" (Flathman 1987, 150).

abled, that it is possible for others (such as governments) to be the cause of these effects, that these effects can be considered harms, and that we value autarchy. From these propositions we can conclude that people have a fairly strong right not to be interfered with in ways that deprive or diminish their autarchy. Moreover, governments have an obligation not to disable the capacity for choice. In liberal states, one of the more important ways to protect autarchy is through a panoply of rights (e.g., rights to privacy, rights to information, consent laws regarding medical procedures). To the extent that liberal democracies protect our capacities as choosers, they respect deeply held beliefs that we have about ourselves. A liberal democratic regime that attempted to eliminate or disable this capacity for choice would fail to live up to some of its deepest obligations and commitments.

We are, indeed, very close to the proposition that liberal democracies not only have a responsibility to protect autarchy but to foster it as well. Is there a kind of soulcraft that is demanded of liberal democracy? Although governments can clearly do all sorts of things to diminish the autarchy of their citizenry, do they have the capacity to foster and encourage autarchy? Allowing people the capacity to exercise their agency may go a great distance in fostering it. On the other hand, those conditions are not necessary insofar as the capacity to choose and act freely has survived during circumstances of "persistent, widespread unfreedom" (Flathman 1987, 149). For example, after close to fifty years of Communist rule, the Chinese people are not automatons. If their daily, mundane actions do not prove that, then Tiananmen Square certainly did.

Perhaps autarchy is as natural as breathing. Under this possibility, we become choosers within a wide set of developmental practices. It is something requiring a minimal degree of decency and care that can be met by a extensive range of cultures and times. We are not forged into agents. It is a capacity that we realize, given an incredible array of circumstances. At most the state has a negative obligation not to interfere with its development. There is no positive obligation on the part of the liberal state to reproduce autarchy. There is, however, an obligation not to foreclose it.

In contrast, the Foucauldian argument claims that human beings must be forged into agents. There is a story to be told of our "agentification." In order to meet Benn's requirements for autarchy we must be subjugated violently and ordered. Through both subtle and not so subtle mechanisms of coercion we are turned into beings with the capacity to judge alternatives on the basis of evidence, alter our preferences in the light of changing beliefs, connect up ends with appropriate means, and so on. Autarchy does not come naturally. We can forge agents. If this "can" is combined with the idea of agency as a necessary condition of value, the state may have a positive obligation to forge agents.[27]

Is the autarchic self itself the result of human practice? Although citizens have a right to have their autarchic actions respected, they do not have a right to be autarchic. There is no right to autarchy in part because there is no guaranteed remedy for the loss of this condition. Liberal governments may be able to prevent harm or allow freedom to flourish, but they cannot insure that someone who is inner impelled or heterarchic will be restored to the status of a chooser. Indeed, in many cases it is impossible to prevent the disabling of autarchy. While we could establish conditions conducive to autarchy by preventing physical and psychological harm, there is no guarantee that they will have the desired effect. Although autarchy is a more deep-seated value than autonomy within liberalism, its existence is far less understood.

This outcome does not mean that there is no obligation to care for those who suffer from schizophrenia or catatonia. But the obligation to provide health care is not the same as an obligation to make everyone healthy. Between these two obligations is an enormous gap. This gap is not only financial and scientific, but in the case of the autarchic self it is also conceptual. Chapter 6 argues that because of the problems associated with the social construction of agency, liberal democracies do not have a responsibility to foster it.

---

[27] Although it admits that agents are made and not found, the genealogical position resists the claim that this is an unmitigated good. They would deny the appropriateness of an obligation to foster agency.

6

Cultivating Agency?

I HAVE ARGUED that the capacity for choice, as expressed in the ideas of autarchy or agency, is an elemental feature of both liberal theory and practice because it is a precondition for much of what we value and its diminution or dissolution is a serious harm. Protecting agency is crucial to liberal democracies. In making this claim, I am not denying that we value certain talents, behaviors, and capacities that we have not chosen. Protecting agency does not rule out the more general protection of human abilities and engagements.

If autarchy is an elemental value, do liberal democracies have a responsibility to foster selves with this capacity? I argue that the liberal state has no such responsibility. Even though agency may be a necessary precondition for a great deal that we value, the liberal state does not have a duty to insure the production of agents. In order for such a responsibility to make sense, the state must be able to cultivate agency. In order to defend the possibility of a state responsibility to cultivate agency, the capacity to exhibit intelligence and make choices must itself be an exhibition of intelligence and the result of choices.

If agency is as natural as breathing, then a state responsibility to cultivate it makes little sense. Although this position supports the conclusion that I am trying to reach with regard to agency, its demonstration is fraught with difficulties. Some of these difficulties lead us back to the problems of understanding nature itself. Another way to defend the conclusion that the state has no responsibility to cultivate agency is to question those positions that suggest that such cultivation is possible. Although this strategy may not be as satisfying as one that presents a knockdown argument for the naturalness of agency, it may support the desired conclusion.

My exploration of this possibility returns us to Foucault's work, for, clearly, Foucault supports the view that the self is constituted through the actions and utterances of other human beings.[1] Although he would

[1] The idea that the self is an exhibition of intelligence is shared widely by those who claim that the self is a social construction. This view goes back at least as far as Rousseau's notion of the perfectibility of human beings. Today, a number of perspectives share this view. Samuel Bowles and Herbert Gintis note that "scorning the notion of the exogenously given individual, Karl Marx championed the view that people produce themselves through their social practices" (Bowles and Gintis 1986, 145). Calling this a realist ontology, Jeffrey

not support the claim that the government had a responsibility to foster agency, his general argument presents a necessary condition for the existence of such a responsibility. The problems raised by and through his position point to the difficulties of seeing agency as the result of human intelligence.

It is important to note that the idea of cultivating agency is ambiguous. It can either refer to the attempt to create agency or it can mean the development of an already-existing potential. For the most part, this chapter explores the former, more radical claim of creating agency itself. Yet, one could argue that given the importance of agency, liberal regimes have an obligation to promote and hone our skills as choosers. From this perspective fostering agency could mean developing the capacity to make rational, responsible, mature judgments. The soil of liberal culture should be good enough to cultivate better choosers. More importantly, if the state has an obligation to protect the capacity to choose, does it not also have an obligation to foster that capacity?

Clearly, governments can do many things to develop better choosers. The ability of the state to act is a necessary condition for a political responsibility to foster agency. For example, requiring education that would provide the cognitive and emotional skills to discipline one's character, judge the feasibility of options, weigh evidence, give reasons and justifications, and imagine new possibilities can all be part of fostering our judgment, as are laws and regulations relating to the free flow of information. In the case of the United States, First Amendment rights, the Freedom of Information Act, the labeling of foods and medicines, campaign financing, product safety regulations, and laws pertaining to truth in advertising all point to the attempt to create better choosers in the political and economic marketplace. In fact, if one becomes a better chooser by exercising choice, then those social, political, and economic institutions that encourage choice could also be cultivating it. A culture that is free of coercion and respects the will of individuals would advance the prospects for a more developed form of agency.

The state can (and does) do a number of things that not only improve the quality of the choices available to us, but that directly attempt to improve our decision-making capacities. Does this mean that the state has an obligation to provide the conditions for such improvement? The problem is that "fostering better choosers" could mean a number of different things. For example, being a better chooser could mean that one

---

Isaac claims that "human agents are both determined and determining, interpreting, reproducing, and transforming historically given structures" (Isaac 1987, 640). Judith Butler argues that the "self is not only irretrievably 'outside,' constituted in social discourse, but that the ascription of interiority is itself a publicly regulated and sanctioned form of essence fabrication" (Butler 1990a, 279).

is choosing autonomously, or that one is choosing authentically, or that one is effectively relating one's means to a given set of ends, or that one is choosing not just what is desired, but what is desirable or good. In other words, beneath the surface of the idea of a "better chooser" is a disputed set of criteria. In the cases of autonomy and authenticity we have already presented the arguments against a state obligation to foster these ideals. Similarly, it is clear that being able to relate means to ends is an important skill in our culture. But agency itself implies that we already have some capacity to exercise practical reason. An individual who was unable to relate means to ends would hardly qualify as an agent. Cultivating this skill, then, implies developing it beyond a minimal threshold needed for agency. Whether there is a state obligation to either instill more sophisticated methods of connecting means to ends (e.g., teaching how to perform cost/benefit analyses or analyze risk) or to foster the kind of managerial self deplored by MacIntyre is unlikely. Individuals capable of the deft and elegant employment of instrumental rationality are not necessarily better choosers. Not only may unjust or evil purposes be served by such reasoning, but we also value spontaneous, intuitive, and tradition-based decisions.

More difficult problems, however, face the association of a good chooser with choosing what is desirable. Here the case for an obligation depends upon desirable ends being readily intelligible and universally shared. Clearly, these claims would run headlong into the kind of pluralism that is generally celebrated by liberal thinkers and liberal cultures. It is only by overcoming that pluralism that identifying a good chooser with choosing the good could work. The larger point is that these disputes over what criteria to employ in judging the development of agency defeat an obligation to cultivate one kind of chooser over another. Ultimately, this defeat does not mean that the attempt to promote our decision-making capacities should be precluded from politics.

The Self as an Exhibition of Intelligence

A different set of problems face the more radical claim that the state has an obligation to create agency itself. At the very least, this claim requires being able to set out the choices, purposes, practices, beliefs, and intentions that explain how a self comes to have the capacity to make choices, pursue purposes, engage in practices, hold beliefs, and formulate intentions. This, of course, is no small feat. This also raises the problem of temporal origins. If agency is constituted by other selves and agents did not always exist, how could this capacity have appeared on the scene? Moreover, if an account in which forging a creature with the capacity for choice and intelligence could be made without appealing to practices, actions, mistakes, and intentions, why could such an account not be given today? The problem of ultimate origins may be intractable. By bracketing it, we can consider the possibility that however this capacity initially arose, the self is currently constituted by other selves. Within this bracket, whether we emerged from a primordial soup or God's pocket may make little difference for what we are now.

Can an appeal to practices, choices, or institutions explain how human beings can exhibit agency and interpret and respond to the world? The general problem that this kind of account faces is that it constantly presupposes that the self already possesses the capacity to exhibit intelligence and understanding, i.e., agency. It is this problem that accompanies Foucault's hermeneutics of the self.

The notion that the self is itself an exhibition of human practice and action is an important theme throughout Foucault's work.[2] He rejects the idea that there is a subject or self existing outside of history and culture. Foucault's objective "has been to create a history of the different modes by which, in our culture, human beings are made subjects" (Rabinow 1984, 7).[3] Throughout his histories Foucault attempts to formulate a hermeneutics of the self (Foucault 1988c, 17). He presents a self that appears to be constituted entirely through the actions and utterances of other human beings. In short, the self has a history in which it constitutes itself.

Simply seeing the self as constructed, however, does not necessarily mean it would possess agency. Indeed, in the normal course of things, the objects, institutions, and actions that are exhibitions of human intelligence do not themselves have the capacity to choose and interpret their world. Moreover, the notion of *construction* is compatible with claims that agency is a result of certain structures and social processes as opposed to human practices and actions.

In contrast, the Foucauldian argument appears to be that social con-

---

[2] Foucault argued that "in the first place, I do indeed believe that there is no sovereign, founding subject, a universal form of subject to be found everywhere. I am very skeptical of this view of the subject and very hostile to it. I believe, on the contrary, that the subject is constituted through practices of subjection, or, in a more autonomous way, through practices of liberation, of liberty, as in Antiquity, on the basis, of course, of a number of rules, styles, inventions to be found in the cultural environment" (Foucault 1988b, 50–51).

[3] Christian Jambet notes that "this is one of the major lessons of Foucault's work: that ontology is susceptible to history. It should be stated not only that there is a multiplicity in the doctrines of being but, more radically, that being *constitutes itself*" (1992, 238). Similarly, Ian Hacking argues that Foucault "wants to know how the subjects themselves are constituted. . . . It is a Foucaultian thesis that every way in which I can think of myself as a person and an agent is something that has been constituted within a web of historical events" (1986, 36).

struction results in the production of agents. On occasion, however, Foucault is read as a structuralist (Isaac 1987). From this perspective, social processes, cultural forces, and psychological laws construct the self. The problem with this interpretation is that it does not account for the ways in which Foucault's argument turns upon human practices and action (Foucault 1984b, 369).[4] To avoid the structuralist interpretation, Foucault's account of the constructed character of the self must tell a story connecting human actions and inactions, intentions and mistakes, practices and procedures to what we are: creatures with the capacity for choice and understanding. Can such a story be told?

In order to analyze the manner in which this constitution of the self occurs, we can draw upon a distinction that Foucault used in describing his own work: "Let's say very briefly that through studying madness and psychiatry, crime and punishment, I have tried to show how we have indirectly constituted ourselves through the exclusion of some others: criminals, mad people, and so on. And now my present work deals with the question: How did we directly constitute our identity through some ethical techniques of the self which developed through antiquity down to now?" (Foucault 1988d, 146; 1993, 202–3). Our question for Foucault is whether his discussion of either the direct or indirect constitution of identity provides a convincing account of the self as autarchic. To answer this question, I focus upon the role that power and resistance play in Foucault's discussions of the indirect constitution of the self and, in the case of the direct constitution of the self, his distinction between knowing oneself and caring for oneself.

Power, Resistance, and the Indirect Constitution of the Self

What does Foucault mean by the indirect constitution of our identities through the exclusion of others? Foucault's histories of the practices of medicine, psychiatry, and criminal justice tell a series of stories about how various procedures, goals, arrangements, and tactics defined not only these particular disciplines but also those within the purview of those practices. All of the practices that he examines entail the exclusion or marginalization of others: the mad, the sick, the abnormal, the criminal, the delinquent. For Foucault, the marginalization of others is an indirect way to define ourselves. For example, our sense of what is healthy, sane, and responsible is defined by establishing what is sick,

----

[4] Foucault also denied this characterization: "Let me announce once and for all that I am not a structuralist, and I confess with the appropriate chagrin that I am not an analytic philosopher—nobody is perfect. I have tried to explore another direction" (1993, 202).

mad, and delinquent. The most visible effects of norms of behavior are to be found in those who fail to live up to them. Hence, Foucault examines those who are marginalized in order better to see the constitution of our selves.

Foucault's histories not only give us a sense of what the exclusion of others has meant for the rest of us, they also try to describe the emergence of these exclusionary practices and how these practices are connected to the constitution of the self. Both of these concerns are intertwined in Foucault's notion of power, which he uses to describe the forging of norms of social practice as well as identities of practitioners. Power—and in modernity, disciplinary power—is at the bottom of our identities and our social practices.

Is this notion of power a social/structural force? Foucault's belief that power is never "in anybody's hands," that it is never "appropriated as a commodity or piece of wealth" (Foucault 1980b, 98), suggests that it is closer to being a causal law than a tool of hermeneutics. However, it is also clear that power is part of and carried by human practices and interactions: There "is no power that is exercised without a series of aims and objectives." "But," he goes on to say, "this does not mean that it results from the choice or decision of an individual subject" (Foucault 1980a, 94–95). As I interpret Foucault, power is a kind of unintended consequence of intentional action. Some of us may have the very specific aim of improving efficiency in the workplace, or of raising the test scores of school children, or creating a better army. Accompanying each of these goals are sets of techniques and practices for disciplining bodies and encouraging subjects to discipline themselves. Foucault's argument is that these modest-seeming actions have had the cumulative effect of establishing a rigorous set of norms for how bodies should act and how minds should think. Although no one group or elite may have set out to establish a more disciplined society, this has been the effect of a whole series of practices, e.g., the training of troops, the punishment of criminals, the organization of factories, the control of diseases, and the education of children.

Power is not a structural force, at least as Foucault understood it.[5] Rather it is part and parcel of human practices and it is linked to the constitution of the self. This linkage occurs when one learns how to judge oneself and how not to behave: One must not look, act, or talk like the marginalized. The line distinguishing normal from abnormal, healthy from sick, mad from sane, delinquent from responsible is itself a social construction, not a biological given. But are these distinctions

[5] For views arguing that Foucault's notion of power gives insufficient weight to agency, see Isaac (1987) and Taylor (1986).

stamped upon our selves as a die casts a piece of metal? We are certainly not stamped in the sense that some of us are predestined to act normally and others abnormally. Neither are these distinctions stamped upon us in such a way that we know automatically where the line of normality falls. These distinctions must be learned, understood, and subscribed to. Hence, they can be traced, challenged, misunderstood, and altered— Foucault's own writings require the first two possibilities. Foucault's argument suggests that both power and the indirect constitution of our identities are practices that presuppose or assume subjects with the capacity to learn, interpret, misunderstand, endorse, and question the norms that they encounter. Power is not so much about forging a self with the capacity to understand, but the forging of norms of behavior that themselves presuppose a wide set of human capacities and abilities.

This interpretation of Foucault's idea of the indirect constitution of our identities is further strengthened if we turn to his notion of resistance. The notion of resistance either comes down to blind forces and impulses or to a form of agency that stands in opposition to power. In the latter case there is a notion of the subject that is independent of and not fully explainable by the prevailing mechanisms of power.

In chapter 4 I argued that the ideal of autonomy does not capture Foucault's notion of resistance. It fails because resistance can take the form of "a centrifugal movement, an inverse energy, a discharge" (Foucault 1980c, 138). In contrast, autonomy implies a careful, reflective questioning of the norms governing one's life. On this view, resistance is a reaction produced by disciplinary power. As such, it looks more like a process, or causal event, than a creation of human practice and action. It has a necessity to it that is intertwined with the logic of power.

But resistance can be more than a "discharge" and still something less than an exercise of autonomy. It can also take the form of an intentional response to a felt imposition. At one point Foucault argues that "there is a plurality of resistances, each of them a special case: resistances are possible, necessary, improbable; others that are spontaneous, savage, solitary, concerted, rampant, or violent; still others that are quick to compromise, interested, or sacrificial" (Foucault 1980a, 96). Foucault's language here moves from processes and behaviors ("possible, necessary, improbable") to more ambiguous characterizations ("spontaneous, savage, solitary") to fairly complex human practices and actions ("quick to compromise, interested, or sacrificial"). At the very least, Foucault uses the notion of resistance to encompass things that are and are not displays of intelligence. The problem here is that if certain resistances are displays of intelligence, then at any given moment the pressures of disciplinary power are not fully determinative. The given relationships of power cannot completely account for agency.

Perhaps Foucault would argue that the capacity for intelligence was itself at one time a product of social practice and power. Prior to the moment of its emergence, resistance could only take the form of reactions. But this suggestion just returns us to the question of how power could have been exercised without presupposing the human capacity to engage in the practices conveying power. Given Foucault's discussion of power and resistance, once the capacity for choice and intelligence is up and running, it appears to provide a point of resistance to and is not fully explainable by the prevailing disciplinary mechanisms. Moreover, before these capacities were up and running, power, as Foucault describes it, could not function. The indirect constitution of the subject is not a story about the constitution of the capacity for agency.

The Direct Constitution of the Self

A similar set of problems attends Foucault's discussion of the direct constitution of our identities found in the practices of knowing and caring for oneself. In these practices the constitution of the self refers to the quality of our choices, interests, desires, and projects and not to the generation of our capacity to have choices, intentions, intelligence, and understanding. On this interpretation, these capacities are already assumed in Foucault's discussions of care for the self and in knowing oneself. The idea of constituting the self comes closer to Benn's notion of autonomy than to the construction of agency.

Knowing Oneself

For Foucault, the practice of knowing oneself as a direct way to constitute the self seems to dominate Western history. The exception to this prevalence occurs during the Hellenistic and Roman periods when, according to Foucault, the idea of care for the self obtained a degree of priority over and perhaps independence of the practice of knowing oneself. Although Platonist and Christian thinkers emphasized knowledge of oneself, Epicurean and Stoic thinkers stressed caring for the self. Foucault argues that we moderns seem philosophically disposed to give priority to the problem of knowing the self before addressing how to care for our selves: "In the modern world, knowledge of oneself constitutes the fundamental principle" (Foucault 1988c, 22; For an example see Norton 1991, 98–100).

Foucault argues that both knowing and caring constitute the self. He is not claiming that all of the thinkers and schools that have contributed to these activities saw themselves as constituting the self. Rather, his claim is that these thinkers may have thought they were discovering the self or the soul, but they were actually considering the ways by which the self has been constituted.[6] Foucault's idea of knowing oneself entails a kind of self-fashioning based upon a conception of what is best. To know oneself, Foucault believes, does not entail a care for a soul-as-substance but rather the establishment of a substantive truth or ideal up to which one tries to live. Knowledge of oneself is not a matter of discovering what one is and then caring for oneself. Rather, it is a matter of constituting oneself through the art of caring for one's soul—a soul that is modeled upon some greater image or truth. Foucault's interpretation of Plato's "Alcibiades I" illustrates the point. What is at stake in the following discussion is whether knowing the self explains the constitution of the capacities to choose and understand.

"Alcibiades I" is relevant because Foucault uses it as a way to set out important themes in the constitution of the self. At one point in the dialogue Socrates asks how we can know the way to improve ourselves, if we are ignorant of what we are.[7] For Socrates, what is called care for the self (i.e., knowing how to improve ourselves) is intimately connected to a question of knowledge. And so Socrates asks, "Come then, in what way might the self itself be discovered? For in this way we might perhaps discover what we are ourselves, while as long as we are ignorant of this it will presumably be impossible for us" (Plato 1987, 129b).[8] The way the self itself is to be discovered is through the dialectic. But the dialectic of the "Alcibiades I" does not appear to yield the "self itself." At the end of the exchange immediately following his question, Socrates speaks of having "passed over" what they were going to consider, namely the "self

[6] The difference between knowing and caring for oneself should not be taken as a difference between discovering and creating the self; it is, rather, a difference in how the self is allegedly being constituted.

[7] Socrates asks, "As to what art makes better oneself, could we ever know it if we were ignorant of what we are ourselves?" (Plato 1987, 128e).

[8] The operative words here are *auto tauto.* Carnes Lord translates the phrase as "the self itself," but acknowledges that it can also be translated as "the same itself." He argues that the "expression refers to self-identity generally" (211n.32). In Lord's translation, Socrates makes a distinction between "the self itself" and "what each thing itself is" (130d), but it is unclear what this actually entails. Like Lord, Foucault relies upon the concept of *the self* to capture Socrates' argument. For Foucault, "Self is a reflexive pronoun, and it has two meanings. *Auto* means 'the same,' but it also conveys the notion of identity. The latter meaning shifts the question from 'What is this self?' to 'What is the plateau on which I shall find my identity?'" (1988c, 25). W.R.M. Lamb translated the phrase to mean "a sudden adumbration of the Platonic 'idea' or form which remains constant, and so 'the same,' behind the shifting objects of sense related to it through its influence or impress" (Plato 1927, 194–95n.1). Following *A Greek-English Lexicon,* this interpretation is reasonable because when the neuter gender of *auto* is attached to a noun it often indicates the Platonic

itself" (130d). "As it is," Socrates says, "we have considered, instead of the self, what each thing itself is. And perhaps this will be enough, for presumably we could not assert there is anything more dominant in ourselves than the soul" (130d). This distinction is far from clear. If we consider what the dialogue at this point has yielded, "what each thing itself is" must refer to the relationship between body and soul. At most, the exchange with Alcibiades has established that the soul is not the body and that the body is dominated by the soul. Consequently, when Socrates says that "what we are has been properly agreed on" (132b), he means merely that they have agreed that we are beings whose soul rules the body. Those who know things of the body, then, cannot be said to know themselves and those who love Alcibiades' body cannot be said to love Alcibiades. From this, Socrates says that we must agree that taking care of the body and of money does not entail taking care of oneself.

Does Socrates offer more? Does he say what the self itself is? At one point, Socrates appears to reverse his position completely, suggesting that if we know how to take care of ourselves, then "we will also know ourselves" (132c). But he backs off from this claim quickly, because it suggests what he takes to be the false idea that we have no notion whatsoever of what the Delphic oracle means.[9] Socrates then offers an interpretation of what "know thyself" entails. His analysis relies on an analogy: just as an eye can see itself by looking in the pupil of another, the soul must look into that which would best mirror it. The part of the soul associated with wisdom "resembles the god, and someone who looks at this and comes to know all that is divine—god and sensible thinking— would thus come to know himself also" (133b). Knowledge of oneself, then, requires knowing a great deal more about other, particularly divine, things. It requires knowing what the soul resembles. This knowledge, moreover, is of a practical sort. Foucault suggests that "in this divine contemplation, the soul will be able to discover rules to serve as a basis for just behavior and political action. The effort of the soul to know itself is the principle on which just political action can be founded, and Alcibiades will be a good politician insofar as he contemplates his soul in the divine element" (Foucault 1988c, 25).

---

idea. On Lamb's translation, when Socrates notes that they have not considered the same-in-itself (the idea—or what Lord translated as "the same itself") but merely "what each single thing is in itself" (130d), he may be drawing a distinction between the universal and the particular. In other words, up to that point in the dialogue Socrates and Alcibiades have been considering the particular relationships between the soul and the body, but not what the soul itself is.

   [9] "For if we know this, it would seem, we will also know ourselves. But in the name of the gods! Do we really not understand the Delphic inscription we mentioned just now, which is so well spoken?" (Plato 1987, 132c).

Clearly, for Plato, knowing oneself has priority over, and is seen as a necessary condition for, caring for oneself (26). So why does Foucault see this idea of knowing oneself as constituting the self and not as a matter of caring for the soul-as-substance (25)? First, the dialogue itself implies that care for the self cannot be care for the soul-as-substance because Socrates never gets to the point of setting out what the soul itself is.[10] He establishes merely that the soul rules the body and that knowing ourselves requires coming to know divine things. Indeed, contrary to Socrates' introduction to this particular part of the dialogue, it appears to be enough to know first that the soul dominates, and next to know *how* we would go about discerning our identity. Indeed, only by searching for what we are and leaving behind what we are not do we come to care for ourselves.

Second, Foucault could argue that there are enormous difficulties with the claim that the soul resembles what is divine. Socrates says that the Delphic oracle tells us to look towards the mirror of the divine (Plato 1987, 132d). It is only in something else that we will discover what we are. This assumes, however, that we already know what the soul looks like in order to see it in something else. In other words, the image of the mirror works only if we assume we can recognize the very thing that we want to find out. An alternative way to understand this claim can draw together the ideas of knowing the self and constituting the self even more closely. Perhaps knowledge of oneself entails the aspiration to be what we believe is best and, calling that divine, we attempt to forge a self along those lines.[11] We try to see ourselves in what is divine by trying to emulate the divine. In either case, the end result could not be described as discovering what we are. Rather, in the pursuit of knowing our selves we come to forge an identity modeled upon our understanding of what is divine.

But even on Foucault's reading is this forging of an identity a matter of constituting the capacity for choice and understanding? Once again,

---

[10] Steven Forde notes that Socrates appears to be dissatisfied with his argument: "Indeed, the argument might be said to have presupposed the existence of a 'hidden artisan' inside the human being rather than demonstrating it. Against the argument Socrates says that it would require an account for the 'self itself' to be conclusive, a mysterious problem that might have to do with our ability to make subtle distinctions between beings precisely, such as that between body and soul" (Forde 1987, 235). While the problem is mysterious, it seems to have less to do with the distinction between body and soul and more to do with the unanswered question of what the soul is.

[11] There are lines within the dialogue that claim that the divine is the best of all possible mirrors: "In looking to the god, therefore, we shall treat him as the finest mirror, and in human things we shall look to the virtue of the soul. In this way above all, we may see and know ourselves" (Plato 1987, 133c). Lord notes that this line may have been added by the Christian apologist Eusebius (217n.37).

the door of Foucault's conception of knowing oneself swings on the hinges of a self that already possesses these capacities. This characterization of the self has a "given-ness" to it. At most, the practice of knowing oneself addresses the ideals or ways of living that are believed to be divine. The idea of a self with the capacity to understand is presupposed and remains undisturbed in order to pursue the activity of knowing and hence caring for oneself. In this sense, knowledge of oneself does not entail the constitution of the self as agent. Indeed, if we interpret knowing oneself as merely a reflexive pronoun, then it may have little to do with knowing something called *the self*. On at least one occasion Foucault seems to recognize this: "The Delphic principle was not an abstract one concerning life; it was technical advice, a rule to be observed for the consultation of the oracle. 'Know yourself' meant 'Do not suppose yourself to be a god.' Other commentators suggest that it meant 'Be aware of what you really ask when you come to consult the oracle'" (Foucault 1988c, 19–20). None of these possible explanations requires that we go very far into how the self is itself constituted. One can say, without fear of contradiction, that the constitution of oneself (using the reflexive sense of *self*) in the activity of knowing oneself turns upon and does not explain the constitution of agency.

Care for the Self

Foucault uses the idea of knowledge of oneself as a way to contrast care for the self. How does he distinguish these two practices? Foucault argues that by late antiquity, Epicurean and Stoic thinkers had detached the notion of care for the self from the Platonic practice of knowing oneself. Along with this detachment, Foucault suggests, came a number of changes: the connection between politics and concern for the self became looser (one can turn away from politics and towards one's self); care for the self expanded to include a lifetime (and not a pedagogical practice that was limited to youth); and there was a change in how this idea of care was conveyed and taught (by quietly listening as opposed to through dialogue) (26). In discussing care for the self, Foucault discusses an art, a style, a form of cultivation, a kind of work, and a way of being—terms that he does not use when discussing knowing oneself. Moreover, practitioners of care for the self were willing to reverse the relationship between body and soul. Instead of the soul ruling the body, care for the self counsels that the soul should submit to the needs of the body (Foucault 1986, 135–36). Finally, there is a sense that the constitution of the self implied by care was less restrictive and more open-ended than Plato's ideal of knowing oneself. While knowledge of oneself began with a truth or a template against which to measure one's progress in coming to know oneself, care for self entailed more subjective, aesthetic criteria.[12]

As important as these changes may be, the central difference between these practices of constitution seems to lie elsewhere. "The change," Foucault suggests in discussing the movement from knowledge to care, "had more to do with the manner in which the individual needed to form himself as an ethical subject" (67). The manner of caring for oneself in the first centuries C.E. included such things as health regimes, physical exercise, measurement of how one's needs were being satisfied, meditation, a focus upon conversation, speaking and writing, as well as turning to private consultants, guides, and advisers to direct one's care (51–52). The difference, however, is not solely a matter of a concern with the details of everyday life—it is also a concern with governing one's life through rules. Knowing oneself, as "Alcibiades I" sets it out, does not entail the kind of rule-governed conduct found in those traditions that advance care for the self. Although rules may issue from coming to know oneself, the project of knowing oneself is connected more intimately to the search for the divine. In contrast, the constitution of the self through care requires rules. Foucault argues that "in the Stoic tradition examination of self, judgment, and discipline show the way to self-knowledge by superimposing truth about self through memory, that is, by memorizing the rules" (Foucault 1988c, 43).[13] In a sense, both Platonic and Stoic practices engage in what Foucault sees as the constitution of the subject through the imposition of a truth or template. In caring for the self, this template emerges through the memorization of rules, while for the Platonists it entails knowing an ideal.

Once again, thinking about the practice of care for the self raises questions about whether Foucault gives an account of the constitution of

[12] However, in the case of Stoicism, it is not clear how far one can take this description. Pierre Hadot has raised a serious objection to Foucault's view of the Stoics. He argues that it is misleading to suggest that the Stoics were attempting to forge a personal identity or something that we would call the self. Hadot claims that the point of Stoics' spiritual exercises was not to forge a self, "but to free oneself from one's individuality, to raise oneself to universality" (Hadot 1992, 229). The point, Hadot suggests, was to go "beyond the self" (226). This can be seen in Seneca's writings, where "Seneca does not find joy just in 'Seneca,' but by transcending Seneca, by discovering that he has a reason in himself, a part of the universal Reason which is within all men and the cosmos itself" (226). Given the difficulties of using such terms as self (as a noun) and subject within antiquity, Hadot argues that the Stoics did not understand themselves as forging, constituting, or cultivating the self.

[13] Foucault also wants "to underscore the fact that in Stoicism, it's not the deciphering of the self, not the means to disclose secrecy, which is important; it's the memory of what you've done and what you've had to do" (1988c, 35).

agency. Consider what Foucault takes to be Seneca's view: "the subject is not the operating ground for the process of deciphering but is the point where rules of conduct come together in memory. The subject constitutes the intersection between acts which have to be regulated and rules for what ought to be done. This is quite different from the Platonic conception and from the Christian conception" (34; see also 1993, 207). What does Foucault mean by saying that "the subject is not the operating ground for the process of deciphering"? He may be claiming that in this view there is no truth to be drawn out of the self. The self does not have its own dark hidden secrets that must be brought to the surface as is understood in certain confessional practices (e.g., Christian and psychoanalytic). Rather, truth is something to be remembered, something that had been learned and could be forgotten through inattention. More important, Foucault says that the subject constitutes the intersection between rules and actions. This suggests two possible readings. If *constitute* is taken as a transitive verb, then this intersection does not constitute the subject. Instead, the self comes upon the scene and creates the intersection between actions and rules. This interpretation presupposes the self and leaves open the question of how it is constituted. On the other hand, if *constitute* is taken as an intransitive verb, then this intersection constitutes the subject. Without rules and without actions to be regulated, there would be no self. But it is not clear that presenting a set of rules and listing a set of actions to be regulated is sufficient to constitute a subject. A great deal must be presupposed before one could follow and understand the rules as well as conceptualize the actions to be regulated.

Foucault's discussion of care does not describe the forging of the capacities to choose and understand. As with knowing oneself, the practice or art of caring for the self postulates, rather than excavates, the ability of human beings to act. Shifting attention to one's own life, being more autonomous, delighting and taking pleasure in one's own capacities, silently listening to teachers, memorizing the appropriate rules for life, recalling for others what you thought and felt are all aspects of care for the self. All of them, however, presuppose autarchy or agency, the capacity to participate in these practices, and understand or misunderstand, accept or reject some or all of their features. If the self has the capacity to choose and understand, it is not constituted through either knowing or caring for the self.

Perhaps a better description of what Foucault is doing is not describing "agentification," but tracing meticulously a complex set of practices and rules that were meant to guide and govern human conduct. One could say that individuals who subscribed to and attempted to follow those rules are engaged in a practice of self-disclosure, but this would not be disclosing something called a self.[14] Rather, it would be a matter of disclosing to others the ends, projects, and desires that one had decided to pursue in light of the given moral rules.

The practice of care for the self could also entail reflecting upon the sentiments that one should choose to adopt in doing whatever one does. This could be called self-enactment, but it would not be enacting a self.[15] Rather, it would entail attending to whether we acted in good faith or bad, generously or with spite, enviously or liberally, shamefully or appropriately, and so on. What is understood, disclosed, and enacted is a complex set of practices, principles, sentiments, desires, and codes.[16] This examination of Foucault's position points to a general problem with seeing the self as having the capacity to act and understand: it is difficult if not impossible to set out the practices that constitute such a self. The relevant capacity for the self to understand and choose is presupposed in the discussion of practices and conventions.

It is important to contrast this argument with another criticism raised against the claim that the self is constituted or constructed: construction is incompatible with agency. In this alternative criticism, if our identities are constructed thoroughly, then there is no room for agency.[17] In contrast, I believe not that agency is irreconcilable with construction, but that it is all too compatible with it. Agency, or the capacity for choice and understanding, is already postulated in the subject that is meant to be explained by the construction.

Butler hints at one response, arguing that

> The question of locating "agency" is usually associated with the viability of the "subject," where the "subject" is understood to have some stable existence prior to the cultural field that it negotiates. Or, if the subject is culturally constructed, it is nevertheless vested with an agency, usually figured as the capacity for reflexive mediation, that remains intact regardless of its cultural

[14] Oakeshott defines self-disclosure as "choosing satisfactions to pursue and pursuing them; its compunction is, in choosing and acting, to acknowledge and subscribe to the conditions intimated or declared in a practice of moral discourse" (1975, 76).

[15] Oakeshott defines self-enactment as "choosing the sentiments in which to act; and its compunctions are conditions of 'virtuous' self-enactment intimated in a language of moral conduct" (1975, 76).

[16] Following Hadot's argument, the Stoics were concerned with the establishment of a moral practice, not the constitution of the self. In so doing, they hoped to replace a set of moral practices that had lost their vitality. What may be distinctive about these first centuries is the level of self-reflection (as opposed to reflection about the self) and care in which people engaged when carrying out this task: "In short, what the Greco-Roman world of this period had to offer was a morality in which the selfconscious pursuit of moral ideals was pre-eminent" (Oakeshott 1991, 483–84).

[17] Those who advance the claim that the subject is constructed appear to be most worried about the charge that their position precludes agency (Butler 1990c, 147; 1992a, 12–13; Hekman 1992, 1099, 1113–14).

embeddedness. On such a model, "culture" and "discourse" *mire* the subject, but do not constitute that subject. This move to qualify and enmire the preexisting subject has appeared necessary to establish a point of agency that is not fully *determined* by that culture and discourse. And yet, this kind of reasoning falsely presumes (a) agency can only be established through recourse to a prediscursive "I," even if that "I" is found in the midst of a discursive convergence, and (b) that to be *constituted* by discourse is to be *determined* by discourse, where the determination forecloses the possibility of agency. (Butler 1990c, 142–43)

How does the position set out in this chapter compare and contrast to the account of agency that Butler rejects in this passage? First, I am not positing autarchy as having a stable existence prior to any kind of cultural field. The claims that agency is a central feature of Western culture, that it can be diminished and destroyed in a variety of ways, and that there may be cultures in which this attribute is not developed or absent (Benn 1975–1976, 121) do not lead to the conclusion that agency possesses an existence outside of the cultural realm. Second, there is, however, something to be said for the argument that in discussions of Western practices and culture, our agency is prefigured in our notions of discourse, rule following, and participation in practices. Does this argument falsely presume the existence of a prediscursive "I" and the elision of the difference between constitution and determination? I do not contend that the problem of determination haunts discursive or practice-based explanations. More generally, the idea that agency is prefigured in our conceptions of practices, discourse, and rule following says more about how we use these terms than it does about agency. For Butler, denying that discourse constructs agency also affirms that agency exists prior to discourse. Yet a failure of the constitution argument is not an affirmation that agency should be understood as a prediscursive or natural entity.

Opacity

> Socrates: Do you understand, then, that going
> wrong in one's actions comes about through
> this sort of ignorance—the ignorance of one
> who supposes he knows when he does not?
>   (Plato 1987, 117d)

If agency is not constituted through human actions, discourses, or practices, then the liberal state cannot have a responsibility to cultivate it. A prediscursive or natural conception of agency would also support this conclusion. But one need not subscribe to Butler's alternatives that either agency is constituted or prediscursive. A third possibility is that agency is, in many respects, opaque. The most important aspects of its opacity would be the failure of either naturalist or discursive explanations to fully account for how we have this capacity.

Without attempting to prove such opacity, consider what effect an opaque form of agency would have on the problem of soulcraft. For example, even though it may settle the problem of the state's responsibility to cultivate agency, the attribution of opacity to agency could not be complete or entire. We do have a fairly good idea that a variety of actions and procedures can diminish and destroy agency: physical trauma, drugs, illness, and so on. These generalizations suggest that whatever opacity attends this conception of the self, it cannot be completely mysterious.[18] In this light, we at least have an obligation *not* to do certain things that disable or harm our capacity for choice and understanding.[19]

Second, an element of opacity within agency may also reinforce the problematic character of positions claiming to present a true conception of the self. One problem with the critics' claims regarding the production of identity is that their alternative standard cannot capture the self as chooser or capable of understanding. Without knowing what the right conception of the self is in this regard, theory cannot elevate and legitimate a particular politics of identity.

Third, such opacity would not only rule out claims that one view or the other is true, but it would also have some effect on whether one view or another is false. Clearly, this conception of autarchy would still rule out understandings that are self-defeating, i.e., views that would undermine the capacity of agency.[20] On the other hand, an opaque conception of agency would permit a fair number of understandings of the self. In other words, this position could not support a procedural neutrality that would exclude these terms from public debate. As Flathman argues, "opacity creates spaces protective of individuality and plurality" (1992, 112). It does this, in part, through its inability to rule out a wide range of

---

[18] Flathman argues that "human action as strong voluntarists conceive and valorize it is only finally or ultimately, not entirely or unqualifiedly mysterious and unpredictable" (1992, 11).

[19] In contrast, Flathman argues that opacity also provides a level of insulation against deep forms of manipulation and control. He writes that "if you (they) do not understand me (us), or do not know whether you understand me or not, your ability to enter into my affairs, certainly your capacity to do so skillfully and especially insidiously, is diminished" (1992, 109). I suppose much depends upon the meaning of "skillful" and "insidious" here. Because our agency can be threatened brutally and invasively, it is unlikely that the opacity of our autarchy is itself much of a protection.

[20] Liberal theory and practice cannot be neutral between a view that denied or devalued agency and a view that assumed such a capacity and sought to protect it.

self-conceptions. A liberal politics, then, should be able to make room for this plurality.

Fourth, as Flathman notes, a failure to understand something need not lead to respect. It could lead to fear: "As Wittgenstein's discussions would suggest . . . we sometimes sanctify and worship that which is beyond our understanding, sometimes contemn and attempt to obliterate it" (115). A characteristic of liberal politics may be that it engenders a constant dispute over and adjustments regarding the procedures, laws, forms of education, and other mechanisms that protect agency. Not only do various liberties and rights presuppose the existence of agency, but they also secure agency against some of the more blatant attempts to diminish or destroy it. What tends to be feared, however, is not the capacity for choice but the specific choices made. This tendency suggests that theory may help very little in responding to specific threats. Ultimately, protecting individuals from forms of power that would destroy agency is a practical, political concern.

Putting aside the question of opacity, the state cannot have a responsibility to cultivate agency as long as the accounts of that cultivation remain unconvincing. Furthermore, although there is a responsibility to protect agency, such protection is not the same as selfcraft. The strong case for liberal selfcraft fails. In the next chapter I examine the strong case against selfcraft.

7

The Liberal Method of Avoidance

SHOULD POLITICS be judged by its effects on our selves or souls? Despite their differences, the thinkers discussed in the previous six chapters agree that such judgments are appropriate and necessary. As we have seen, some judge that liberal regimes harm our selves or souls in a variety of ways while for others this regime holds out the promise of cultivating certain ideal conceptions of the self. For the critics and defenders of liberalism a political responsibility exists either to engage directly in selfcraft or to mitigate the perceived effects of this culture.

When taken together, these positions compose only one of two broad views that dominate the dispute over selfcraft. The problems associated with these positions appear to push us toward the second dominant view of selfcraft: not only do liberal democracies lack a responsibility to engage in selfcraft, but also such judgments are inappropriate, unacceptable, and illiberal. This second perspective has been expressed under the rubric of liberal neutralism. In examining some of the important formulations of this position, I will argue that they are not strong enough to preclude selfcraft and soultalk from politics. In other words, the problems raised by those who see a political responsibility to engage in selfcraft need not lead us to embrace liberal neutralism.

Neutrality of Effect and Intent

Liberal writers have offered a number of arguments for precluding selfcraft from politics. A recent set of arguments strives to circumvent these concerns by having liberal theory and practice adopt a neutral stance vis à vis problems of the self. Neutrality, however, can mean many things and be applied in many ways. Charles Larmore, John Rawls, and Richard Rorty have argued that at the level of theory conceptions of the self or soul have no place in our understandings of and justification for liberalism. Neutrality at this level means simply that certain sorts of arguments should carry little or no weight in our philosophical explorations of politics. At the level of political practice, by contrast, the issue of neutrality is more complicated. The central difficulty here is that neutrality can be applied to the intentions and effects of both procedures and sub-stantive policies. When applied to our intentions in the formulation of policies and procedures, neutrality means that we should not justify par-ticular political procedures or policies by appealing to conceptions of the self. When it is applied to effects, neutrality means that procedures and policies should be either equally burdensome (or favorable) or they should have little or no effect upon different self conceptions.

Of these various uses, neutrality of effect has only an oblique connec-tion to precluding concerns of selfcraft. Obviously, selfcraft has not been precluded from political deliberations if neutrality of effect demands that policies and procedures be equally burdensome to diverse concep-tions of the self. Even when neutrality is interpreted as requiring little or no effect on different self conceptions, it has the potential to bring selfcraft into politics. At the very least, neutrality would require that pol-itics be open to claims that pernicious forms of selfcraft have been the result of particular procedures or policies. Paradoxically, neutrality of effect may not be a principle of preclusion as much as a particular kind of selfcraft.

Perhaps because neutrality of effect has the potential for bringing selfcraft back into politics, liberals rarely demand it of political proce-dures and policies. Indeed, in order for our intentions and justifications of political arrangements to be neutral, it may be necessary to stipulate that such effects are irrelevant to politics and not that they are merely neutral. For example, Judith Shklar writes, "no system of government, no system of legal procedures, and no system of public education is with-out psychological effect, and liberalism has no reason at all to apologize for the inclinations and habits that procedural fairness and responsible government are likely to encourage" (1989, 33). More broadly, Rawls argues that "it is surely impossible for the basic structure of a just consti-tutional regime not to have important effects and influences on which comprehensive doctrines endure and gain adherents over time, and it is futile to try to counteract these effects and influences" (1988, 262).[1] Rorty goes a step further and argues that it is imprudent to counteract biased effects upon our selves. He believes that those unfortunate effects upon our selves are actually an acceptable tradeoff. Conceding that the "typical characters of liberal democracies *are* bland, calculating, petty, and unheroic," Rorty nevertheless feels that "the prevalence of such peo-ple may be a reasonable price to pay for political freedom" (1991a, 190).

---

[1] Along somewhat similar lines, Charles Larmore argues that "it is a general truth that what the state does, the decisions it makes and the policies it pursues, will generally benefit some people more than others, and so some conceptions of the good life will fare better than others" (1987, 43).

All things considered, the last man really is not such a bad deal. The fairness of this price for Rorty is most apparent in his response to MacIntyre's claim that the central character types of modernity are rich aesthetes, managers, and therapists: "I would welcome a culture dominated by 'the Rich Aesthete, the Manager, and the Therapist' so long as *everybody* who wants to gets to be an aesthete (and, if not rich, as comfortably off as most—as rich as the Managers can manage, guided by Rawls's Difference Principle)" (Rorty 1991b, 159).

What is interesting about Rorty's position is not only that it abandons neutrality of results, but that it also actively defends those results. The underlying assumption of that defense is that if a regime attempted to foster less petty, more vibrant, less normalized characters, it would decrease freedom. Although this is certainly possible, Rorty has not shown that the tradeoff is necessary. If the tradeoff is not necessary, then forms of selfcraft that did not violate freedom could be permitted. For those who seek to preclude selfcraft, it is not necessary to rule out policies and procedures that could conceivably have some effect upon our selves or souls.

For the most part, liberal neutralists are far more concerned with the character of our justifications for theories, procedures, and policies than with neutrality of effect. In other words, reasons given in support of liberal theory, decision-making mechanisms, and public policies should be neutral vis à vis particular conceptions of the self or soul. At the policy level, this means that we should not be saying various things about selves and souls when supporting or criticizing particular policies. For example, justifying aboriginal rights with the claim that native peoples' self-conceptions were intimately linked to the group would violate the provision of neutrality. This provision would also be violated if a president or a member of Congress justified a bill by claiming that funding certain educational projects would encourage autonomy or the rule of reason in the souls of our children. Similarly, neutrality would be violated if a genealogist, in arguing for prison reform, claimed that the prison system unavoidably produced its own form of resistance in the form of delinquency. According to Rorty, central to the conduct of a liberal politics is "a vocabulary which is no more relevant to one's individual private self-image than to another's. In a liberal society our public dealings with our fellow citizens are not *supposed* to be Romantic or inventive; they are supposed to have the routine intelligibility of the marketplace or the courtroom" (196). The liberal vocabulary of "justice is necessarily public and shared, a medium for argumentative exchange" (Rorty 1989, xiv). Although statecraft may have all sorts of effects upon souls and selves, those effects should not then become part of the justification for theories, institutions, and policies.

The Appeal to What Is Shared

Why should our theoretical and political discourses be this constrained? One frequent justification is that the existence of a liberal public/political realm depends upon society sharing both a set of norms and a certain vocabulary. What is not held in common should not form the basis of theoretical conclusions or political actions. As Bruce Ackerman, Charles Larmore, and Rorty have argued, ideas of the good life and conceptions of autonomy are not shared, and should not form part of our justificatory discourse (Ackerman 1989; Larmore 1987, 1990; Rorty 1989, xiv). This argument is easily expanded to include general disputes over the self. Liberalism's critics and defenders are divided over what constitutes harm and, more importantly, what constitutes an unharmed self or soul, and these controversies undermine the claim that the state has an obligation to engage in a particular form of selfcraft. In contrast, the neutralists would draw a stronger conclusion: these controversies are reason enough to banish selftalk completely from politics and philosophy.

The appeal to what is shared can be found in Rawls's understanding of political philosophy. He argues that as members of large, industrialized, heterogeneous democracies we do not share a conception of the self. Because claims about the self are deeply divisive, liberal theory should avoid appealing to them when conceiving regulative principles for the just state. If liberal theory is to get us anywhere, its postulates and assumptions must be shared widely. According to Rawls, the function of political philosophy is to help direct political practice by finding the common features already implicit in our practices. Rawls writes:

> There are periods, sometimes long periods, in the history of any society during which certain fundamental questions give rise to sharp and divisive political controversy, and it seems difficult, if not impossible, to find any shared basis of political agreement. . . . One task of political philosophy in a democratic society is to focus on such questions and to examine whether some underlying basis of agreement can be uncovered and a mutually acceptable way of resolving these questions publicly established. Or if these questions cannot be fully settled, as may well be the case, perhaps the divergence of opinion can be narrowed sufficiently so that political cooperation on a basis of mutual respect can still be maintained. (Rawls 1985, 226)

When political philosophy is based upon controversial ideas of the self, it cannot support the kind of overlapping consensus needed to sustain liberal democracy. What is not shared should not be incorporated into theory because theory must legitimize and sustain democracy. Without the discovery of shared norms to serve as philosophical backup, liberal democracy cannot be justified.

As long as one subscribes to Rawls's vision of political philosophy, his case for excluding views of the self appears convincing, but this vision is itself controversial. Not all political practitioners and theorists see political philosophy as a consensus builder that tries to find agreement in times of trouble. Furthermore, it is not at all clear that practice should look to theory to reinforce its founding assumptions and shore up its basic principles. Even if this role were offered to philosophers, many would argue that it could not be taken up without risking confusion and disaster. For example, Michael Oakeshott sees political philosophy as a mode of abstract understanding that is entirely distinct from the engagements of political activity. In contrast, Leo Strauss sees political philosophy as challenging common beliefs in the pursuit of truth. Strauss, however, would reject the claim that these challenges could be directly converted into political action. Marx, of course, offered a far more radical understanding: philosophy should not only challenge our common opinions but also seek to transform the world.

In light of these different conceptions of what political philosophy is all about, Rawls's position is either self-defeating, or he must show an underlying consensus to our views of political philosophy. His position is self-defeating when one combines his view that that which is not shared should be excluded from political philosophy with the existence of diverse conceptions of political philosophy. The second alternative requires arguing that beneath these controversial conceptions of political philosophy we actually share a view of political philosophy that resembles Rawls's own. Not only has Rawls not made this argument, it is unclear whether it could be made. In short, the controversial character of Rawls's view of political philosophy undermines his position of excluding from political philosophy whatever is not shared.

There is another more general problem with the appeal to what is shared. Such an appeal may be too weak to support a principle of preclusion. As William Galston notes, it is "overwhelmingly likely that there will be no moral proposition on which all groups agree"; public discourse, therefore, should be able to accommodate serious and deep disagreements (Galston 1991, 103–4). The controversial nature of a reason is not enough to exclude it from political discourse. The neutralist's best case cannot rest solely upon what is shared and what is not. Writers such as Rorty, Gutmann, Thompson, and Rawls offer other ways to justify the exclusion of selfcraft from politics. The rest of this chapter examines each of their positions, beginning with Rorty's.

Rorty and the Preclusion of Selfcraft

Several arguments can be drawn out of Rorty's writings to support the case for precluding selfcraft from politics.[2] Rorty's appeal to the liberal hatred of cruelty, his attempt to show the limits of conversations, his detachment of politics from philosophy, and his desire to surpass the present philosophical debates suggest different ways to exclude concerns of self from political theory and practice. None of these arguments provides a strong enough case for preclusion.

The Question of Cruelty

To see how Rorty's appeal to the liberal hatred of cruelty could support an argument for excluding selfcraft, we must begin by examining a character he calls the ironist. According to Rorty, the ironist is somebody who "has radical and continuing" doubts about the vocabulary she uses to justify her actions and beliefs. The ironist not only believes that these doubts cannot be resolved in her present vocabulary, but that there is no universal criterion distinguishing a right vocabulary from a wrong one (Rorty 1989, 73). In addressing these doubts the ironist may rethink, challenge, and disrupt the prevailing vocabulary that she once used to make sense of her life. Her pursuit of autonomy and self-creation may ultimately lead her to reject the prevailing vocabulary and scorn those who rely upon it. The ironist seems to thrive upon revealing inconsistencies in prevailing opinion, inverting or leveling its hierarchies, or blurring its distinctions. In effect, the ironist tells those of us who subscribe to the prevailing vocabulary that our language is "up for grabs by her and her kind." At the very least, this means that ironists are constantly redescribing other people and the world around them. Rorty suggests that there is something cruel about that activity, "for the best way to cause people long-lasting pain is to humiliate them by making the things that seemed most important to them look futile, obsolete, and powerless" (89). This potential for moral cruelty leads Rorty to argue that "irony seems inherently a private matter" (87).[3] The activity of continually call-

---

[2] It is unlikely that Rorty would describe these statements so formally as arguments.

[3] He does say, however, that, "whereas Habermas sees the line of ironist thinking which runs from Hegel through Foucault and Derrida as destructive of social hope, I see this line of thought as largely irrelevant to public life and to political questions" (Rorty 1989, 83). He also writes, "Irony is, if not intrinsically resentful, at least reactive" (88). Rorty reframes the argument yet again by suggesting that the real reason why people are suspicious of the ironist is not her ability to redescribe, but her "inability to empower.... For she cannot

ing into question the justificatory vocabulary that underlies social inter-action ipso facto calls into question the life plans and projects of other individuals.

This employment of the public/private distinction could relegate to the private sphere some of liberalism's critics as well as those who seek autonomy or authenticity. For even if they do not all qualify as ironists, they are willing to encourage forms of redescription. Just as the ironist worries that "the process of socialization which turned her into a human being by giving her a language may have given her the wrong language, and so turned her into the wrong kind of human being," many of those who are concerned with selfcraft believe that the language and nurtur-ing given to us by this regime has failed us (75). This element can cer-tainly be found in the writings of communitarians, classical political ra-tionalists, and genealogists.[4] To some extent, it can also be found in the critical stance of those who pursue autonomy. If the engagement of re-description is what is relevant, then quite a number of writers concerned with selfcraft open the possibility for humiliation.[5] "We should," Rorty argues, "stop trying to combine self-creation and politics, especially if we are liberals" (120). Because of the potential moral cruelty that attends the pursuit of self-creation and autonomy, these activities must be kept private. Consequently, Rorty advocates privatizing "the Nietzschean-Sartrean-Foucauldian attempt to authenticity and purity, in order to prevent yourself from slipping into a political attitude which will lead you to think that there is some social goal more important than avoiding cruelty" (65).

---

offer the same sort of social hope as metaphysicians offer" (91). The final transformation of the argument occurs when Rorty claims that the liberal ironist can indeed empower to the extent that redescriptions can increase our chances of being kind (91). This compati-bility with liberalism, however, does not mean that ironism is not potentially cruel.

[4] Not everyone, however, would meet Rorty's additional requirement that ironists reject any criterion distinguishing a right vocabulary from a wrong one. Clearly, classical political rationalists or those who advance the idea of authenticity reject wholeheartedly the an-tiessentialism that this lack of any criterion implies. Nevertheless, Rorty does believe that "redescription and possible humiliation are no more closely connected with ironism than with metaphysics" (90).

[5] Rorty's account of the relationship between ironism and liberal democracy, however, is somewhat more ambiguous than the above portrayal suggests, for he argues there are actually two varieties of ironism. On the one hand there are ironists who write books to help us become more autonomous or realize our selves; on the other hand there are liberal ironists who write books to help us become less cruel (141). To an extent, liberal (private?) ironism is congruous with liberal democracy. Its redescriptions are not intended to foster autonomy and self-creation, but to make us aware of the cruelties of our own public institu-tions and private practices. Liberal irony seeks to redescribe these things and consequently expand our understanding of "we" by showing us the ways in which our intentional and unintentional actions humiliate others or make them suffer. To this extent, Rorty holds

Can Rorty's public/private distinction serve as a basis for excluding concerns of selfcraft from politics? Much of the normative force of this argument is drawn from his use of the idea of cruelty. To a great extent, Rorty's understanding of the term appears to be drawn from Judith Shklar's interpretation of Montaigne and Montesquieu, the core of which is that cruelty is the worst of all vices, and it is the central purpose of liberal government to alleviate and prevent this vice. But Shklar also makes a fairly sharp distinction between physical and moral cruelty. Physical cruelty refers to brutality and physical suffering. Moral cruelty entails "deliberate and persistent humiliation, so that the victim can eventually trust neither himself nor anyone else" (Shklar 1984, 37). Shklar argues that there is something compelling about putting physical cruelty ahead of moral cruelty. By this, she means that we should be unwilling to permit the use of physical coercion to prevent moral cruelty. Even though moral cruelty results in humiliation and may ultimately precede physical cruelty, Shklar notes that "painful as humiliation is, it does no bodily damage" (37). Furthermore, a system in which moral cruelty is put first opens up enormous vistas for justifying physical cruelty. Shklar writes that, "If one . . . puts moral cruelty first, whether it be injustice as revolutionaries sometimes do, or self-torment as Nietzsche did, one can readily adopt every one of Machiavelli's cruelest maxims" (42).[6]

Shklar's distinction between physical and moral cruelty suggests that while she would not tolerate physical cruelty in either the public or private sphere, she might be willing to tolerate some moral cruelty. At the very least, she would be unwilling to devote the state's coercive apparatus

---

that private irony can be seen as compatible with the liberal hope for a world with less and less cruelty.

This compatibility, however, requires the liberal ironist to remain liberal and not to push her ironic stance very far. The benefits of opening up other vocabularies and worlds must outweigh the costs of her redescriptions. Thus, the liberal ironist limits her irony. She knows when to stop being ironic and start politicking in other kinds of ways. It is not clear, however, where Rorty places liberal ironism in his public/private distinction, nor whether liberal ironism is, in some sense, publicly sanctioned.

[6] For Shklar, cruelty is a *summum malum* (1989, 29). She grounds the notion that cruelty is the worst of all vices upon a "moral intuition based upon ample observation" (30). She also seems to suggest that cruelty is a summum malum because the fear of systematic cruelty is universal (i.e., shared). Earlier liberals may have thought cruelty itself an absolute evil, "an offense against God or humanity" (23), but we can simply begin with the fact that we have this fear. This fact, however, does not sufficiently justify what Shklar calls a liberalism of fear. She argues that "one cannot rest on this or any other naturalistic fallacy" (30). The avoidance of cruelty, then, must be elevated to a principle of political morality. One way to do this is through Kantian universalism. Another way is through utilitarian justification. Shklar seems to suggest that either approach is compatible with liberalism and that there is consequently no need for liberalism to choose between them (30).

to the alleviation and prevention of moral cruelty in public or private life.

In many respects, Rorty's argument simply follows Shklar's lead. At times, Rorty, like Shklar, seems to appeal to the idea that cruelty is a universally shared *summum malum*. Rorty argues that "it is a historical contingency whether we are socialized by Neanderthals, ancient Chinese, Eton, Summerhill or the Ministry of Truth. Simply by being human we do not have a common bond. For all we share with all other humans is the same thing we share with all other animals—the ability to feel pain" (1989, 177). But this is not quite true, as Rorty admits a few sentences later, because humans seem to have a special kind of pain. For humans "can all be humiliated by the forcible tearing down of the particular structures of language and belief in which they were socialized (or which they pride themselves on having formed for themselves)" (177). The special pain that humans share is not a susceptibility to physical pain but to the destruction of their language and belief structures. To inflict this kind of pain, however, is not physical but moral cruelty. Perhaps it is because of this further claim that Rorty is willing to take the additional step of arguing that moral cruelty should be excluded from the public realm. This outcome does not mean that Rorty puts moral cruelty first. Rather it means that neither form of cruelty has a place in a liberal politics.

If both physical and moral cruelty should be excluded from the public sphere, and selfcraft brings with it moral cruelty, then perhaps selfcraft should have no place in the public realm. It does, however, have a place in the private sphere, which should tolerate the pursuit of perfectionism, autonomy, and authenticity. The redescriptions that are part of this kind of ironism are nobody's business, particularly the state's. But if the kind of cruelty that accompanies selfcraft can be so severe that it should be relegated to the private realm, then it is unclear why it should be tolerated even there, i.e., why the state should not interfere to prevent it. Rorty's response is twofold. On the one hand, moral cruelty should be tolerated in private because to try to prevent it would require the use of physical force.[7] Individuals should not be restricted from pursuing their own conception of perfection and self-creation, "so long as they do it on their own time—causing no harm to others and using no resources needed by those less advantaged" (xiv). On the other hand, the possibilities for physical cruelty are far greater if the power of the state reinforces the pursuit of a particular self-conception. That possibility is diminished significantly when one is left to one's own devices in the private realm.

[7] Rorty sees Mill as providing the last word on this matter: Governments should "devote themselves to optimizing the balance between leaving people's private lives alone and preventing suffering" (Rorty 1989, 63).

The problem with the first response is that the same argument that permits moral cruelty in the private sphere could also be used to permit it in the public. That is, any attempt to exclude self-creation from politics would require the use of coercion and the violation of freedom. Perhaps it is because of this risk that Rorty does not advocate using state institutions to prevent individuals from advancing their own conceptions of self-creation in the public realm. He does not defend a discourse police. Indeed, directing the state's resources against individuals who deploy their favored self-conception in public-policy disputes looks very much like giving priority to moral cruelty over physical cruelty. If moral cruelty should be permitted in the private realm because preventing it comes at too high a price, the same argument can apply to moral cruelty in the public sphere.

It is conceivable that Rorty really wants to do nothing more than convince us to be liberals, not ironists, in public debate. At best, neutrality becomes a weak hortatory device. If this is true, then the weight of the argument would appear to depend upon the risks associated with mixing politics and selfcraft. But are the risks great enough to convince those pursuing autonomy or perfection to keep their demands out of the public realm? Do these risks present good reasons for adopting public self-restraint and private self-creation?

The answer to this question depends upon the risk that seems to accompany the incorporation of selfcraft into statecraft. Rorty believes that that risk is enormous: justifying public action on the basis of a particular conception of the self, or upon a notion of a healthy soul, or upon an ideal of autonomy starts us down the road toward total revolution. For Rorty, the risk is large because those who are concerned with the character or ordering of the self or soul are attempting to impose their own understanding of personal perfection on the rest of society. But this portrayal is not entirely accurate. It is, of course, true that the critics of liberalism as well as those advancing autonomy and authenticity, do have preferred conceptions of the self or soul. Nevertheless, those conceptions remain entwined in much of the liberal project. For example, none of the authors discussed here have advocated the dismantling of the kinds of rights and guarantees provided by the Bill of Rights in the Constitution of the United States. From what can be discerned in their writings, they do not seek to use the state to silence or censure alternative self-conceptions. Moreover, as we saw in chapter 5, liberals are themselves willing to trade some freedom for the pursuit of autonomy and the protection of agency. The only way to demonstrate that the risk is significant is to assess the political programs and desires of those who see statecraft as soulcraft. This kind of assessment is absent in Rorty's writings.

And there is still another problem in judging the risks of mixing selfcraft with statecraft. Rorty claims that liberals should not want people to take up publicly forms of discourse that redescribe others and portray what is important to them as futile or obsolete. The problem with this argument is that in Rorty's desire to keep this kind of language out, he opens up the liberal regime to the very charge he levels at many of its critics. Communitarians, classical political rationalists, and genealogists contend that liberal democratic culture does not keep these redescriptions successfully within the private realm. They see themselves as somehow redescribed by the public order. Classical political rationalists view liberal, public discourse as openly hostile to a notion of human excellence. Communitarians perceive liberal democratic politics as undermining essential kinds of communities and forms of unity. And finally, genealogists see the prevailing order as naturalizing and disciplining whatever differences they happen to embody. In one way or another, classical political rationalists, communitarians, and genealogists could argue that the kind of cruelty that Rorty believes their own positions have the potential to create is actually being cultivated if not enacted by liberal democratic institutions. The thrust of the critics' arguments is that the prevailing political and cultural discourses are already highly intrusive. More importantly, the vocabulary that liberal political theorists have devised over the past few centuries is not, in fact, neutral regarding certain self-understandings. Indeed, the critics claim that this vocabulary depreciates their own self-images.

The risks associated with mixing selfcraft and statecraft are not necessarily significant enough to justify excluding selfcraft from politics. The potential for moral cruelty should not exclude concerns of identity from either the public or private sphere. Furthermore, the claim that the present set of political and social arrangements already favors certain self-conceptions over others weakens the argument that it is more prudent to preclude than permit selfcraft. The desire to preclude moral cruelty in politics is an insufficient basis for precluding selfcraft.

Cutting off the Conversation

Aside from drawing upon the liberal hatred of cruelty, Rorty offers another way to justify excluding certain issues from our theoretical and political discourse. The basis of this argument is that there are limits to how far one has to go when conducting a conversation. Rorty believes that after a certain point, even liberal democrats are justified in cutting off an exchange. This termination, he argues, seems to be justified vis à vis those who argue that the kinds of persons cultivated by liberal democracies are objectionable. Rorty uses various reasons to support such a cutoff: one concerns the nature of the opponent; another entails Rorty's desire to push the conversation beyond the philosophical concerns of the self. In general, he argues that liberal political theory and practice can avoid philosophical controversies surrounding the self.

Evading the critics by simply cutting off the conversation seems rather drastic, if not illiberal. Indeed, Rorty admits that this strategy places liberals in a dilemma:

> To refuse to argue about what human beings should be like seems to show a contempt for the spirit of accommodation and tolerance, which is essential to democracy. But it is not clear how to argue for the claim that human beings ought to be liberals rather than fanatics without being driven back on a theory of human nature, on philosophy. I think that we must grasp the first horn. We have to insist that not every argument needs to be met in the terms in which it is presented. Accommodation and tolerance must stop short of a willingness to work within any vocabulary that one's interlocutor wishes to use, to take seriously any topic that he puts forward for discussion. (Rorty 1991a, 190)

Before discussing why Rorty believes that we should grasp the first horn of the dilemma, we should note that he may not be holding it very firmly himself: Rorty is a writer fully engaged in the philosophical debates of his time. Moreover, he occasionally leaps into other vocabularies and values multiple and diverse discourses. Rorty argues that such gestalt switches improve our ability to see and expand our self-understandings. Indeed, "leaping" may be the best one can do when confronted by a different vocabulary. Rorty is explicit about this: "We do have a duty to talk to each other, to converse about our views of the world, to use persuasion rather than force, to be tolerant of diversity, to be contritely fallibilist" (67).

Having said this, Rorty has also branded as mad or fanatical the positions of some of liberal democracy's opponents. As examples, Rorty uses Nietzsche and Ignatius Loyola. Both are fanatics because they would be unwilling to sacrifice their personal accounts of perfection for public expediency. Nietzsche expresses this in his disdain for liberal democracy and Loyola in his willingness to subsume all aims under one conception of the good.[8] Rorty argues, "one imagines these two rejoining that they are quite aware that their views unfit them for citizenship in a constitutional democracy and that the typical inhabitant of such a democracy would regard them as crazy. But they take these facts as further counts

[8] Rorty picks this argument up from Rawls. In referring to Loyola, Rawls writes, "Although to subordinate all our aims to one end does not strictly speaking violate the principles of rational choice . . . it still strikes us as irrational, or more likely mad" (Rawls 1971, 554).

against constitutional democracy. They think that the kind of person created by such a democracy is not what a human being should be" (190). According to Rorty, the best response to this kind of charge is no response. This disregard seems especially appropriate if one's opponent is of a particular nature. For example, if one's opponent is like O'Brien, Winston Smith's torturer in George Orwell's *1984*, then one should not respond because O'Brien rejects the whole idea of being answered (Rorty 1989, 176). Refusing to speak may be the best response to those who cannot be persuaded either through normal argumentation or through paradigmatic leaps. Even if one's opponent is not an O'Brien, but a Nietzsche or Loyola, however, one may still cut off the conversation because, after a certain point, there is nothing to exchange. Rorty argues that one can reach this conclusion "only after extensive attempts at an exchange of political views have made us realize that we are not going to get anywhere" (Rorty 1991a, 191). Only then may we conclude that there just is not enough "overlap . . . to make possible agreement about political topics, or even profitable discussion of such topics" (191). Rorty argues that liberals may find themselves in a genuine confrontation, in which there are "people whose beliefs on certain topics overlap so little with ours that their inability to agree with us raises no doubt in our minds about the correctness of our own beliefs" (30–31n.13). Rorty suggests that this is not a problem of untranslatability, "but simply a practical problem about the limitations of argument; it is not that we live in different worlds than the Nazis or the Amazonians, but that conversion from or to their point of view, though possible, will not be a matter of inference from previously shared premises" (30–31n.13).

In responding to Rorty's argument, it may be useful to distinguish between talking to thugs (O'Brien) and talking to theorists (Nietzsche and Loyola). In the case of thugs, breaking off the conversation may be a necessary part of action. If thugs are so defined because they seem willing to cause physical or psychological harm, spending time talking would clearly be less advantageous than preparing for what could come next (assuming one is not in Winston's helpless position). Or one may break off what little communication there is in order not to dignify one's adversary or because one wants to signal a seriousness of intent to stand one's ground. On the other hand, occasions may occur in which one may try to respond to thugs in order to buy time, or to demonstrate to the rest of the world a willingness to negotiate. In practice, how one responds to a thug, or to anyone who refuses fundamentally to be answered, depends upon the particular situation.

At the level of theoretical engagement, cutting off the conversation seems bizarre. This is not to say that every theorist must entertain every position and every possibility when considering any matter whatsoever. No one would argue that. There are, after all, limits to time and expertise, not to mention what publishers will publish and what audiences will read. Yet Rorty's argument is more demanding than the claim that one not reach beyond one's expertise or fatigue one's audience. Mere fatigue may require suspending a conversation, but not closing it down altogether. Rather, Rorty must be saying that liberal democratic theorists simply do not need to engage in dialogue where either agreement is impossible or discussion is unprofitable. Rorty believes that liberal democratic theory has reached this point with regard to positions claiming that liberal democratic culture produces a deeply objectionable kind of person. Nothing more can be said to the critics than what has already been said.

There are a number of obvious problems here. The first is that liberal democratic theorists are not of one mind in responding to these criticisms. For Rorty's argument to hold, there must be agreement that liberals of every stripe cannot conduct a reasonable conversation with any of the critics. Second, even if such agreement existed, it is not clear whether we have reached the end of dialogue or the limits of our own imaginations. How can one demonstrate that a point has been reached beyond which further conversation is impossible? If talking with a Jesuit is not like trying to read Etruscan, then it is unclear why one would ever close down the conversation. Third, at the level of theoretical inquiry, why would one even want to close off the possibility of conversation? Is there something that theorists should do that corresponds to war preparation when responding to thugs? Moreover, even if one claimed that people who attempted to subordinate all their aims under one end are mad, this characterization would not imply that somebody who reflected upon this submission was also mad. What may be mad in practice may be a legitimate consideration in theory. Finally, the idea of cutting off conversation when progress is deemed impossible implies that unless conversations are conducted in certain ways, they should not be conducted at all. This dictum violates the spirit of liberalism. To dismiss and ignore an adversary who has taken one to a draw in the *agon* is, at the very least, not very generous or liberal. Rather, liberalism would seem to call for quite a high level of respect and toleration at the level of theorizing. Rorty's first impulse is correct: grabbing the first horn of the dilemma does violate the liberal spirit of accommodation and tolerance.

The Irrelevance of Philosophy to Politics

The first argument we looked at for precluding selfcraft was based upon Rawls's understanding of the role of political philosophy. According to Rawls, because the role of political philosophy is to find a shared basis for political practice, controversial views of the self should be excluded. In contrast, Rorty rejects this role of political philosophy and argues that philosophy is largely irrelevant to politics. Rorty claims that liberal democrats have reached a point at which we can give priority to democracy over philosophy and still sustain and support the regime. Just as Western liberal societies in the past two hundred years have been able to move questions of whether there is one god or twenty off the political agenda, we should also move questions of whether we are petty, docile subjects with the "souls of tourists" out of discussion of political theory. Rorty sees Jefferson as offering a position in which "politics can be separated from beliefs about matters of ultimate importance—that shared beliefs among citizens on such matters are not essential to a democratic society" (175).[9] These matters, in other words, are simply irrelevant to both the theory and practice of democratic government. Even if all or most of us believed that there were twenty gods, we still would not need to appeal to such a belief in organizing or thinking about our political life. We can found democratic political institutions, discuss public policy, write legislation, as well as engage in social theory without philosophical backup.

The heart of Rorty's argument is that philosophy (as he uses the term) is no longer necessary to either the theory or the practice of liberal democracy. Rorty argues that liberal democracy does not rest upon philosophical consensus but upon practical agreement. We do not need philosophical backup to support society's central opinions and conventions: the rejection of slavery, the belief in religious toleration, the idea that justice is the first virtue of society, and the notion that freedom is a fairly significant social good. Rorty argues:

> Such a society will become accustomed to the thought that social policy needs no more authority than successful accommodation among individuals, individuals who find themselves heir to the same historical traditions and faced with the same problems. It will be a society that encourages the "end of ideology," that takes reflective equilibrium as the only method needed in discussing social policy. . . . For such a society will view such accounts [drawn from philosophical accounts of the self or of rationality] not as the foundations of political institutions, but as, at worst, philosophical mumbo jumbo, or, at best, relevant to private searches for perfection, but not to social policy. (184)

We do not need philosophical backup to engage in political practice because we twentieth-century liberals are content with what liberal democracy can provide. Citizens of liberal democracies, Rorty argues, can

---

[9] This position differs somewhat from that of Rawls and Larmore. Both argue that because questions regarding the nature of the self are not shared, they are disqualified as a basis for liberal democratic regimes. The implication of their positions is that if we did share beliefs on these matters, then they could form the basis for politics and political discussion. The implication of Rorty's position is that even if we shared these beliefs, they should still be separated from politics.

get along without the satisfaction that liberal democracy is the best of all possible regimes. Liberal democratic citizens will pay for, work for, and die for a regime whose reason for being rests upon nothing more than the values derived from their own history and culture.[10] As Rorty notes, much of practical political discourse gets along quite well without raising questions concerning selfhood and human nature.

Rorty's argument is that disputes over the self should be excluded from politics because they are unnecessary to the conduct of our political life. If by *unnecessary* Rorty means that people do not appeal to particular self-conceptions in justifying procedures and policies, he is wrong. Both critics and defenders of liberalism justify procedures and policies by appealing to particular conceptions of the self.[11] The existence of these positions conflicts with Rorty's portrayal of liberal democracy.

On the other hand, Rorty could be making a deeper claim about the relationship between liberal political theory and philosophical disputes over identity. Such a claim emerges most clearly in Rorty's antiessentialism. Since *Philosophy and the Mirror of Nature* (1979), Rorty has argued that knowledge is not a matter of getting reality "right," or having our language correspond to a world out "there." If this argument is convincing, then the critics of liberalism, for example, cannot claim that it has produced the wrong kind of human being. Philosophy is no longer necessary to liberal theory because philosophy as the pursuit of essences and forms can be abandoned. Whatever is the result of a large-scale, conflict-ridden, pluralistic, industrial, representative democracy cannot be said to be objectionable in the deep sense of not corresponding to what human beings really are. In other words, Rorty's antiessentialism erodes the deepest claims of those who wish to deploy critically the idea of the self: "It is no more evident that democratic institutions are to be measured by the sort of person they create than that they are to be measured against divine commands. It is not evident that they are to be measured by anything more specific than the moral intuitions of the particular historical community that has created those institutions"

---

[10] Clearly the problem with this statement by Rorty is that there may very well be certain metaphysical commitments that are a part of our historical and cultural values. Rawls openly acknowledges this possibility: "One might also say that our everyday conception of persons as the basic units of deliberation and responsibility presupposes, or in some sense involves, certain metaphysical theses about the nature of person as moral or political agents. Following the method of avoidance, I should not want to deny these claims" (Rawls 1985, 240n.22).

[11] Rorty's own candidate for this position is an understanding of the self as a centerless, socially constituted entity. He believes that this conception "does in fact comport better with liberal democracy than does the Enlightenment conception of the self" (Rorty 1991a, 178). In saying this, however, Rorty denies that a notion of the self is necessary to justify democracy.

(190). Insofar as the bases of those who advocate selfcraft are drawn from a "natural order of premises from which moral and political conclusions are to be inferred" (190), they are swept aside along with all other forms of representational thinking.

It is unclear, however, how far the antiessentialist argument goes. Even if philosophy is not up to the task of showing us a reality standing independently of human experience and language, we may still have to take arguments about the self seriously, although the antiessentialist argument diminishes the status of these disputes. Instead of arguing that their favored conception of the self is right—in the sense of corresponding to what human beings *really* are—antiessentialists can only claim that their conception of self better accords with all of the other assumptions and beliefs that we have about our selves. As Wittgenstein argues in his own approach to philosophy, antiessentialism leaves things pretty much the way they are. Rorty seems to recognize this when he says, "We pragmatists do not see the end of logocentrism or the death of God as requiring us to adopt a new self-image. For us, no argumentative roads lead from antiessentialist philosophy to the choice of such an image" (Rorty 1991b, 132). While Rorty takes antiessentialism as an abandonment of a "correct" conception of the self, we must abandon only the notion of correct as a form of correspondence.[12] This does not mean that the idea of correct as appealing to arguments, reasons, and beliefs also falls away.

Surpassing the Present Debate?

Perhaps realizing that his antiessentialism would not get him very far, Rorty offers another defense of the proposition that self-conceptions are unnecessary to theory. This defense is based upon Rorty's desire to surpass the current terms of philosophy. Rorty argues that his pragmatic position should distinguish itself "not by arguing against their answers, but against their questions" (Rorty 1991a, 52). Part of Rorty's reason for wanting to get beyond the present debate is clearly related to the above arguments regarding the dangers to the public realm that he believes this debate creates. Another part of Rorty's ground for leaving this debate behind is his belief that the quarrels that the big questions raise are just not very interesting anymore. These kinds of quarrels depend upon the use of "familiar and time-honored" vocabularies (Rorty 1989, 8). At best these disputes attempt to "show that central elements in that vocab-

---

[12] Rorty claims that to abandon the idea of a "correct" description of the self requires that the world and the self be de-divinized. This appears to be a good thing because, "both . . . have power over us—for example, the power to kill us" (Rorty 1989, 40).

ulary are 'inconsistent in their own terms' or that they 'deconstruct themselves.' But that can *never* be shown" (8). For Rorty, a more interesting philosophical approach is not to set out the "pros and cons of a thesis," but rather to abandon those vocabularies and do something else (9). What is interesting philosophy for Rorty is not normal science, to put it in Kuhnian terms, but those great paradigm shifts. Indeed, this dissatisfaction with normal science gives us a sense of Rorty's own strategy in responding to traditional philosophical debates: "So my strategy will be to try to make the vocabulary in which these objections are phrased look bad, thereby changing the subject, rather than granting the objector his choice of weapons and terrain by meeting his criticisms head-on" (44).

Abandoning the argument and trying to make one's opponents' vocabularies "look bad" is to try to outflank or end-run those criticisms. In Rorty's view this strategy of avoidance is an attempt to do more interesting philosophy. Rorty wants to push our discussions to the point where philosophers are no longer talking about certain issues. Just as our public behavior no longer turns upon the difference between *homoousios* (of the same substance) and *homoiousios* (of a similar substance), our theoretical debates should abandon issues of whether the self is essentially constituted by its relations with others or is contingently constituted by those relations. Although this is not meant to be an argument, it is meant to sway us. In quoting John Dewey, Rorty argues that "'intellectual progress usually occurs through sheer abandonment of questions together with both of the alternatives they assume—an abandonment that results from their decreasing vitality and a change of urgent interest. We do not solve them; we get over them'" (Rorty 1991a, 96n.2).

To encourage this overcoming, Rorty adopts a strategy of light-mindedness. He writes, "Moral commitment, after all, does not require taking seriously all the matters that are, for moral reasons, taken seriously by one's fellow citizens. . . . It may require trying to josh them out of the habit of taking those topics so seriously" (193). Joshing one's opponents and discarding the "'spirit of seriousness'—has been an important vehicle of moral progress" (194).

It is difficult to know how to respond to this kind of claim without being a wet blanket. Even attempting to respond seems to open oneself to the charge of being a metaphysician (that great "other" to Rorty's ironist): "The metaphysician thinks that there is an overriding intellectual duty to present arguments for one's controversial views—arguments which will start from relatively uncontroversial premises" (Rorty 1989, 78). But I believe that even if Rorty wants to surpass the old debates and arguments, his newfangled liberal theory still relies upon very old distinctions, such as between the public and private realms and between violence and persuasion, that will not go away and thus remain open to discussion and dispute. It is unlikely that even Rorty has successfully surpassed the present debate and circumvented the problem of selfcraft.

A Lockean Principle of Preclusion

Amy Gutmann and Dennis Thompson provide other arguments for precluding topics from politics. These arguments are gathered under what they call the Lockean principle of preclusion. Although Gutmann and Thompson do not articulate this principle with a view to selfcraft, we can still consider whether selfcraft would pass the tests included in the principle of preclusion and, more generally, whether the principle is itself convincing.

As set out by Gutmann and Thompson, the Lockean principle of preclusion establishes three criteria (Gutmann and Thompson call them premises) that an issue or position must meet if it is to be permitted into the political domain: it must be morally valid, it must entail matters with which the government can be trusted, and it must be subject to rational deliberation. If a position or issue fails to meet any one of these criteria then it is not an appropriate concern for politics. In order to establish whether an appeal to particular conceptions of the self would pass these conditions, it is necessary to explore what these premises entail.

Moral Validity

The first condition, that of moral validity, serves the function of a gatekeeper, establishing that about "which reasonable citizens might morally disagree" (Gutmann and Thompson 1990, 129). If a policy is not a valid moral position, then it should not be placed on the public agenda. This first condition, however, is rather complex. For whether a policy proposal is morally valid itself depends on three requirements: it must "presuppose a disinterested perspective," it must rest upon "generally accepted methods of inquiry" to support its empirical claims, and finally, it must avoid premises that are "radically implausible" (130). A failure to meet any one of these three requirements rules out a position as even prima facie moral and hence precludes it from politics.

Would the engagement in selfcraft pass these three requirements of moral validity? Gutmann and Thompson's first requirement entails that positions that are supported for purely self-regarding or self-interested reasons are neither disinterested nor moral (130). In other words, the arguments supporting soulcraft must have a certain generality to them. For the most part, the positions of the critics and defenders of liberal democracy who raise the issue of selfcraft seem to adopt such a perspective. Because their claims regarding the self or the soul are not merely prudential or self-regarding, it appears they would meet this first requirement of moral validity.[13]

The second requirement of the Lockean validity premise raises more difficult questions. This requirement would demand that the empirical arguments supporting soulcraft be "in principle open to challenge by generally accepted methods of inquiry" (130). There is no solid empirical evidence that liberal democratic culture and politics harms identity. Moreover, fairly complex empirical connections would have to be established for soulcraft to be defensible. Would these problems be enough to exclude soulcraft?

On the one hand, those who advocate selfcraft could argue that their positions are in principle "open to challenge." Whether they actually meet that challenge is a different matter and perhaps one that need not be met in order to satisfy this second requirement. If the second requirement requires that claims regarding selfcraft be open to challenge, then they clearly meet it.

On the other hand, there is a more demanding interpretation of this requirement. Under a stricter interpretation a position must already be backed up by solid empirical evidence before it enters the political realm. The basis for this more restrictive reading can be found in Gutmann and Thompson's discussion of why laws against homosexuality do not pass this condition. They argue that "the common claims that homosexual sex causes various kinds of harms have not been supported with solid empirical evidence" (133). In part, it is for this reason that such laws are seen to fail the test of moral validity. Even though positions advocating selfcraft are clearly open to challenge, it is similarly not clear that they are backed up by solid empirical evidence.

But this version of the requirement for empirical evidence is too demanding as it leaves open the problem of who should decide whether evidence is solid enough and it rules out of bounds political actions based upon partial or contestable evidence. Moreover, given the diffi-

---

[13] Even if these positions regarding selfcraft were purely self-regarding, however, it is not clear that they should be precluded from politics. This first requirement of moral validity suggests that moral disagreements are the only appropriate topics for political concern. Would decisions to fund and build a town pool, or establish price supports for corn, or deregulate the airline industry be necessarily moral issues? If these things were merely matters of competing interests, then the validity premise would keep them off the political agenda. Gutmann and Thompson's requirement of moral validity may itself be too stringent (Galston 1991, 114).

culties of predicting effects, the relevant, solid evidence emerges frequently only after the state has acted. If the state should not act before such evidence is available, then it may discourage a degree of experimentation.

Although selfcraft may not meet the requirement of solid empirical evidence, that requirement is too restrictive. The absence of such evidence may surely make us think twice about engaging in particular forms of selfcraft. But that merely means that such proposals should be, in principle, subject to challenge. The questionable character of such evidence should not be enough to exclude a matter from politics. To accept a more restrictive definition may have the effect of legitimizing technocratic guardians of the political domain.

The final requirement of moral validity may be more apropos for the problem of soulcraft. Under this requirement, "premises for which empirical evidence or logical inference is not appropriate should not be radically implausible" (130). Throughout this book I have expressed skepticism about what the critics and defenders take to be a preferred conception of the self or the soul. I do not argue that their notions of souls and selves are radically implausible, and although I acknowledge there is an opacity that accompanies aspects of our agency, I do not argue that this settles all questions regarding selves and souls. What I do show are the difficulties of publicly conveying a set of truths regarding the ordering and character of the self and using those beliefs to ground a generalizable claim of harm and political responsibility. Past chapters have not shown that defenders and critics of liberal democracy rely on radically implausible premises. Indeed, each camp possesses quite a bit of initial plausibility. This discussion of the three requirements of moral validity suggests that proposals raising the possibility of selfcraft could pass Gutmann and Thompson's first criterion of the Lockean principle of preclusion. Although questions can be raised about the stringency of the requirements that compose this first criterion, the issue of selfcraft does pass the hurdle of moral validity.

Governmental Trust and Rational Deliberation

Aside from moral validity, Gutmann and Thompson also argue that in order to be politically permissible, an issue must be one with which the government can be trusted. For example, they argue that the problem with allowing the state to legislate religious matters is that "it is just as likely to favor the false as the true religion" (128). Because of this possibility, they conclude (following Locke), that religion should not be legislated. Could one not say the same about soulcraft, namely, that the state is as likely to advance a false conception of the self as a true one?

This question presupposes that disputes over the self are similar to religious disputes. This presupposition is mistaken for two reasons. First, there is the difference in the form of harm implied by the two disputes. According to Locke, the harm that would result if the state imposed the wrong religion is damnation. To permit the state to legislate religious matters is to make heavenly salvation dependent upon one's place of birth. Framing the problem in terms of true versus false religion is convincing if one subscribes to the belief that adherence to the true religion leads to salvation. Indeed, this argument works only if one sees eternal life as an end that everyone seeks and its loss as a harm that everyone should avoid. The same kind of harm does not accompany the secular problem of selfcraft. Within certain broad parameters, it is not clear what getting the self "wrong" means because it is not clear what constitutes a harmful ordering of the self or soul.

The parallel between the establishment of a religion and the fostering of selfcraft falters for a second reason. Controversies over the character and ordering of the self do not generate the kinds of ruthless, antagonistic divisions that have historically accompanied religious controversies. There is no historical precedent of political power being divided along the lines of how many parts the soul or self possesses.[14] Because selfcraft has not raised the same kind of intense reaction, its entrance into politics may not have the same kind of tendency to destroy civil society. Advancing the "wrong" conception of the self does not have the same ramifications for politics as advancing the wrong religion.

Still, one can argue that this is merely a historical contingency. According to Rorty, to allow the problem of soulcraft into political life is to start down the road to totalitarianism. Even though there is nothing to correspond to the wars of religion with regard to selfcraft, there is, nevertheless, a great deal at stake in the attempt to craft selves. Because of these stakes, it is possible that those whose selfcraft was being implemented would never relinquish power and that those who disagree would never acquiesce. Soulcraft could generate resentment and intransigence. To avoid this problem, questions regarding selves and souls must be kept out of politics.

At least three obstacles can be placed on the road to totalitarianism. The first obstacle concerns the protection of agency. However selfcraft is

---

[14] In contrast, consider the virulence generated by religious disputes regarding the number of gods or the number and order of parts into which they should be divided, e.g., monotheists and polytheists, Manicheans and Christians, Arians and the Orthodox, Unitarians and Trinitarians.

conceived of in a liberal polity, it should guard our capacity to make choices, formulate projects, have desires, and so on. The conception of ourselves as agents is both a necessary condition for and a central value of liberal democracy. Political projects to mold the self like clay violate a fundamental liberal commitment to protect agency.

A second obstacle to totalitarian selfcraft is that a particular ordering or understanding of the self could not be engendered through direct political intervention. As Raz notes, "it is the special character of autonomy that one cannot make another person autonomous" (1986, 407). I differ from Raz in suggesting that this "special character" may also apply to such ideals as a diachronically united self, a reason-governed soul, a complex but connected identity, and an authentic self. In each of these cases, the self, soul, or subject is understood as something more than clay. Because these selves cannot be imposed, the most politics can do is provide the conditions that are either favorable or unfavorable to particular self-conceptions. In very general terms, selfcraft amounts to the creation of the conditions under which a particular view of the self could be cultivated. To use Galston's terminology, selfcraft would be a form of opportunity-oriented as opposed to conduct-oriented public policy (Galston 1991, 179). To the extent that the politics attempted to go beyond the establishment of an opportunity, it would encounter the first obstacle regarding the protection of agency.

A final obstacle to those who would use public institutions to encourage only one or a few self-conceptions inheres in institutional arrangements that facilitate the revision of policies of selfcraft. Given the absence of an obligation to engage in selfcraft, no form of selfcraft can be seen as an essential goal of liberal democracy. To prevent any form of selfcraft from being seen as essential, such policies should be revisable if not revocable. Clearly, the demand to revise or revoke a set of policies could find expression at many institutional decision points within liberal democracies: electoral politics, bureaucratic decision making, adjudication, executive orders, and legislation. Each of these institutions addresses the possibility for change differently. How claims for change should be made and what kinds of policies should follow from these claims are questions that depend upon time and place and theory may be of little help.

I am suggesting, then, that it is possible to trust government with certain forms of soulcraft that do not jeopardize rights, undermine agency, or depend upon radically implausible empirical claims. At the very least, government must be expected to protect agency from private and public interference. But it may also be trusted to provide the conditions, open to political adjustment and reconsideration, for particular conceptions of self. Along with these requirements, Gutmann and Thompson also argue that collective moral judgments must be a matter of rational deliberation. It is not clear, however, how this serves as a principle of preclusion. Perhaps the argument is that those who believe issues are to be decided by force should not have their positions placed on the public agenda. But why would such people want their positions placed before public judgment? More importantly, I have not argued that questions concerning soulcraft could not be subject to rational deliberation.

Although the Lockean principles of preclusion have problems (particularly with the meaning of the first and third premises), they do not exclude selfcraft decisively. In order to strengthen the case for soulcraft, however, empirical questions regarding the effects of policies would have to be more extensively and intensively considered. For the most part, these kinds of issues have been bracketed in this analysis. It may be the case that a permission to engage in selfcraft, at least under the Lockean principles, ultimately turns on their resolution.

Rawls and the Duty of Civility

The final argument that I will consider for excluding certain topics from public discourse is found in Rawls's *Political Liberalism*. Rawls argues there that public reason imposes certain limits on what we may talk about and appeal to in our public discourse. These limitations, he suggests, do not exclude "all political questions but only . . . those involving what we may call 'constitutional essentials' and questions of basic justice" (Rawls 1993, 214). These kinds of constitutional questions include concerns with voting rights, religious toleration, equality of opportunity, and property rights. When we try to decide who should vote, worship, or hold property, then our discourse should be limited to a shared, public conception of justice and not to what anyone sees as "the whole truth." With regard to certain procedures and substantive matters our intentions should be neutral.

Part of what could be seen as "the whole truth" are understandings of the character and ordering of the self or soul. Such views of the self should not be brought to bear in the discussion of certain political rights or essential constitutional matters. For example, a waiting period for abortions should not be justified as an attempt to foster autonomy by limiting freedom. Similarly, attempts by certain indigenous peoples to change residency requirements for voting should not be grounded upon a desire to protect their group authenticity. Rawls's notion of public reason appears to exclude such justifications. In these cases, "reasons given explicitly in terms of comprehensive doctrines are never to be introduced into public reason" (247).

It is important to note both the status and justification of this duty of civility. For Rawls, civility is a moral and not a legal duty (217). Violations of this duty should not trigger the coercive powers of the state. For example, this duty does not override the right to free speech, but is rather a matter of political self-restraint.

The justification for this duty of self-restraint is connected to how we legitimize the exercise of political power. According to Rawls, "our exercise of political power is proper and hence justifiable only when it is exercised in accordance with a constitution the essentials of which all citizens may reasonably be expected to endorse in the light of principles and ideals acceptable to them as reasonable and rational" (217). Once again we see Rawls appealing to what is shared. Because metaphysically controversial conceptions of selves and souls will not be seen by everyone to be reasonable and rational, they should be ruled out of deliberations about constitutional essentials; their disputed character prevents them from serving as grounds for political legitimacy.

Furthermore, it is important to note that in nonideal circumstances the duty does not exclude all appeals to metaphysically controversial conceptions and in an ideal setting the duty is redundant. Rawls argues that it is only in the ideal case that public reason will exclude all appeals to more comprehensive views of the world and our selves. Only in the well-ordered society are citizens not "stirred by any deep disputes," and have "no great interest in introducing other considerations" (248). But in this ideal case, there is no need to talk about a duty of civility—no need to refer to a *duty* in order to restrain discourse—because discourse would already be self-restrained.

To fill out his position, Rawls distinguishes between two nonideal cases that illustrate the variability of the duty of civility. Disputes in a "nearly well-ordered" society, where opposing groups do deploy comprehensive doctrines, Rawls argues that these groups should explain how their comprehensive doctrines support fundamental political values. It appears that as long as metaphysical or comprehensive doctrines are compatible with our deepest political values they can be included in public debate. Rawls's hope may be that, in the long run, people will put aside the need to appeal to larger belief systems and accept the justice of the given set of political values on its own. Even if this does not happen, however, it appears that comprehensive doctrines are acceptable as long as they can be portrayed as just.

In other words, in a nearly well-ordered regime the duty of civility is really a duty not to advance proposals and reasons that violate the two principles of justice. But this would appear to be part of the more general duty to justice that Rawls assumes. The duty of civility does not, in fact, preclude comprehensive doctrines as long as they affirm fundamental political values.[15]

Rawls's second nonideal case involves a society divided deeply over constitutional essentials. Here he employs as examples the abolitionist and civil-rights movements, where appeals were made to God's law against current social and legal practices. He argues that abolitionists and civil rights activists did not violate the ideal of public reason "provided they thought, or on reflection would have thought (as they certainly could have thought), that the comprehensive reasons they appealed to were required to give sufficient strength to the political conception to be subsequently realized" (251). In these examples we see that the problem is not with comprehensive doctrines as such, but with how they are held in relation to political values. These political values are not just because they are grounded upon a comprehensive doctrine, unless such an appeal is necessary to give sufficient strength to those political values. If one truly believes that political values must pass muster before a comprehensive doctrine, then that doctrine should not be advanced in public discourse. In certain circumstances, as an expedient that bolsters political values, turning to a comprehensive doctrine is acceptable. As a form of legitimation, it is not.

To what, then, does the duty of civility amount? First, it does not apply to ordinary, day-to-day political discourse. Although Rawls believes that it would be highly desirable if it did apply in such circumstances, he is primarily concerned with its application to fundamental political questions (215). Second, the duty of civility also rules out comprehensive doctrines that do not support constitutional values. Finally, it excludes judging constitutional doctrines against the demands of comprehensive doctrines unless those judgments are meant ultimately to strengthen political values.

When Rawls's duty of civility is put in terms of our immediate concerns it clearly permits soultalk in wide areas of political life. Unlike Rorty (as well as Larmore and Ackerman), Rawls would allow these considerations to enter into ordinary political discourse, precluding them only when they undermine constitutional principles. In other words, we should not appeal to particular conceptions of the self or soul to support programs that debilitate an essentially just constitution. The duty of civility bars judging the quality of fundamental political values and constitutional

---

[15] "Affirm," however, could mean a number of things. In its strongest sense, to affirm means to actively support. In a weaker sense to affirm could mean not to detract from or undermine. Thus, in the word's weaker sense, fairly wide appeals to particular conceptions of the self or soul could be rendered consistent with Rawls's conception of fundamental political values.

principles by their effects on our souls and selves, unless those judgments are meant to ultimately reinforce and strengthen just political
values. Without that strengthening motive, a conception of self should
not be used as a criterion in assessing political values.

Of the above prohibitions, a moral duty to refrain from advancing
conceptions of the self that would support unjust laws seems to follow
from a general duty to be just. This duty, of course, depends upon those
essential values and fundamental political principles meeting the demands of justice. If basic constitutional arrangements do not meet this
demand, then conceptions of the self (or comprehensive doctrines) can
be brought in only if one intends (or would intend, upon reflection) to
use them to strengthen appropriate political values.

The duty of civility may come down ultimately to a judgment of intentions. We should keep quiet if we believe that a just state is justified
because it ultimately serves our comprehensive doctrines. For example,
if we believed that the soul should be ordered in a particular way to
express human excellence, that belief could be deployed in a political
debate only if its end was to establish a just regime. Alternatively, if we
believed that what made a state just was its capacity to foster human
excellence, that would be prohibited by the duty of civility.

This duty is applicable in only a limited set of circumstances. It seems
to operate fully only during constitutional crises. But even within these
situations, the duty is moral and not legal. Given its limited, weak character, is the duty problematic?

One problem is that the duty is meant to preclude arguments that
reject just constitutional arrangements on the basis of larger truths and
doctrines. In order to prevent people from being provoked to repudiate
a well-ordered society for such reasons, Rawls is willing to exclude arguments for a just set of political arrangements based on comprehensive
values. The trouble with this tradeoff is that those who are rejecting a just
set of arrangements on the grounds of larger truths are also going to be
impervious to a duty of civility. The duty has the chance of being effective only for those who support a just regime on the basis of its service to
larger truths. But instead of accepting their support, the duty of civility
chastises them for relying upon inappropriate reasons. For example, to
the extent that Martin Luther King, Jr., actually believed that "just law is
a man-made code that squares with the moral law or the law of God," he
was being unreasonable. King and his supporters were not merely mistaken in appealing to God's law, they were being uncivil.

In other words, those whom Rawls would most want to be self-restrained will be unconvinced by the argument for such a duty, and those
who would back the regime may be alienated by it. If the ultimate goal is
to garner support for a just regime, the duty of civility may have the

opposite effect. The terms "unreasonable" or "uncivil" would themselves escalate the temperature of the rhetoric.

Second, the duty of civility seems to be unworkable in connection with a wide variety of legal and social issues that can, very easily, be portrayed as fundamental. Abortion, euthanasia, surrogate motherhood, the ownership of genetic innovations, and animal rights involve controversial scientific, moral, and metaphysical questions. A highly rarefied public reason would leave these questions dangling in an unaddressable state. Rawls's response is that public reason is complete: we need not appeal to anything outside its bounds to settle constitutional issues. But without evidence that public reason is complete, Rawls's position appears unduly optimistic.

Third, the duty of civility may be not only impractical but undesirable. From a Millian perspective, allowing reasons, whatever their character, their day in court serves a variety of purposes. On the one hand, permitting comprehensive doctrines in public debate leaves open the possibility that a noncontroversial comprehensive doctrine could be found. On the other hand, allowing such controversy reminds us that these doctrines are indeed controversial. Prohibiting reliance upon comprehensive doctrines may also foster greater adherence to them. Whereas calling those who appeal to such doctrines uncivil or unreasonable may alienate such individuals, allowing these doctrines into political discourse could function as a safety valve. Even given its limited character, we should not adopt Rawls's duty of civility to preclude certain kinds of appeals in political discourse.

This discussion of liberal neutralism leads to the following conclusions. First, the argument that political practice should either have no effect or the same effect upon different conceptions of human identity is not only too demanding, but would require that concerns of the self enter into political discourse. Second, the idea that our theorizing about liberalism should exclude controversial views of the self makes sense only if we accept the controversial belief that theory should appeal only to what is shared. Third, neutrality of intent has been supported by a variety of claims: the appeal to what is shared, the avoidance of cruelty, the limits of conversations, the irrelevance of philosophy to politics, the desire to surpass the present debate, the requirement of moral validity, the problem of governmental trust, and the duty of civility. None of these arguments successfully precludes selfcraft. In light of these conclusions, neither of the dominant ways for dealing with the problem of selfcraft is convincing. Those who argue that we should judge the quality of politics by its effects on our selves and those who argue that such judgments are inappropriate are both mistaken. At best, these approaches possess only part of what is necessary to sort out the problem of soulcraft. The liberal neutralists are correct in arguing that liberal democracies have no responsibility or obligation to engage in selfcraft. However, the critics and defenders are correct in believing that to exclude these judgments from politics completely is unwarranted. A more defensible solution, combining these two elements, is that liberal democracies have a qualified permission to engage in soulcraft.

8

A Permission to Cultivate the Self

BEHIND THE LIBERAL NEUTRALISTS' attempt to preclude selfcraft from politics is a fear of dissolving the private into the public. If not merely the personal but the person is political, then what space is left to protect from the collective, unwanted intrusions of others? For those who seek to establish a political responsibility to engage in selfcraft, the problem looks very different. To the extent that this culture deforms or misrecognizes us, we risk losing or mistaking the very point of our lives. Surely there must be a political responsibility to abate if not avoid such harms?

I have argued that we should be suspicious of both of these claims. The basis for this suspicion is twofold. First, the case for a political obligation or responsibility to mitigate or cultivate particular forms of selfcraft is overdrawn. Second, the attempt to justify the total exclusion of selftalk from politics and theory is unsuccessful. This does not, however, also imply that we should deny the importance of the self to political judgments. Nor does it mean that we should ignore the risks of fusing the public with the private. Between the dominant positions of the debate over the politics of the self, there may be just enough room to talk about a qualified permission to engage in selfcraft. The qualified character of the permission emanates from the fears raised by liberal neutralists. The actual existence of the permission arises from the absence of either an obligation or a prohibition to engage in selfcraft. In other words, claims regarding selves and souls should be allowed to enter politics.

What's at Stake?

Before examining the justification for a permission to engage in selfcraft, it may be useful to consider briefly what this permission would entail in practice. In chapter 7, I argued that our intentions in the formulations of policies and programs need not be neutral vis à vis competing conceptions of the self. In light of the failure of the neutrality argument, a permission would mean that policies could be justified and pursued in the attempt to foster particular conceptions of the self or soul. For example, representatives should be able to pass laws in the belief that they will encourage community, reason, respect for difference, authenticity, or autonomy. Citizens should be permitted to support candidates and causes in the belief that particular forms of soulcraft will be advanced. More specifically, the wishes of the people or their representatives should not necessarily be deemed inappropriate, illiberal, or unacceptable solely because they are based upon controversial ideas of the self or soul. A legislator would not violate the basic tenets of liberalism by advocating an education bill (say to subsidize storybooks for a Headstart program) in the belief that it will cultivate more authentic, autonomous, or reason-governed adults. Citizens would not act inappropriately by supporting candidates who attempt to encourage greater participation in politics or who wish to diminish economic inequalities in the hope that it will cultivate a shared communal identity. The justification for policies and laws need not preclude the terms of self-development or creation.

I also suggested that selfcraft could try to establish the conditions for the cultivation of particular self-conceptions. Public policies could be opportunity oriented in the sense of providing a conducive environment for the development of particular conceptions of the self. To the extent, however, that a form of soulcraft entails an attempt at branding or brutal imposition, it would violate the obligation of the state to protect agency and freedom. In general, the permission to engage in selfcraft is framed by the larger obligations and responsibilities that define a liberal democratic regime. A response to the perceived effects of liberalism should not run roughshod over the rights and liberties associated with liberal society. Protecting or providing the opportunities for cultivating diverse self-conceptions is probably as far as a permission to engage in selfcraft could extend. In other words, citizens and representatives are not ultra vires when introducing conceptions of the self or the soul into politics.

Finally, it is important to note that in any given situation all sorts of reasons (other than the protection of civil liberties and agency) may prevent soulcraft from being a state concern: resources may not be available; the opportunity costs may be too high; institutional support may be lacking; the program itself may be perceived as ineffectual; the causal connection between policy and identity may be dubious. Some of these problems bear directly upon the ends that a policy of soulcraft could pursue. Others are related to its implementation. It is unclear, however, whether theory can sort out the details of which programs should be implemented. To say that a concern with soulcraft could get this far, however, is to say that these kinds of policy disputes are within the general purview of liberal democratic practice. A permission to engage in soulcraft, however, does not guarantee against impolitic, imprudent, or irresponsible proposals.

The justification for a permission to engage in this conditional form of selfcraft is largely implicit in the previous chapters. In order to make this justification explicit, I will consider four general arguments that are part of the earlier discussions. The first argument is that the permission to consider questions of selfcraft is upheld by the general freedoms and procedures associated with liberal democracy. The second argument is that this permission is implied by the logic of rejecting prohibitions and obligations to engage in selfcraft. The third reason in favor of selfcraft follows from the impossibility of devising procedures and policies that have neutral effects vis à vis differing conceptions of the self. The final argument is that the difficulties of identifying harm in matters of the ordering of the self open space for a permission.

Rights and Procedures

The first argument appeals to the rights and procedures that are generally associated with liberal democracy. The values implied or suggested by those practices do, at least, initially favor selfcraft. When we look at the kinds of procedures and constitutional arrangements that are part of liberal democracies, we find neither attempts to exclude self talk from politics, nor explicit prohibitions for state action based upon such talk. An equally important omission is the absence of state obligations to cultivate a particular conception of the self. This is not to say that selftalk is absent from our political life. After all, we set out standards for mental competence, support education in the desire of improving our children, and send criminals to prison in the hopes of reform. But these explicit and implicit concerns with the self are given expression within a larger set of rights and procedures. For example, a public expression of the importance of autonomy, authenticity, communal identity, the place of reason, and the respect for difference is protected (at least in the United States) by a guarantee of free speech. Furthermore, the notion of a government of and by the people implies a set of procedures that are sensitive to their opinions and demands. Assuming these demands do not violate the rights of other individuals, the desire to cultivate particular conceptions of the self or respond to policies that are seen as harmful to one's self should have their chance in the political process.

The argument that the institutional character of liberal democracy supports a permission to engage in selfcraft can be challenged on the basis of its adequacy. For the problem of selfcraft is not merely a problem of whether we should judge the quality of politics by its effects upon our selves. Historically, it has also included the question of whether a particular kind of person is necessary to establish a particular kind of regime.

These two concerns are not unrelated: the issue of prerequisites can affect whether the engagement of soulcraft is merely a permission. If liberal democracy rests upon a particular ordering of the self or soul, then the survival of the regime would require the cultivation of that self-conception. If the regime is itself worthy of being sustained, then to talk of a permission is much too weak.

For the most part I have focused upon the effects of a regime upon our selves as opposed to whether a particular kind of self is a prerequisite for liberal democracy. The question of prerequisites, however, has made a brief appearance in my discussion of agency. There I argued that although agency is a prerequisite for politics, it is not something that politics can create. Furthermore, I have also argued that to the extent that agency can itself be fostered, it gives rise to competing conceptions of what constitutes a better chooser.

Of the positions I have considered in the previous chapters, it is not clear that Bloom's reason-governed soul, Taylor's conception of authenticity, or Benn's idea of autonomy is a necessary condition for liberal democracy. The citizenry in a liberal democracy need be neither autonomous nor authentic. The formal nature of autonomy and the rarefied quality of authenticity indicate that neither could serve as a necessary condition for this kind of regime. Aside from these general comments, the claim that a particular form of selfcraft is needed to sustain liberal democracy is an empirical question that cannot be broached fruitfully without a great deal more evidence. It may very well be the case, however, that questions concerning deep psychic prerequisites for a regime may go the way of religious prerequisites. Arguments that Christianity is incompatible with civic virtue, that Catholics and Jews have sovereign allegiances elsewhere, that atheists cannot be trusted to uphold their oaths, have all fallen away (at least in liberal societies). Without serious evidence linking particular orderings or configurations of the self or soul to liberal democracy, these arguments for soulcraft will remain deeply disputed.

Obligations, Prohibitions, and Permissions

A second argument in favor of a permission for selfcraft is implied by the following logic: that which is neither prohibited nor obligatory is permitted. In much of this book I have responded to those who advocate a political responsibility to engage in or respond to forms of selfcraft, likewise to those who would insulate politics from the whole issue. The juxtaposition of these two arguments implies that space still exists for the state to engage in selfcraft.

The strict logic behind a permission seems to work only if "prohibitions," "obligations," and "permissions" exhaust the possibilities. But perhaps the alternatives are not as stark as I have portrayed them. There are, after all, many things that we are legally permitted to do, but that we still should not do. Similarly, we possess a variety of moral obligations that are not legally or politically enforced. For example, although we can act ill-manneredly and rudely within the confines of the law, we ought not to do so. Moreover, we should be fair and trustworthy in our personal relations, although these are not necessarily legal obligations. In light of such examples, selfcraft may entail a similar kind of moral prohibition or obligation. For example, Rawls's duty of civility involves a moral prohibition against bringing certain matters into politics. As we have seen, Rawls does not see this as a legal duty, enforceable through state action. Instead he is arguing that it is simply inappropriate to bring comprehensive doctrines into the political realm. Similarly we can ask whether we should view selftalk as a form of politically tolerated but morally inappropriate behavior.

To adopt the last line of reasoning inevitably raises the question of why selftalk is morally inappropriate. As we have seen, the answers offered by the liberal neutralists—that selfcraft is deeply divisive, necessarily cruel, and imprudent—are unconvincing. Indeed, liberals have not argued successfully for a blanket prohibition against selfcraft. And, if they are propounding a weaker, fallback moral prohibition, they must still offer an argument. The basis for this fallback position has yet to be expounded.

A similar problem accompanies attempts to formulate a moral obligation to engage in selfcraft. One example of this kind of obligation can be found at the end of the discussion of authenticity in chapter 6 where I discussed whether there was a general obligation for the state to do whatever it can to cultivate this ideal. The problem with this formulation of the obligation to cultivate one form of the self is that it still excludes competing conceptions of the self. Certain views of the self are mutually exclusive. This can be seen not only in the alternatives to authenticity, but also in the other self-conceptions we have encountered. For example, the highly unified ideal of the self offered by communitarians directly conflicts with the fragmented version offered by Parfit. The reason-governed soul of the classical political rationalists runs headlong into a soul governed by faith or desire. The performative, inexhaustible self of the genealogists obviously conflicts with the earlier two schools. One couldn't devise a weaker moral obligation to cultivate mutually exclusive self conceptions without the obligation being self-defeating. On the other hand, without being able to show the superiority of one view of the self over the other, a moral obligation to advance any of these conceptions is too demanding. If there is a moral obligation to engage in selfcraft it is part of a larger, more general obligation that a democratic state possesses in taking seriously the claims of its citizens. In light of my earlier arguments, if no one is interested in judging politics on the basis of what it does to their selves, then the state would have an obligation to respect that disinterest.

Neutrality of Effect and Revision

A third justification for a permission for selfcraft is linked to the claim that liberal regimes inevitably affect the character and ordering of our selves or souls. We encountered this claim not only in the discussion of the critics, but in the discussion of neutrality of effect. The critics, of course, argue that this regime inevitably cultivates and forges a particular set of (objectionable) identities. Similarly, no liberal neutralist believes this regime is without impact on alternative self-conceptions, nor that it has equally advantageous (or burdensome) effects upon all. Paradoxically, all sides agree that whatever social and political practices we devise, some conception of the self will be perceived as advantaged or disadvantaged. Despite this agreement, where the critics want a politics that faces up to its consequences to the self, the liberal neutralists want a politics in which those consequences have no public salience.

If the liberal method of avoidance fails and if neutrality of effect is impossible to obtain, then perhaps the best that can be done is to provide people with an opportunity to change policies and practices they find incompatible with their self-conceptions. The absence of a neutrality of effect points to a permission to provide relief to those who object to the effects of the current policies and procedures. The absence of neutrality of effect also points to the conditions under which that permission should be realized. As a serious response to intentional or inadvertent forms of selfcraft, the democratic process should be open to alternative conceptions of the self or soul. If the procedures are not open, then a permission to engage in selfcraft is no more than a permission to engage in some forms of selfcraft and not others.

This permission is connected to the accessibility of political procedures to alternative self-conceptions. This understanding of the permission raises two problems. The first concerns its implications for how we understand those "open" or "accessible" procedures. If the problem is an absence of neutrality of effect, the solution appears to rely upon procedures that are neutral vis à vis those alternative self-conceptions. In other words, does a permission to engage in selfcraft reinsert an appeal to neutrality? The second problem concerns the political reality of liberal democracies, a reality in which accessibility appears to be lacking for a variety of self-understandings. Does a permission to engage in selfcraft set a standard that liberal practice does not (and perhaps cannot) meet?

Are open, accessible political procedures also covertly neutral? Once again, the answer depends upon what we mean by neutrality. The issue at hand points to a form of neutrality in which procedures do not discriminate against inputs on the basis of their content. Surely open and accessible procedures must be neutral in terms of how they treat inputs. For example, a majoritarian-decision procedure will obviously be less favorable to minority positions (or it may yield no determinative outcome), but the procedure itself is neutral if it does not predetermine which proposals or policies are decided upon or placed on the agenda. In the case of selfcraft, political procedures are open and accessible if they do not themselves predetermine which self-conceptions are going to win out.

Should political procedures be neutral with regard to all self-conceptions? Given the importance of agency, a strong case could be made that not all self-conceptions should be placed on an equal footing. Because the destruction or abridgment of agency is a serious harm, procedures that filtered out harmful forms of selfcraft would be justified. To some extent, this could be accomplished by protecting a wide range of rights and liberties. By protecting freedom, one also prevents things such as torture, classical conditioning, lobotomies, or brainwashing. Although a tamperproof filtering mechanism is not possible, a number of institutional mechanisms do militate toward impartiality and freedom. For example, legislators, administrators, and executives filter proposed items for the agenda as they interpret constitutional documents and attempt to protect rights and liberties. Under most liberal democratic systems filtering can also come at the end of the legislative process through legal challenges. Given the importance of protecting agency, the political process need not treat neutrally every proposal for selfcraft.

The notion that political procedures should be open and accessible to competing forms of selfcraft is, at best, an ideal bounded by the obligation to protect agency and liberty. It is also, however, an ideal given the fact that the choice of procedures can itself dictate outcomes. What cannot be approved in a consensus system may be approved in a majoritarian system. In cases of voting cycles, who gets to structure the decision process may also get to control the results. As with any program or policy, forms of selfcraft may win or lose given the ability of individuals or groups to dictate the decision procedure itself. The potential for manipulation, however, does not mean that we should give up on the idea that procedures should be open and accessible. Rather, it means that we have to listen closely to those who argue that a given set of rules and procedures systematically penalizes particular self-understandings.

To a certain extent, the critics do argue just this: liberal politics are systematically biased against particular conceptions of the self. Critics claim that liberal politics are mired in forms of selfcraft that are extremely difficult to change. Contemporary democracies too easily freeze out some self-understandings while elevating and reifying others. The ability to revise or rescind policies and programs that one believes are affecting one's self adversely is largely nonexistent in practice. For the most part, alternatives are crushed by prevailing self-understandings. To focus upon the idea of a permission is to ignore this reality of liberalism.

This charge must be clarified before it can be answered. Very generally, it could mean either that the regime (broadly understood) stigmatizes people and discourages them from expressing alternative self-conceptions, or it could mean that the regime fails to cultivate these alternatives. These two interpretations, although related, are distinguishable. Under the first interpretation the emphasis is less on selfcraft and more on freedom, for it implies that the regime is impeding people from doing something that they want to do. The question then becomes whether those barriers to freedom are justified. If they are unjustified, then the regime has a responsibility to hinder those hindrances. In the absence of a right to a particular conception of being, the fact that what one wants to do is connected to a deeper self-conception may have very little relevance. Liberal regimes still have an obligation to protect freedom and hence to protect the freedom to actualize a particular self-conception.

For our purposes, the more interesting question is whether liberal institutions are failing to cultivate a particular mode of being that some desire. If this is what is at issue, then a further clarification is required. The failure to advance one's own preferred form of soulcraft may be a systemic failure or it may be part of the contingencies of politics. If the claim is that there are institutions that exclude completely or are slow to respond to perfectly legitimate preferences, alternative institutional mechanisms must be invented. For example, Foucault attempts to show how central institutional structures (prisons, classrooms, workplaces, clinics) systematically reinforce certain self-understandings and penalize others. If the claim cannot be made that these marginalized self-understandings require urgent relief (i.e., that there is a serious harm being perpetrated), then the best response to these institutions is to offer alternatives that provide greater possibilities for augmentation and revision. To have any teeth, charges of systemic institutional biases must presuppose and offer better ways to live up to the demand of responsiveness. But, of course, the capacity for change is never going to be the only desideratum. Institutions have other functions and purposes. The concern will always be a matter of balancing the ability to revise policies with other aims, such as efficacy.

As the earlier discussion implied, a system with majoritarian features will not result in equally advantageous or burdensome outcomes. Conceptions of the self that are in the minority are going to have a difficult time advancing their preferred conception of the self or soul. By failing to accord special urgency to these claims (e.g., through the notions of moral or legal rights), this position appears to leave such individuals with little more than the refrain, "That's politics." Although a variety of institutional mechanisms may empower such individuals (representation, federalism, separation of powers, local autonomy, the intensive petitioning of the government), there can be no guarantee that all claims will ever be satisfied. Majoritarian democracy does not guarantee neutrality of effects. Hopefully, a failure of the political regime to advance one conception of the self or another is political in the sense that one is not prohibited from advancing one's cause another day. The character of the permission, with its emphasis upon revision, suggests that neither a win nor a loss should ever be total or complete. But this may be nothing more than a reminder of how politics should be conducted in liberal democracies.

Moral Harm and the Setback of Interests

A final argument supporting the permission to engage in selfcraft can be drawn out of the discussion that dominates much of this book: in most cases we have no clear sense of what constitutes a harmful ordering or understanding of the self. If we had a defensible conception of harm regarding these matters, then the case for prohibiting harmful views of the self or cultivating preferred conceptions would also be strengthened. We are not completely at sea in our understanding of harm. In chapter 6, I argued that we have good reasons for prohibiting actions that would deprive or diminish agency, being harmed if our capacity to choose is impaired or destroyed. The permission to engage in selfcraft is, as I have noted all along, bounded by an obligation not to deprive persons of agency. Within this boundary, however, the idea of harm loses its footing. Consequently, the argument that we have no more than a permission to engage in selfcraft is connected to the unsettled (and perhaps unsettleable) character of harm in these matters.

Joel Feinberg's study of the moral limits of criminal law provides one way to redescribe and challenge my argument. Within his study, Feinberg discusses four senses of "harm," the first of which he dismisses, finding it largely derivative because it applies to objects and things (e.g., "frost does harm to crops"). A second sense of harm is also derivative, but it possesses elements that are important to what Feinberg means by causing harm. This view refers to the violation of distinct rights or duties and, Feinberg notes, can be encompassed more readily under "wrongs" instead of harm (e.g., trespassers may "harm" a property owner's rights even though they may improve the land).[1] The third and most important view portrays harm "as the thwarting, setting back, or defeating of an interest" (1984, 33). He goes on to define interests as "all those things in which one has a stake" (34). The fourth and final view of harm is moral harm. Feinberg writes that "no doctrine was more central to the teachings of Socrates, Plato, and the Stoics than the thesis that a morally degraded character is itself a harm quite independently of its effect on its possessor's interests" (66). Feinberg restricts his discussion of harm primarily to the third sense and wholeheartedly and abruptly rejects the idea of moral harm.

Feinberg's typology offers an opportunity to formulate my argument in a different way. Although the translation is not perfect, many of the critics of liberalism allege what Feinberg calls "moral harm." For example, similar to a morally degraded character, communitarians see a fragmented, divided self, and classical political rationalists see an ignoble, desire-driven soul. Even Connolly's writings suggest harm is implied by a failure to be open to whatever life exceeds our identities. Like Feinberg, I question the validity of the notion of moral harm. Unlike him, however, I do not reject the notion entirely, but see it as depending upon a clear and credible view of what an unharmed self or soul looks like. In the absence of such a view, arguments based upon moral harm will be unconvincing. Because the critics fail to offer such a conception, their respective understandings of moral harm also fail.

Feinberg's typology not only sets out a conception of moral harm, but also challenges implicitly the comprehensiveness of what I have taken to be harm. For Feinberg, moral harm is neither the only nor the most defensible understanding of harm. Because harm can also be defined as a setback to interests, rejecting the claim of moral harm may not settle the matter of selfcraft. It is possible that the critics' claims can be reformulated as a setback to interests. Feinberg himself suggests that if one has a stake in the improvement of one's character, then a setback to that improvement could be understood as a harm (69–70). A failure to realize a particular conception of one's self is a harm only if one has an interest or a stake in this matter.

It is certainly the case that communitarians, classical political rationalists, genealogists, and some liberals think we have a stake in how their selves, souls, and subjectivity are ordered and understood. Although many in these schools would find it peculiar to talk about having a stake

---

[1] Feinberg goes on to note that "there *can* be wrongs that are not harms *on balance*, but there are few wrongs that are not *to some extent* harms" (1984, 35).

in one's self or soul, this formulation does present a challenge to my argument.[2] For it is a plausible reformulation of the argument that practices and policies thwarting the realization of one's preferred self-conception are harmful. This reformulation seems to reopen the question of whether the state does not, after all, have an obligation to address these claims of harm.

Let us begin by conceding Feinberg's definition of harm as a setback to interests and agreeing that people can have a stake in how their selves are ordered. These concessions, however, do not necessary lead to an obligation on the part of the state to mitigate or engage in selfcraft. As Feinberg himself notes, simply because one's interests have been set back does not mean that the behavior that caused the harm should be regulated or prohibited. Some harms can occur when we knowingly engage in risky behavior (e.g., breaking a leg when skiing) or participate in a competitive practice in which someone's interest is going to be set back (e.g., the market). We may also harm ourselves (e.g., give up on a project) or consent to sacrifice our interests for others. These kinds of harms fall into the category of wrongless harms.

The fact that not all harms are wrongs is important to Feinberg's central project of discerning the moral limits of the criminal law. He is concerned with formulating a principle that would help guide lawmakers in deciding whether to criminalize conduct. Feinberg argues that wrongless harms should not be subject to statutory prohibitions. In contrast, a wrongful harm constitutes a good (although not sufficient) reason for prosecution under a criminal statute. Wrongful harms require more than a setback of interests; they also require that A intentionally, negligently, or recklessly acted in a morally indefensible manner such that B's rights are violated (105–6). Even though Feinberg's notion of *wrongful harm* is meant to guide criminal law, it may also serve as a tentative way to guide the discussion over an obligation to engage in selfcraft.

Feinberg's distinction between acceptable and unacceptable setbacks of interests is important. Although we shall see that his formulation of a wrongful harm may not be directly applicable to the question of discerning a state responsibility to engage in or mitigate selfcraft, a consideration of whether a failure to realize one's preferred self-conception is a wrongful harm will help sort out these matters. On Feinberg's definition, such a failure could be considered a harm only if there was an iden-

[2] Part of the peculiarity may be that to have a stake in a particular self-conception seems to imply a degree of voluntariness that many of these positions would reject. But Feinberg's notion of interest extends beyond the goals and projects we may choose. It also includes a conception of a welfare interest, something that is shared by nearly everyone (37). As we shall see, the question then becomes whether a concern with one's self can be interpreted as a welfare interest.

tifiable A who unjustifiably violated a right of B to realize a particular self conception. We must consider not only whether concerns of selfcraft meet these prerequisites but also whether they *should* meet them.

An initial problem is that whereas a wrongful harm assumes some identifiable A as the cause of the harm, not all causes of harm to the self are linked to identifiable agents. It is true, of course, that the state or other institutions may play the role of just such an agent. Nevertheless, democratic cultural and social practices are also portrayed as impoverishing or misconstruing the self, and practices are not agents. We may wonder, then, whether the criminal law (or the law of torts, for that matter) is an appropriate model for our inquiry. The criminal law's preoccupation with blaming an identifiable agent, so necessary when we abridge liberties in order to prevent harm, may be inappropriate where the alleged sources of harm are amorphous norms and practices. At the very least, some adjustment is needed. Here I am less concerned with "who done it" and more concerned with whether there is a political responsibility to respond to the alleged harm. Identifying a culprit would be important only to the extent that it helped address the problem. The possibility that an obligation exists to take up the problem of selfcraft does not itself depend upon finding a specific agent who caused the harm.

A second adjustment is also required. Feinberg's notion of a wrongful harm necessitates that A's *actions* are morally indefensible. Because the identification of a causal agent is not a necessary condition for the form of state action with which we are concerned, we must convert the word "actions" into "effects." This means that we are less concerned with indefensible conduct (which would require a causal agent) than with unjustifiable effects. To put it another way, even if we admit that the effects of certain practices and politics are harms, can we justify their continuation? As we saw in the previous chapter, Rorty argues that liberals can justify the effects of liberalism upon our selves by providing a straightforward comparison of the benefits of the current arrangements with the costs of attempting to correct unfortunate effects upon ourselves. For Rorty, our characters are a good exchange for our freedoms. As I have mentioned earlier, it is not clear that this exchange is necessary. Nor is it clear that liberals, at least in practice, are never willing to contain freedoms in order to advance the ideal of autonomy. In general, we should be open to the possibility that these effects upon our selves are unjustifiable harms.

The final condition for Feinberg's notion of a wrongful harm is that A's action must violate a right that B possesses not to be treated in a particular way. Along with the claim that the harm be unjustifiable, the idea that one has a moral right to realize a particular conception of the self would also seem to be a necessary condition for a state obligation. The political responsibility to protect and cultivate a particular conception of our selves would, in part, turn upon such a right. Two ways exist to establish such a right, neither of which is successful. The first goes back to the notion of moral harm. The idea of a right to be autonomous, authentic, reason-governed, or unified would be strengthened if a convincing argument could be made for a moral harm in failing to realize any of these ideals. The difficulties in making that case, in turn, weaken the argument for a particular right to be something.

Feinberg, however, offers another way to support moral rights. He bases moral rights upon the idea of welfare interests. According to Feinberg, "welfare interests . . . are the grounds for valid claims against others (moral rights) *par excellence*. They are reasonable interests reasonably ascribed, if not to every person in the world without exception, at least to the standard person that must always be before the legislator's eye" (112). Included on his list of welfare rights are such things as physical health and vigor, the absence of obsessive pain, the absence of grotesque disfigurement, intellectual competence, emotional stability, economic sufficiency, a tolerable environment, and minimal political liberty (60). Could a particular view of the self or soul also be understood as a welfare right?

Whether one agrees with everything on Feinberg's list, none of those items is as controversial as the dispute over the correct view of the self, soul, or subject. The depth of disagreement over these matters suggests that a particular view of the self could not meet the criterion of generality that Feinberg sets out for a welfare interest. A welfare interest that was not general could hardly qualify as a welfare interest. Consequently, the second route for establishing a moral right also fails. Because the citizenry has no right to expect that a preferred self-conception should be fostered, there is no obligation or responsibility on the part of liberal democracies to cultivate a particular ordering of the self or soul.

It is possible to argue that people have a stake or interest in a particular conception of the self or soul. Moreover, insofar as those interests are set back through the intentional and unintentional policies and practices that comprise a liberal regime, those who have such interests are being harmed. This reformulation, however, does not then create an obligation upon the state to mitigate or rectify that harm. Even if the harm is unjustified, that does not mean that it entails a moral right to some political remedy. The case for an obligation is weak whether one sees harm as a setback to interests or in terms of moral harm.

Given the character of liberal democracy as well as the failure of obligations and prohibitions, the impossibility of neutral effects and the problematic character of harm, there *is* a permission to engage in selfcraft. It is important, however, to reemphasize that this permission is qualified in a number of respects. Questions regarding rights, implementation, empirical evidence, and causality must be dealt with before the state could pursue selfcraft as an opportunity-oriented policy. More generally, the permission is bounded by the requirement of protecting the capacity of agency and by the revisable character of such programs and policies. As democratic attempts to promote autonomy and group authenticity have shown, however, these heavy burdens can be carried. Still, this may be little comfort for those who believe that this regime produces an odious kind of person. Although the expression of that belief should not be excluded from politics, neither should it be accorded special weight in a democratic process. In other words, the absence of an obligation to judge the quality of our political life by its effects upon our selves or souls does not proscribe making those judgments. There is no theoretical reason why individuals should not vote for candidates or policies on the belief that it will encourage a particular kind of soulcraft. Nor is there sufficient a priori reason to prohibit representatives from justifying legislation in the hope that it will encourage some ideal ordering of the self. The problem of selfcraft must be left to the vicissitudes of politics.

References

Ackerman, Bruce. 1989. "Why Dialogue?" *The Journal of Philosophy* 86:5–22.

Alcoff, Linda. 1988. "Cultural Feminism Versus Post-Structuralism: The Identity Crisis in Feminist Theory." *Signs* 13:405–36.

Aristotle. 1976. *The Ethics of Aristotle.* Trans. J.A.K. Thomson. Harmondsworth: Penguin.

Austin, J. L. 1975. *How to Do Things with Words.* 2d ed. Cambridge, Mass.: Harvard University Press.

Barber, Benjamin. 1988. "The Philosopher Despot." *Harper's Magazine,* Jan., 61–65.

Barry, Brian. 1973. *The Liberal Theory of Justice.* Oxford: Clarendon Press.

Beiner, Ronald. 1990. "Hannah Arendt and Leo Strauss." *Political Theory* 18:238–54.

————. 1992. *What's the Matter with Liberalism?* Berkeley and Los Angeles: University of California Press.

Bellah, Robert, Richard Madsen, William M. Sullivan, Ann Swidler, and Steven M. Tipton. 1985. *Habits of the Heart.* New York: Harper & Row.

————. 1991. *The Good Society.* New York: Vintage.

Benn, Stanley I. 1975–1976. "Freedom, Autonomy and the Concept of the Person." *Proceedings of the Aristotelian Society* 76:109–30.

————. 1988. *A Theory of Freedom.* Cambridge: Cambridge University Press.

Berlin, Isaiah. 1969. "Two Concepts of Liberty." In *Four Essays on Liberty.* Oxford: Oxford University Press.

Bloom, Allan. 1968. "Interpretive Essay." In *The Republic of Plato. See* Plato 1968.

————. 1975. "Justice: John Rawls vs. the Tradition of Political Philosophy." *The American Political Science Review* 69:648–62.

————. 1977. "Response to Hall." *Political Theory* 5:315–30.

————. 1987. *The Closing of the American Mind.* New York: Simon and Schuster.

————. 1993. *Love and Friendship.* New York: Simon and Schuster.

Bordo, Susan. 1992. "Postmodern Subjects, Postmodern Bodies." *Feminist Studies* 18:159–75.

Bowles, Samuel, and Herbert Gintis. 1986. *Democracy and Capitalism: Property, Community and the Contradictions of Modern Social Thought.* New York: Basic Books.

Buchanan, Allen E. 1989. "Assessing the Communitarian Critique of Liberalism." *Ethics* 99:852–82.

Burnyeat, Myles. 1985. "Sphinx Without a Secret." *New York Review of Books,* May 30, 30–37.

Butler, Judith. 1989. "Foucault and the Paradox of Bodily Inscriptions." *The Journal of Philosophy* 86:601–7.

————. 1990a. "Performative Acts and Gender Constitution: An Essay in Phenomenology and Feminist Theory." In *Performing Feminisms,* ed. Sue-Ellen Case. Baltimore: Johns Hopkins University Press.

————. 1990b. "Gender Trouble, Feminist Theory, and Psychoanalytic

Discourse." In *Feminism/Postmodernism,* ed. Linda J. Nicholson. New York: Routledge.

———. 1990c. *Gender Trouble.* New York: Routledge.

———. 1992a. "Contingent Foundations: Feminism and the Question of 'Postmodernism.'" In *Feminists Theorize the Political,* ed. Judith Butler and Joan W. Scott. New York: Routledge.

———. 1992b. "Discussion." *October* 61:108–20.

———. 1993. *Bodies That Matter.* New York: Routledge.

Christman, John. 1989. "Introduction." In *The Inner Citadel,* ed. John Christman. Oxford: Oxford University Press.

Connolly, William E. 1988. *Political Theory & Modernity.* Oxford: Basil Blackwell.

———. 1991. *Identity/Difference.* Ithaca: Cornell University Press.

———. 1993a. "Beyond Good and Evil: The Ethical Sensibility of Michel Foucault." *Political Theory* 21: 365–89.

———. 1993b. *The Augustinian Imperative: A Reflection on the Politics of Morality.* Newbury Park, Calif.: Sage.

———. 1993c. "Epilogue to the 1993 Edition: Modernity, Territorial Democracy, and the Problem of Evil." In *Political Theory and Modernity.* Ithaca: Cornell University Press.

Cornford, F. M. 1971. "The Doctrine of Eros in Plato's *Symposium.*" In *Plato II. See* Vlastos 1971.

Cropsey, Joseph, Harry V. Jaffa, Allan Bloom, Ernest J. Weinrib, Thomas L. Pangle, Clifford Orwin, Robert Gordis, and M. F. Burnyeat. 1985. "The Studies of Leo Strauss: An Exchange," *New York Review of Books,* Oct. 10, 41–44.

Dahl, Robert A. 1957. "The Concept of Power." *Behavioral Science* 2:201–15.

———. 1989. *Democracy and Its Critics.* New Haven: Yale University Press.

Derrida, Jacques. 1986. "Declarations of Independence." *New Political Science* 15:7–15.

Deutsch, Kenneth L., and Walter Soffer, ed. 1987. *The Crisis of Liberal Democracy.* Albany: State University of New York Press.

Diamond, Peter. 1993. "A Commonsense Defense of the Liberal Self." Presented at the annual meeting of the American Political Science Association, Washington, D.C.

Digeser, Peter. 1992. "The Fourth Face of Power." *Journal of Politics* 54:977–1007.

———. 1994. "Performativity Trouble: Postmodern Feminism and Essential Subjects." *Political Research Quarterly* 47: 655–73.

Di Stefano, Christine. 1990. "Dilemmas of Difference: Feminism, Modernity, and Postmodernism." In *Feminism/Postmodernism. See* Butler 1990b.

———. 1991. "Who the Heck Are We? Theoretical Turns Against Gender." *Frontiers* 12:86–108.

Donner, Wendy. 1991. *The Liberal Self.* Ithaca: Cornell University Press.

Drury, Shadia B. 1988. *The Political Ideas of Leo Strauss.* New York: St. Martin's.

Dworkin, Gerald. 1988. *The Theory and Practice of Autonomy.* Cambridge: Cambridge University Press.

———. 1989. "The Concept of Autonomy." In Christman 1989.

Feinberg, Joel. 1984. *Harm to Others.* Oxford: Oxford University Press.

———. 1989. "Autonomy." In Christman 1989.

————. 1990. *Harmless Wrongdoing.* Oxford: Oxford University Press.

Flathman, Richard E. 1973. "Introduction." In *Concepts in Social and Political Philosophy,* ed. Richard E. Flathman. New York: Macmillan.

————. 1980. *The Practice of Political Authority.* Chicago: University of Chicago Press.

————. 1987. *The Philosophy and Politics of Freedom.* Chicago: University of Chicago Press.

————. 1992. *Willful Liberalism.* Ithaca: Cornell University Press.

Flax, Jane. 1990. *Thinking Fragments: Psychoanalysis, Feminism, and Postmodernism in the Contemporary West.* Berkeley and Los Angeles: University of California Press.

————. 1992. "The End of Innocence." In *Feminists Theorize the Political. See* Butler 1992a.

Forde, Steven. 1987. "On the *Alcibiades I.*" In *The Roots of Political Philosophy,* ed. Thomas L. Pangle. Ithaca: Cornell University Press.

Foucault, Michel. 1977. *Discipline and Punish: The Birth of the Prison.* Trans. Alan Sheridan. New York: Random House.

————. 1979. "On Governmentality." *Ideology & Consciousness* 6:5–21.

————. 1980a. *The History of Sexuality, An Introduction.* Vol. 1 of *The History of Sexuality.* Trans. Robert Hurley. New York: Random House.

————. 1980b. "Two Lectures." In *Power/Knowledge: Selected Interviews and Other Writings 1972–1977,* ed. Colin Gordon. New York: Pantheon.

————. 1980c. "Power and Strategies." In ibid.

————. 1980d. "The Politics of Health in the Eighteenth Century." In ibid.

————. 1983. "The Subject and Power." In *Michel Foucault: Beyond Structuralism and Hermeneutics,* 2d. ed., ed. Hubert Dreyfus and Paul Rabinow. Chicago: University of Chicago Press.

————. 1984a. "Nietzsche, Genealogy, History." In *The Foucault Reader. See* Rabinow 1984.

————. 1984b. "On the Genealogy of Ethics: An Overview of Work in Progress." In ibid.

————. 1984c. "Politics and Ethics." In ibid.

————. 1986. *The Care of the Self.* Vol. 3 of *The History of Sexuality.* Trans. Robert Hurley. New York: Pantheon.

————. 1988a. "The Dangerous Individual." In *Michel Foucault: Politics Philosophy Culture,* ed. Lawrence D. Kritzman. New York: Routledge.

————. 1988b. "An Aesthetics of Existence." In ibid.

————. 1988c. "Technologies of the Self." In *Technologies of the Self,* ed. Luther H. Martin, Huck Gutman, and Patrick H. Hutton. Amherst: University of Massachusetts Press.

————. 1988d. "The Political Technology of Individuals." In ibid.

————. 1991a. "Politics and the Study of Discourse." In *The Foucault Effect,* ed. Graham Burchell, Colin Gordon, and Peter Miller. Chicago: University of Chicago Press.

————. 1991b. "Questions of Method." In ibid.

————. 1993. "About the Beginning of the Hermeneutics of the Self: Two Lectures at Dartmouth." *Political Theory* 21:198–227.

Frankfurt, Harry. 1989. "Freedom of the Will and the Concept of the Person." In Christman 1989.

Fraser, Nancy. 1985. "Michel Foucault: A 'Young Conservative'?" *Ethics* 96:165–84.

Galston, William A. 1991. *Liberal Purposes.* Cambridge: Cambridge University Press.

Gildin, Hilail. 1987. "Leo Strauss and Liberal Democracy." In Deutsch and Soffer 1987.

Gordon, Colin. 1991. "Governmental Rationality." In *The Foucault Effect. See* Foucault 1991a.

Gourevitch, Victor. 1987. "The Problem of Natural Right and the Fundamental Alternatives in *Natural Right and History.*" In Deutsch and Soffer 1987.

Gruber, David F. 1989. "Foucault's Critique of the Liberal Individual." *The Journal of Philosophy* 86:615–21.

Gunnell, John. 1985. "Political Theory and Politics: The Case of Leo Strauss." *Political Theory* 13:339–61.

Gutmann, Amy. 1985. "Communitarian Critics of Liberalism." *Philosophy & Public Affairs* 14:308–22.

Gutmann, Amy, and Dennis Thompson. 1990. "Moral Conflict and Political Consensus." In *Liberalism and the Good*, ed. R. Bruce Douglas, Gerald R. Mara, and Henry S. Richardson. New York: Routledge.

Habermas, Jürgen. 1987. *The Philosophical Discourse of Modernity.* Trans. Frederick Lawrence. Cambridge, Mass.: MIT Press.

Hacking, Ian. 1986. "The Archaeology of Foucault." In *Foucault: A Critical Reader*, ed. David Couzens Hoy. Oxford: Basil Blackwell.

Hadot, Pierre. 1992. "Reflections on the Notion of 'The Cultivation of the Self.'" In *Michel Foucault: Philosopher*, trans. Timothy Armstrong. New York: Routledge.

Hall, Dale. 1977. "The *Republic* and the 'Limits of Politics.'" *Political Theory* 5:293–313.

Hardin, Russell. 1989. "Autonomy, Identity, and Welfare." In Christman 1989.

Hartsock, Nancy. 1990. "Foucault on Power: A Theory for Women?" In *Feminism/Postmodernism. See* Butler 1990b.

Hekman, Susan. 1992. "The Embodiment of the Subject: Feminism and the Communitarian Critique of Liberalism." *Journal of Politics* 54:1098–1119.

Heller, Agnes. 1992. "Death of the Subject?" In *Constructions of the Self*, ed. George Levine. New Brunswick, N.J.: Rutgers University Press.

Hill, Thomas E., Jr. 1989. "The Kantian Conception of Autonomy." In Christman 1989.

———. 1991. *Autonomy and Self-Respect.* Cambridge: Cambridge University Press.

Holmes, Stephen Taylor. 1979. "Aristippus in and out of Athens." *American Political Science Review* 73:113–28.

———. 1993. *The Anatomy of Antiliberalism.* Cambridge, Mass.: Harvard University Press.

Honig, B. 1991. "Declarations of Independence: Arendt and Derrida on the Problem of Founding a Republic." *American Political Science Review* 85:97–113.

———. 1992. "Toward an Agonistic Feminism: Hannah Arendt and the Politics of Identity." In *Feminists Theorize the Political*. In Butler 1992a.

———. 1993. *Political Theory and the Displacement of Politics*. Ithaca: Cornell University Press.

Hutton, Patrick H. 1988. "Foucault, Freud, and the Technologies of the Self." In *Technologies of the Self. See* Foucault 1988c.

Irwin, Terence. 1977. *Plato's Moral Theory*. Oxford: Clarendon Press.

Isaac, Jeffrey C. 1987. "On the Subject of Political Theory." *Political Theory* 15:639–45.

Jaeger, Robert A. 1977. "Am I in the World?" *American Philosophical Quarterly* 14:239–45.

Jaffa, Harry V. 1984. "The Legacy of Leo Strauss." *Claremont Review of Books*, Fall, 14–21.

Jambet, Christian. 1992. "The Constitution of the Subject and Spiritual Practices." In *Michel Foucault. See* Hadot 1992.

Jones, Kathleen B. 1993. *Compassionate Authority: Democracy and the Representation of Women*. New York: Routledge.

Kateb, George. 1990. "Walt Whitman and the Culture of Democracy." *Political Theory* 18:545–600.

Kent, Christopher A. 1986. "Michel Foucault: Doing History, or Undoing It?" *Canadian Journal of History* 21:371–95.

Klosko, George. 1986. "The Straussian Interpretation of Plato's *Republic*." *History of Political Thought* 7:275–93.

Kotz, Liz. 1992. "The Body You Want." *Artforum* 31:82–89.

Kukathas, Chandran. 1992a. "Are There Any Cultural Rights?" *Political Theory* 20:105–39.

———. 1992b. "Cultural Rights Again: A Rejoinder to Kymlicka." *Political Theory* 20:674–80.

Kymlicka, Will. 1989. *Liberalism, Community and Culture*. Oxford: Clarendon.

———. 1992. "The Rights of Minority Cultures." *Political Theory* 20:140–46.

Larmore, Charles E. 1987. *Patterns of Moral Complexity*. Cambridge: Cambridge University Press.

———. 1990. "Political Liberalism." *Political Theory* 18:339–60.

Lasch, Christopher. 1978. *The Culture of Narcissism: American Life in an Age of Diminishing Expectations*. New York: W. W. Norton.

Levine, David Lawrence. 1991. "Without Malice but With Forethought." *Review of Politics* 53:200–218.

Lindley, Richard. 1986. *Autonomy*. Atlantic Highlands, N.J.: Humanities Press International.

Lomasky, Loren E. 1987. *Persons, Rights, and the Moral Community*. Oxford: Oxford University Press.

Löw-Beer, Martin. 1991. "Living a Life and the Problem of Existential Impossibility." *Inquiry* 34:217–36.

Lowenthal, David. 1985. "Leo Strauss's *Studies in Platonic Philosophy*." *Interpretation* 13:297–320.

Lukes, Steven. 1973. *Individualism.* Oxford: Basil Blackwell.

MacIntyre, Alasdair. 1984. *After Virtue.* 2d ed. Notre Dame: University of Notre Dame Press.

———. 1988. *Whose Justice? Which Rationality?* Notre Dame: University of Notre Dame Press.

Mansfield, Harvey C., Jr. 1978. *The Spirit of Liberalism.* Cambridge, Mass.: Harvard University Press.

———. 1988. "Democracy and the Great Books." *The New Republic,* Apr. 4, 33–37.

———. 1991. *America's Constitutional Soul.* Baltimore: Johns Hopkins University Press.

Mapel, David R. 1990. "Civil Association and the Idea of Contingency." *Political Theory* 18:392–410.

Markus, R. A. 1971. "The Dialectic of Eros in Plato's *Symposium.*" In *Plato II. See* Vlastos 1971.

Mill, J. S. 1948. "Representative Government." In *On Liberty and Considerations on Representative Government,* ed. R. R. McCallum. Oxford: Basil Blackwell.

———. 1962. "Utilitarianism." In *Utilitarianism, On Liberty, Essay on Bentham,* ed. Mary Warnock. New York: Mentor.

———. 1975. *On Liberty.* New York: W. W. Norton.

Morris, Colin. 1972. *The Discovery of the Individual 1050–1200.* New York: Harper Torchbooks.

Mosher, Michael A. 1991. "Boundary Revisions: The Deconstruction of Moral Personality in Rawls, Nozick, Sandel and Parfit." *Political Studies* 39:287–302.

Mouffe, Chantal. 1992. "Feminism, Citizenship, and Radical Democratic Politics." In *Feminists Theorize the Political. See* Butler 1992a.

Neal, Patrick, and David Paris. 1990. "Liberalism and the Communitarian Critique: A Guide for the Perplexed." *Canadian Journal of Political Science* 23:419–39.

Nichols, Mary P. 1988. "Spiritedness and Philosophy in Plato's *Republic.*" In *Understanding the Political Spirit: Philosophical Investigations from Socrates to Nietzsche,* ed. Catherine H. Zuckert. New Haven: Yale University Press.

Nietzsche, Friedrich. 1966. *Thus Spoke Zarathustra.* Trans. Walter Kaufmann. New York: Viking.

Nisbet, Robert. 1962. *Community and Power.* New York: Oxford University Press.

Norton, David L. 1991. *Democracy and Moral Development.* Berkeley and Los Angeles: University of California Press.

Nussbaum, Martha. 1987. "Undemocratic Vistas." *New York Review of Books,* Nov. 5, 20–26.

Oakeshott, Michael. 1975. *On Human Conduct.* Oxford: Oxford University Press.

———. 1991. "The Tower of Babel." In *Rationalism and Politics.* Indianapolis: Liberty Press.

Pangle, Thomas L. 1983. "Introduction." In Strauss 1983.

———. 1987. "Nihilism and Modern Democracy in the Thought of Nietzsche." In Deutsch and Soffer 1987.

———. 1989. "Introduction." In Strauss 1989.

———. 1992. *The Ennobling of Democracy.* Baltimore: Johns Hopkins University Press.

Parfit, Derek. 1984. *Persons and Reasons.* Oxford: Clarendon Press.

Plato. 1927. "Alcibiades I." In *Charmides, Alcibiades, Hipparchus, The Lovers, Theages, Minos, Epinomis.* Vol. 12 of *Plato, The Loeb Classical Library.* Trans. W.R.M. Lamb. Cambridge, Mass.: Harvard University Press.

————. 1968. *The Republic of Plato.* Trans. Allan Bloom. New York: Basic Books.

————. 1980. *The Laws of Plato.* Trans. Thomas Pangle. New York: Basic Books.

————. 1987. "Alcibiades I." Trans. Carnes Lord. In *The Roots of Political Philosophy,* ed. Thomas L. Pangle. Ithaca: Cornell University Press.

————. 1991. *The Symposium.* Vol. 2 of *The Dialogues of Plato.* Trans. R. E. Allen. New Haven: Yale University Press.

Podhoretz, John. 1987. "An Open Letter to Allan Bloom." *National Review,* Oct. 9, 34–37.

Rabinow, Paul. 1984. "Introduction." In *The Foucault Reader,* ed. Paul Rabinow. New York: Pantheon.

Rawls, John. 1971. *A Theory of Justice.* Cambridge: Belknap Press.

————. 1985. "Justice as Fairness: Political not Metaphysical." *Philosophy & Public Affairs* 14:223–51.

————. 1988. "The Priority of Right and Ideas of the Good." *Philosophy & Public Affairs* 17:251–76.

————. 1993. *Political Liberalism.* New York: Columbia University Press.

Raz, Joseph. 1986. *The Morality of Freedom.* Oxford: Clarendon Press.

Reeve, C.D.C. 1988. *Philosopher-Kings.* Princeton: Princeton University Press.

Rogin, Michael. 1992. "Blackface, White Noise: The Jewish Jazz Singer Finds His Voice." *Critical Inquiry* 18:417–53.

Rorty, Richard. 1979. *Philosophy and the Mirror of Nature.* Princeton: Princeton University Press.

————. 1989. *Contingency, Irony, and Solidarity.* Cambridge: Cambridge University Press.

————. 1991a. *Objectivity, Relativism, and Truth.* Vol. 1 of *Philosophical Papers.* Cambridge: Cambridge University Press.

————. 1991b. *Essays on Heidegger and Others.* Vol. 2 of *Philosophical Papers.* Cambridge: Cambridge University Press.

Rosen, Stanley. 1987. *Hermeneutics as Politics.* Oxford: Oxford University Press.

Rothman, Stanley. 1962. "The Revival of Classical Political Philosophy: A Critique." *American Political Science Review* 56:341–52.

Salkever, Stephen G. 1974. "Virtue, Obligation and Politics." *American Political Science Review* 68:78–92.

————. 1987. "The Crisis of Liberal Democracy: Liberality and Democratic Citizenship." In Deutsch and Soffer 1987.

————. 1990. *Finding the Mean.* Princeton: Princeton University Press.

Sandel, Michael J. 1982. *Liberalism and the Limits of Justice.* Cambridge: Cambridge University Press.

————. 1992. "The Procedural Republic and the Unencumbered Self." In *The Self and the Political Order,* ed. Tracy Strong. New York: New York University Press.

Shklar, Judith. 1984. *Ordinary Vices.* Cambridge: Belknap Press.

————. 1989. "The Liberalism of Fear." In *Liberalism and the Moral Life,* ed. Nancy L. Rosenblum. Cambridge, Mass.: Harvard University Press.

Storing, Herbert J. 1981. *What the Anti-Federalists Were for*. Chicago: University of Chicago Press.

Strauss, Leo. 1953. *Natural Right and History*. Chicago: University of Chicago Press.

———. 1959. *What Is Political Philosophy?* Glencoe, Ill.: The Free Press.

———. 1963. *On Tyranny*. New York: The Free Press of Glencoe.

———. 1964. *The City and Man*. Chicago: Rand McNally.

———. 1965. *Spinoza's Critique of Religion*. New York: Schoken Books.

———. 1968. *Liberalism Ancient and Modern*. Ithaca: Cornell University Press.

———. 1975. "Three Waves of Modernity." In *Political Philosophy: Six Essays*, ed. Hilail Gildin. Indianapolis: Pegasus.

———. 1983. *Studies in Platonic Philosophy*. Ed. Thomas L. Pangle. Chicago: University of Chicago Press.

———. 1989. *The Rebirth of Classical Political Rationalism*. Ed. Thomas L. Pangle. Chicago: University of Chicago Press.

Tarcov, Nathan. 1991. "On a Certain Critique of 'Straussianism.'" *Review of Politics* 53:3–18.

Taylor, Charles. 1976. "Responsibility for Self." In *The Identities of Persons*, ed. A. Rorty. Berkeley and Los Angeles: University of California Press.

———. 1985. "Connolly, Foucault and Truth." *Political Theory* 13:377–85.

———. 1986. "Foucault on Freedom and Truth." In *Foucault: A Critical Reader. See* Hacking 1986.

———. 1989a. *Sources of the Self*. Cambridge, Mass.: Harvard University Press.

———. 1989b. "Cross-Purposes: The Liberal-Communitarian Debate." In *Liberalism and the Moral Life*, ed. Nancy Rosenblum. Cambridge, Mass.: Harvard University Press.

———. 1991a. *The Ethics of Authenticity*. Cambridge, Mass.: Harvard University Press.

———. 1991b. "Comments and Replies." *Inquiry* 34:237–54.

———. 1992. "The Politics of Recognition." In *Multiculturalism and "The Politics of Recognition,"* ed. Amy Gutmann. Princeton: Princeton University Press.

Thalberg, Irving. 1989. "Hierarchical Analyses of Unfree Action." In Christman 1989.

Thiele, Leslie Paul. 1990. *Friedrich Nietzsche and the Politics of the Soul*. Princeton: Princeton University Press.

Tocqueville, Alexis de. 1969. *Democracy in America*. Ed. J. P. Mayer. Garden City, N.J.: Doubleday.

Vlastos, Gregory. 1971. "Justice and Happiness in the *Republic*." In *Plato II,* ed. Gregory Vlastos. Notre Dame: University of Notre Dame Press.

Walzer, Michael. 1977. *Just and Unjust Wars*. New York: Basic Books.

———. 1986. "The Politics of Michel Foucault." In *Foucault: A Critical Reader. See* Hacking 1986.

———. 1990. "The Communitarian Critique of Liberalism." *Political Theory* 18:6–23.

Watson, Gary. 1989. "Free Agency." In Christman 1989.

West, Thomas G. 1984. "Introduction." In *Four Texts on Socrates*. Trans. Thomas G. West and Grace Starry West. Ithaca: Cornell University Press.

————. 1991. "Leo Strauss and the American Founding." *The Review of Politics* 53:157–72.

Wittgenstein, Ludwig. 1958. *Philosophical Investigations.* Trans. G.E.M. Anscombe. New York: Macmillan.

Wolf, Susan. 1989. "Sanity and the Metaphysics of Responsibility." In Christman 1989.

Wolff, Robert Paul. 1970. *In Defense of Anarchism.* New York: Harper and Row.

Wood, Gordon S. 1988. "The Fundamentalists and the Constitution." *New York Review of Books,* Feb. 18, 33–40.

Yack, Bernard. 1988. "Liberalism and Its Communitarian Critics: Does Liberal Practice 'Live Down' to Liberal Theory?" In *Community in America,* ed. Charles H. Reynolds and Ralph V. Norman. Berkeley and Los Angeles: University of California Press.

Young, Iris Marion. 1990. *Justice and the Politics of Difference.* Princeton: Princeton University Press.

Young, Robert. 1986. *Personal Autonomy: Beyond Negative and Positive Freedom.* New York: St. Martin's.

Index

Abelard, Peter, 103, 103n.5
Ackerman, Bruce, 217
agency, 6, 53, 53n.36, 54n.38, 82–83, 191–213, 249; and autarchy, 171n.7; and autonomy, 171; Butler and, 54n.38, 210–11; characteristics of, 171, 171n.7; cognitive, 71–73; and communitarianism, 193; conditions for, 194–95; and Foucault, 201n.5; and harm, 191–92, 251; and heterarchy, 191; and liberal democracy 194–96; meaning of cultivating, 196–98; obligation to cultivate, 196–213; obligation to protect, 192–94, 235–36, 244; opacity of, 211–13; as a product of power, 202; value of, 192–94; voluntaristic, 73, 73n.8. *See also* self; soul; subject
agonistic democracy, 53n.36, 56–57
Aristophanes, 114
Aristotle, 27
Austin, J. L., 151, 151n.13
autarchy. *See* agency
authenticity, 6, 182–91, 198, 223; defined, 144–45; fostering, 183–86; and harm, 187–91; and horizon of meaning, 184, 188–89; individual vs. cultural, 187; and liberalism, 186; a right to, 186–91; value of, 182–83
autonomy, 6, 166–82, 198, 223; and agency, 171; and community, 179–82; and decisive identification, 173–75; defined, 148–49, 167–69; formal vs. substantive, 167–69; vs. freedom, 177–78, 181; and harm, 177–82; instrumental value of, 169–70; intrinsic value of, 170–75; and liberal democracy, 181–82; and revising preferences, 175–77; and second-order preferences, 172–74

Barber, Benjamin, 30n.16
Barry, Brian, 166n.1
Beiner, Ronald, 20
Bellah, Robert, 4, 12, 19–22, 62–63, 63n.3, 65–66
Benn, Stanley I.: on agency (autarchy),

191–93; on autonomy, 148, 167–68, 170–71, 171n.7, 175, 175n.12, 180, 182
Berlin, Isaiah, 178–79
Bloom, Allan, 4, 10, 24–27, 30, 33–37, 65, 65n.5; and eros, 106, 106n.9, 111; and knowing the self, 103–4, 103n.6; on Plato's *Republic*, 115–30
Bowles Samuel, 196n.1
Burnyeat, Myles, 31n.19
Butler, Judith, 5, 38, 48–55, 131–35, 135nn. 3 and 4, 150–65, 197n.1; and agency, 54n.38, 210–11; on citation, 51–52, 55, 150–52, 155, 157–59; on coherence, 49–50, 160–62; and competing roles of the self, 131–32; on essentialism, 162–65; and a feminist genealogy, 39–40; and harm, 156–65; and matter, 154–55; and naturalization, 46, 48–52, 133, 154, 156–57, 160; on Nietzsche, 134n.2; and parodic subversion, 53–55; and performativity, 50–53, 53n.37, 133, 150–54, 157, 157n.17, 159–63; and politics, 53, 55, 162–64; and resistance, 135

Christman, John, 173, 174
citation, and authorization of practices, 51–52, 55, 150–52, 155, 157–59
classical political rationalism, 4, 5, 23–37, 96–130, 247; and best regime, 24–26; and communitarianism, 23–24, 58–60; and crisis of the West, 28–31, 31n.18, 35; and education, 32, 33, 37, 37n.29; empirical support for, 64–65; and epistemology, 102–4; and genealogy, 38, 58–60, 61n.1; and intellectual virtue, 31–36; and knowing nature, 96–102; and liberal democracy, 4, 5, 24–37, 96, 130; and moral virtue, 27–31; and Nietzsche, 28–30, 30n.16; and place of reason in the soul, 104–10; and revelation and reason, 108–10, 114; and the self vs. the soul, 24, 103–4; and Tocqueville, 28–30
coherence, 49–50, 160–62
communitarianism, 4, 5, 12–23, 69–95, 193,